Praise for

DISQUIET TIME

"This is a sturdy book, a thoroughly satisfying and totally credible book. Well conceived and well executed, it offers honest words about holy things, which means that it is also a brave book. I, for one, am grateful."
— Phyllis Tickle, author, *The Age of the Spirit*

"DISQUIET TIME takes us down a thrilling, provocative, and often beautiful path that leads to the deepest parts of ourselves, and the deepest parts of Christ. This book is for folks who don't just want to read the Bible; they want to laugh, wrestle, and cry with the Bible. And that's just the place God wants us to be."
— Joshua DuBois, former head of the White House Office of Faith-Based and Neighborhood Partnerships and author of *The President's Devotional*

"DISQUIET TIME is a devotional for humans, a daily reading for the messy, doubt-filled, sometimes irreverent people who love God or hope to someday. Though hinged on some of the Bible's most deranged narratives, [the book]...is strangely comforting, a spiritual hodgepodge that is deep and convicting, hopeful and honest, quirky and wise. For believers, cynics, and misfit souls, DISQUIET TIME is a welcome invitation to doubt, laugh, fight, debate, and trust."
— Matthew Paul Turner, author of *Our Great Big American God* and *Churched*

"This rich collection of essays is thoughtful, engaging, and provocative. A must-read."
— Margaret Feinberg, author of *Wonderstruck*

"Cathleen and Jennifer are wonderful writers as well as wonderful people and this collection of wonderful essays is, in a word, *lovely*. You thought I was going to say *wonderful*, didn't you? I'm AN ENIGMA!!"

—Pete Holmes, comedian and talk show host

DISQUIET TIME

Rants and Reflections on
the Good Book by the Skeptical,
the Faithful,
and a Few Scoundrels

Jennifer Grant and
Cathleen Falsani

GENERAL EDITORS

Foreword by Eugene H. Peterson

JERICHO
BOOKS™

New York   Boston   Nashville

Jericho Books
Hachette Book Group
1290 Avenue of the Americas
New York, NY 10104

www.JerichoBooks.com

Printed in the United States of America

RRD-C

First Edition: October 2014

10 9 8 7 6 5 4 3 2 1

Jericho Books is an imprint of Hachette Book Group, Inc.
The Jericho Books name and logo are trademarks of Hachette Book Group, Inc.

The Hachette Speakers Bureau provides a wide range of authors for speaking events. To find out more, go to www.HachetteSpeakersBureau.com or call (866) 376-6591.

The publisher is not responsible for websites (or their content) that are not owned by the publisher.

Library of Congress Cataloging-in-Publication Data has been applied for

For our children
Theo, Ian, Isabel, Mia, and Vasco

May you engage with God's word throughout your life;
May you be in community with other people of faith;
May you dare to ask tough questions;
May you be content not knowing all the answers;
May you always be real before God in the joys
and sorrows of living;
May you be still enough to hear God's voice;
May you have the eyes to see God's grace all around you
and extend it to others;
And may you ever rest in God's immeasurable, unchanging
love for you.

Contents

Contents

Contents

The weight of this sad time we must obey;
Speak what we feel, not what we ought to say.

—William Shakespeare, *King Lear*, act 5, scene 2

Foreword
Fitting Our Stories into God's

Many years ago I wrote a phrase that keeps coming back to me from various sources: "Stories are verbal acts of hospitality."

This gathering of stories, *Disquiet Time*, is fresh confirmation of that notion. The stories all have two things in common. They all take the Bible seriously, and, like Jacob at the river Jabbok, they take it seriously enough to wrestle with its meaning in the context of their own lives. More often than not, also like Jacob, they leave the river alive and safe but "limping."

An enormous authority and dignity have, through the centuries, developed around the books of the Bible. Through those centuries they account for a truly astonishing amount of reading and writing, study and prayer, teaching and preaching. God is the primary concern of what is written in the Bible. That accounts for the authority and dignity.

But it is not only God; we get included, too. That accounts for the widespread and intense human interest. We want to know what's going on. We want to know how we fit into things. We don't want to miss out. But this also accounts for the difficulties that most of us have with the Bible from time to time.

Sometimes the difficulties are introduced by our parents—they have found a rule or command or practice that, taken out of context, they feel obligated to impose on other members of the family. Sometimes the difficulties come from well-meaning friends who have adopted an interpretation of one or two texts that they are convinced we need to follow if we want to escape the wrath of God. And sometimes it is a pastor or TV preacher who, as a self-appointed policeman for God, arrogantly bullies us.

But the voices in this book—the ones that interact with biblical texts in their "disquiet times"—seem to be quite free of polemical rhetoric. The voices are conspicuous for not requiring an enemy in order to establish their identity as persons of faith as they read and meditate on the Scriptures.

The Holy Scriptures are made up mostly of stories and signposts. The stories show us God working with and speaking to men and women in a rich variety of circumstances. God is presented to us not in ideas and arguments and abstract "principles" but rather in events and actions that involve each of us personally. The signposts provide immediate and practical directions for behavior that is appropriate to our humanity and the honoring of God but are never isolated in themselves, outside the larger context of the story.

Primarily the Bible comes to us in the form of story—narrative that draws us into a story-shaped life. Not infrequently, though, our lives feel less like a story than like a pile of disconnected fragments that have no relation to one another, a bone pile that leaves no clue as to whether the knee bone is connected to the neck bone or to the finger bone. In our culture, a lot of people spend a lot of time and money on psychologists, psychiatrists, and other experts to put the "bones" together and help give them some sense of identity.

There is also this to be said about story: if you are going to get it right, you need the entire story. You open a book at random, say, at page 257, happen on a beautiful sentence (or an ominous one), copy it out, and then spend the next half hour being either superficially happy or neurotically scared to death. You need the whole Bible in order to understand and interpret rightly every single sentence or paragraph in it.

The men and women who wrote these *Disquiet Time* stories have done it from many different personal contexts but always in the context of the larger biblical story. I sense that they are not trying to fit God into their stories but rather fit their stories into the comprehensive God story of creation, salvation, and community.

I was reading a novel recently and in the middle of a page began to get angry with the author. The main character was a thoroughly unlovely person, although nearly everyone around her thought she was charming. She was interfering in other people's lives in the most intolerable and insensitive ways, making a thorough mess of emotions and relationships.

"She can't do that!" I found myself saying to the author (although she has been dead for two hundred years). "You can't let her get by with that!"

And then I noticed that I was only on page 103, with 115 pages left to read. I recalled that in other novels by this author things always get sorted out in the end, leaving me with a feeling of completion.

I was tempted to turn to the last chapter and get to the end of the story. I resisted, however, remembering that much of the satisfaction of the conclusion comes from giving my imagination over to the contradictions and ambiguities of the plot. I was not absolutely sure that the novel was going to turn out satisfactorily, but since I had read four other books by this writer and in each one she had managed to put it all together for me, I had fairly good expectations. Right then, though, I was thoroughly fed up with Jane Austen's *Emma*.

Just as I get thoroughly fed up at times with God's *Eugene*.

I find myself involved in this comprehensive story of salvation. Sometimes I don't like the position I have in the plot, don't like what I do and say, don't like what other people do and say to me, don't like the way things are going at all, and get angry with the author: "If you are writing a story of salvation, surely you can make it go more satisfactorily than this!"

And then it occurs to me (not for the first time) that my life is a narrative with connections all over the place, not an obscure item on the inside page of last week's newspaper. And the story is obviously not yet finished. When you are in a story you never know how near you are to the end. There may be a surprise ending on the next page, or it may go on for a thousand pages. But for as long as I am conscious of there being a story at all, it is not finished.

It also occurs to me (and how often I forget this) that I am not the only character in the story. Everybody I know and don't know is in it (the Scriptures in their entirety don't let me forget this). I calm down and see that the contradictions, the inconsistencies, the impossibilities, the unresolved tensions, the lack of balance between reward and punishment, disappointment and blessing—all these are in the process of being given a kingdom-of-God shape, which, I have good reason for believing, includes my own and the world's salvation in it.

A good friend calls this honest wrangling with our faith and God "good work." I agree. I hope as you read these *Disquiet Time* stories you will find permission to be honest, move past pat answers, and freely engage with Scripture, maybe for the first time.

Eugene H. Peterson
Translator of *The Message*
Professor Emeritus of Spiritual Theology
Regent College, Vancouver, British Columbia
Montana, September 2013

Introduction
Greetings from the Land of Misfit Toys

An ethicist who can't make the right choices.

A yogi who's tempted to pray the Jesus prayer over her children.

A poet at the helm of a global corporation.

A buttoned-up suburban parent with a penchant for Eminem.

A Hollywood producer who dons a superhero costume and proclaims, *"Sola Scriptura!"*

A female professor at one of the nation's most religiously conservative schools who has a passion for tattoos and scatological literature.

These are but a few of the souls you will hear from in the pages that follow.

The voices collected in this book are those of nonconformists and oddballs—not-too-distant cousins, perhaps, to the denizens of the Island of Misfit Toys from the classic Rankin/ Bass stop-motion animation television special *Rudolph the Red-Nosed Reindeer.*

Not unlike the tiny cowboy who rides an ostrich instead of a horse, the toy train with square wheels on its caboose, and Hermey the Elf—who would rather pursue a career in dentistry than make toys in Santa's workshop—most of us are well acquainted with the itchy, out-of-place feelings wrought by the spiritual subcultures in which we sometimes find ourselves.

Some of us self-identify as orthodox (with a small *o*) Christians, while others feel a flush of pride when called liberal, mainstream, or conservative. Some of us used to identify as Christians or Jews, but now answer "none of the above" (or "all of the above," as the case may be) when asked to choose a religious label. Whatever our spiritual predilections, each of us seeks an end to the divisiveness and name-calling that too often surround discussions of the Bible.

As diverse as our voices are, they harmonize; and we hear echoes of our own stories in those of the "other." We learn something new when we hear how a particular biblical passage sustains some people, while other folks continually stumble over (or are repulsed by) the same passage.

We see God's spirit shining through each other's eyes as we grant ourselves permission and a safe space to, as Edgar says in *King Lear*, "speak what we feel, not what we ought to say"—even (and especially) when it's messy.

All the contributors to this book are personally connected to one or both of us. You'll meet our pastors, professors, mentors, chosen families, and some of our dearest friends, as well as thinkers and artists who have long inspired us.

While we like to say that *Disquiet Time* is "not your mama's *Our Daily Bread*," we do hope it nourishes, sustains, and even invigorates you as you encounter the full array of these diverse writers' authentic experiences with holy writ.

Please consider this book an invitation to join a conversation that has been going on for millennia—one that asks only for you to listen and respond with an open heart. We pray that, through reading it, you will grant *yourself* permission to express your own faith and doubts about the Good Book, honestly and without caveat.

Remember: even if you end up feeling like a cowboy riding an ostrich into the sunset, you are not alone in this. And when it comes to the greatest concerns, biggest questions, and gravest doubts about the Bible, you have the right and freedom to voice them.

God can take it.

Really.

We *promise.*

With grace in our hearts (and sometimes flowers in our hair),

Jennifer Grant and Cathleen Falsani

DISQUIET TIME

Just as I Am

Cathleen Falsani

O Lord, you have searched me and known me!
You know when I sit down and when I rise up;
you discern my thoughts from afar.
You search out my path and my lying down
and are acquainted with all my ways.
Even before a word is on my tongue,
behold, O LORD, you know it altogether.
You hem me in, behind and before,
and lay your hand upon me.
Such knowledge is too wonderful for me;
it is high; I cannot attain it.

For you formed my inward parts;
you knitted me together in my mother's womb.
I praise you, for I am fearfully and wonderfully made.
Wonderful are your works;
my soul knows it very well.
My frame was not hidden from you,
when I was being made in secret,
intricately woven in the depths of the earth.
Your eyes saw my unformed substance;

1

in your book were written, every one of them,
the days that were formed for me,
when as yet there was none of them.

—Psalms 139:1–6, 13–16 ESV

I don't think you're an idiot at all. I mean, there are elements of the ridiculous about you. Your mother's pretty interesting. And you really are an appallingly bad public speaker. And, um, you tend to let whatever's in your head come out of your mouth without much consideration of the consequences...But the thing is, um, what I'm trying to say, very inarticulately, is that, um, in fact, perhaps despite appearances, I like you, very much. Just as you are.

—Mark Darcy (to Bridget Jones) in *Bridget Jones's Diary*

In the decade I spent as a teenager attending Sunday services (morning and evening) at the Southern Baptist church in which I largely was reared spiritually, I must have witnessed (and occasionally participated in) hundreds of altar calls.

Invariably, while we waited for the Holy Spirit to move us at each of these altar calls, we, the congregation, sang all six verses of Charlotte Elliott and William B. Bradbury's hymn, "Just as I Am." In fact, I believe I've sung the words to that hymn more often than any other song in my lifetime. Even more often than "The Star-Spangled Banner," the Eagles' "Desperado," and Sir Mix-a-Lot's "Baby Got Back"—*combined*.

The second verse, then as now, sometimes puts a lump in my throat:

Just as I am—and waiting not
To rid my soul of one dark blot,

2

To Thee, whose blood can cleanse each spot—
O Lamb of God, I come, I come!

The idea that God knows me—all of me—and loves me anyway moves me deeply and in ways for which I have no words.

I did not grow up with a God who was ready to smite me the moment I toed the first blades of grass on the slippery slope of sin. Rather, the God the Southern Baptists introduced me to was a God of grace, mercy, and unconditional love.

My understanding of salvation—what we called the born-again experience, back in the 1980s—was that it was a "one-and-you're-done" transaction. All I needed to do was open the door of my heart to Jesus and let him in, and I would be forgiven for all sins past, present, and future. My salvation would be assured.

Forever.

No backsies.

I was about ten years old when I opened the door to Jesus. In he came with his forgiveness and grace, and he set up shop in my heart's kitchen, making peanut-butter-and-banana sandwiches served with Ovaltine and slices of Gala apples on the side. Last time I checked, he was still there doing his thing, and in return I've adopted an orthopraxis that can be summed up nicely in a slogan I probably stole from Anne Lamott: striving daily not to horrify Jesus.

I am not perfect.

Far from it.

I am neither pious nor disciplined, neither patient nor particularly long-suffering. I try to start good habits but usually give them up before the requisite twenty-eight days. I've never kept a journal for more than a fortnight or successfully awakened

3

early in the morning to have my "quiet time" with the Lord. I've never read the Bible all the way through (even though I hold a degree from a Christian seminary of some repute), and I've never kept a fast or discipline for all forty days of Lent.

I have a temper. I swear like an Irish lumberjack. I shout at other drivers. I sometimes drink vodka gimlets and make promises I don't remember the next day. I probably show more cleavage than I should. I've never followed a diet I didn't cheat on. And I'm pretty sure I once got out of a Columbia House music subscription contract by telling the collector that I had died.

I do things I know are wrong; I say things I know I shouldn't say. My ethics are shaky, my morals are worse, and I am, most assuredly, not a very good Christian.

I'm telling you this because God already knows. God knew about the gimlet thing before I was even a flirtatious wink in my father's eye. And God knows about the ridiculous thing I'll say next week, and the lie I'll tell when I'm eighty, and the reason why the sound of Uilleann bagpipes makes me cry, and why I can't wheel a shopping cart back to its parking lot corral without hearing my uncle Dodi's voice say, "You and your brother are good citizens."

God knows me. All of me. Every inch. Every hair. Every thought. Every zit. Every fart. Every step. Every breath. Every hope, fear, sorrow, joy. Every everything.

King David knew this, and that brother was a major fuckup. He did some horrible shit, and he suffered the harsh consequences, but they didn't include God throwing up God's hands and stomping away in a huff. God was there when David made epic mistakes, God was there for the ensuing heartbreak, and God was there when David got back on his feet, righted his course, and walked on.

4

And God loved David the whole time.

So I tend to believe David when he writes in Psalm 139:

O Lord, you have searched me and known me!
You know when I sit down and when I rise up;
you discern my thoughts from afar.
You search out my path and my lying down
and are acquainted with all my ways.

[I]n your book were written, every one of them,
the days that were formed for me,
when as yet there was none of them. (v. 1–3, 16 ESV)

There is a freedom in being known. God sees me. The real me. All of me. All the time. Just as I am.

And even with all that data to go on, even though God sees everything, God loves me. Just as I am. God is Mark Darcy to my Bridget Jones. God loves me—even when I show Daniel Cleaver my enormous granny panties. God fights for me. God pursues me. God never gives up on me. God never stops loving me.

I bring all that I-am-ness with me when I read the Bible, which, frankly, I do more now than I ever have in the past. Perhaps that's because I stopped trying to read it "right." I used to believe that I wasn't educated enough to engage well with Scripture. I wouldn't get it. I'd misunderstand. I'd do it wrong.

Nowadays, here on the other side of forty, I don't care as much about right or wrong. I lean more into authenticity and figure there's nothing I can misunderstand or dislike in the Bible that someone before me—eons before me—hasn't thought, felt, and expressed already.

A few years ago, while I was visiting with Elie Wiesel at his home in New York City, we talked about how he studies the Bible daily. For hours at a time. It's something he's done for most of his life to hold both himself and God accountable. In the Jewish tradition, he told me, people have the right—some might go so far as to say it's an *obligation*—to take the tough questions directly to God. God can handle it. Hebrew Scripture recounts how Jeremiah shook his fists at God and angrily accused the Almighty of taking advantage of him. And dude was a prophet.

Maybe that's why in those rare moments when I've been pissed off at God, I've also felt, strangely, closest to God. There's an intimacy in anger expressed. You shout, you tell the truth, you say how you feel, and you work it out.

God wants to be in a relationship with us, and in order to do that, we have to keep talking. The Bible is one of the ways the dialogue continues. And unlike dining etiquette, polite conversation with God puts no topic off-limits. Go ahead and put your elbows on the table. Use the wrong fork. It's okay. (Whom are you trying to impress?)

God knows us. All of us. God knows everything about every single one of us.

Still, God loves us. Madly. Just as we are.

And there's nothing we ever could do to make God love us less—or more.

Selah.

Of Feet and Angelic Netherbits

Tripp Hudgins

When Boaz had eaten and drunk, and he was in a contented
mood, he went to lie down at the end of the heap of grain.
Then she came stealthily and uncovered his feet, and lay
down. At midnight the man was startled, and turned over,
and there, lying at his feet, was a woman!
—Ruth 3:7–8 NRSV

I'm a latecomer to Christianity, and I missed that all-
important, formative time in church that most people experience: adolescence. I never had the chance to sit in the pews
making stupid jokes about the preacher, the hymns, that
god-awful soprano soloist, or the Scriptures themselves. And
I missed out on the opportunity to find sexual innuendo in
everything I heard at church, all the time.

Don't try to pretend you aren't familiar with the snigger-
ing humor to which I am referring. If you are honest with
yourself, you know that you, too, have an inner voice that
makes a dirty joke out of everything. Now that middle age
is upon me, I have decided to make it my spiritual discipline

to give voice to my inner eighth grader. I am claiming it loud and proud.

So let's talk about feet.

Yes, *feet*.

Snort! He said "feet"!

In the year that King Uzziah died, I saw the Lord sitting on a throne, high and lofty; and the hem of his robe filled the temple. Seraphs were in attendance above him; each had six wings: with two they covered their faces, and with two they covered their feet, and with two they flew. And one called to another and said:

Holy, holy, holy is the LORD of hosts;
the whole earth is full of his glory. (Isaiah 6:1–3 NRSV)

Angels cover their *feet*? What's that all about?

The first time I noticed this quizzical turn of phrase was in Isaiah 6. I was in college, taking a class in Old Testament literature, and this passage came up. The professor read the verses and looked up at the class. He waited.

Eventually one intrepid student asked, "Um, Professor, *why* are they covering their *feet*?"

"An excellent question. What do you think?" dear Dr. So-and-So replied.

We postulated a great many things that day about purity, including angels' inability to touch the ground with their feet and other foolishness. We were digging deep into our mythological memories and our collective cosmological imagination.

But the professor kept saying, "No. That's not it. Next?"

Eventually we gave up.

8

Finally the professor spoke: "'Feet' is a euphemism for genitalia."

No one said a word for what seemed like an eternity until someone giggled.

"He said 'feet.'" And it was all over. We laughed and laughed and then started quoting other Scripture verses that featured feet while the patient professor of Hebrew literature let us get it all out of our systems.

Clearly he had witnessed this particular brand of disillusionment before.

I always had assumed that angels were genderless. (Frankly I don't know why I ever gave it any thought at all.) Celestial beings don't *need* to procreate, right? I had presumed the heavenly hosts' private bits were a lot like my giant-size Luke Skywalker action figure. (Admit it: you went there when you read "giant-size," didn't you?)

I was a young kid when a large plastic Luke turned up under the Christmas tree. My action figures often needed to join me at bath time. That's right, folks. Luke and me in the bathtub with Chewy and a small phalanx of regular-size Jawas. It was a wild time in the old town, I tell you what. If memory serves, although I never mentioned anything about it to my parents, I found it curious that Luke—even the supersize Luke—was not...well...*anatomically correct*. Not that I wanted him to be, per se, but if you are going to spend that kind of money on plastic...Still, that wasn't the point of the action figure. Luke was a hero. He had his light saber (I was too young to make the Freudian connection there), and he was ready to take on Darth Vader!

Somewhere along the line, I decided that angels were a lot like Luke Skywalker, at least where their netherbits were concerned. They had other work to do. God didn't need to give them those bits. Nope. They were fully equipped to deal with the poor prophets of the Hebrew Scriptures with their swords and wings and tongs with coals. Who needs genitalia when you are a six-winged seraph wielding the holy rapier of justice?

Alas, I was wrong.

Did you know that angels have sex? (And I don't just mean that they have a gender.) I'm talking about knocking boots—or wings, at least. Yessiree. It's right there in the Bible.

> When people began to multiply on the face of the ground, and daughters were born to them, the sons of God saw that they were fair; and they took wives for themselves of all that they chose. Then the LORD said, "My spirit shall not abide in mortals forever, for they are flesh; their days shall be one hundred twenty years." The Nephilim were on the earth in those days—and also afterward—when the sons of God went in to the daughters of humans, who bore children to them. These were the heroes that were of old, warriors of renown. (Genesis 6:1–4 NRSV)

In this passage the "sons of God" are angels. And their progeny, the Nephilim, are the offspring of angelic inter-course with mortal women. Now, let's move past the fact that these must have been some powerfully good-looking women to draw God's own angels out of heaven and consider the fact that the angels actually have sexual intercourse with these women to boot (pun intended). Angels can procreate with their, um, "feet." And their kids are like the demigods, giants, and heroes of Greek mythology.

Those are some potent feet.

As I began to look a little deeper into these two stories from the Bible, it got me to wondering why this particular euphemism—*feet*, of all things—was favored. I mean, we have lots of euphemisms for human reproductive organs in our contemporary parlance. (I won't recite them here, but you may choose to do so as part of your own spiritual discipline.) With all the myriad euphemisms available to us, however, why "feet"?

So I did what any self-respecting twenty-first-century scholar of religion would do. I crowdsourced the answer via my friends on Facebook. Now, before you become outraged, I have some friends who have thought about biblical feet a great deal. These folks are scholars and professional linguists whose work it is to make sense of ancient literature on behalf of all the faithful. Happily, more than a few of them have put in a great deal of time and reflection on the esoteric nature of angels' "feet."

Here's a bit of what I learned from my scholarly friends:

- Biblical authors wrote more than just a few verses about angelic feet (or at least the euphemistic potential therein). The Hebrew word for "feet" is *regel*, which can mean "feet" or "leg"; as a root word, it can have many other permutations and possible meanings as well.

- A quick walk (sorry) through a respected lexicon shows us how the word *regel* is used, variously, as "feet," "leg," "sole," and "hoof." *Regel* also has something to do with traveling, e.g., in phrases such as "to foot it," "on foot," "go about," "explore," and "follow" (as in "obey," or "belong to").

- There are a few more poetic meanings to *regel*, including "to slander" (see 2 Samuel 19:28) or "to make a movement," as in "lift the foot."

• And then there's this: the word for the hair of one's private parts (male or female) also incorporates the same root word, *regel*.

And we're not done yet—*regel* is a very busy word.

There are some ritual habits associated with feet in the Bible. One washes one's feet when one enters the tabernacle, for instance. Scholars are pretty certain this practice involves *actual* feet and not the netherbits, but the associations were so intertwined that to wash one's feet may have been a symbol or metaphor for washing all of one's self.

According to at least one scholar, it was important to comport oneself in such a way in temple worship as to avoid accidentally flashing the Almighty with your *feet*. Here we are using the word in its sexy, euphemistic sense. Apparently this was before the era of ubiquitous undergarments. Purity codes abound in Hebrew Scripture, so it's no wonder that the ancient believers needed a more polite way to talk about human—and angelic, of course—genitalia.

Now that we've moved from angelic netherbits to the mortal variety, let's talk about Ruth and Boaz. This is perhaps the most famous of all "feet" scenes in the Hebrew Scriptures. Ruth's mother-in-law, Naomi, told her:

> "My daughter, I need to seek some security for you, so that it may be well with you. Now here is our kinsman Boaz, with whose young women you have been working. See, he is winnowing barley tonight at the threshing floor. Now wash and anoint yourself, and put on your best clothes and go down to the threshing floor; but do not make your-

self known to the man until he has finished eating and drinking. When he lies down, observe the place where he lies; then, go and uncover his feet and lie down; and he will tell you what to do." She said to her, "All that you tell me I will do."

So she went down to the threshing floor and did just as her mother-in-law had instructed her. When Boaz had eaten and drunk, and he was in a contented mood, he went to lie down at the end of the heap of grain. Then she came stealthily and uncovered his feet, and lay down. At midnight the man was startled, and turned over, and there, lying at his feet, was a woman! (Ruth 3:1–8 NRSV)

(After all this talk of innuendo, it doesn't take a whole lot of ingenuity to figure out what was going on in Boaz's bedchamber.)

So here are a few serious questions for you:

- Does sexual innuendo make any difference in our faith life?
- Does it encourage you to use your imagination in ways that might be surprising?
- Does your internal (and eternal) junior-high self have anything to offer the grown-up you?

I think so.

The ancient writers were not afraid to talk about *every* aspect of life—including netherbits (human or otherwise). God is invested in all of it. Heaven isn't some faraway place. Angelic beings are (or at least *were*) among us, and heaven is a very real part of life.

Human life is complex, and one aspect of that complexity is sexuality. We will wonder about seduction. We will ponder purity. We will try again and again to navigate and make sense of the confoundingly beautiful reality of our earthly experiences and expressions of holiness.

And from time to time, the questions and answers will make us titter like eighth graders.

Snort!

(He said "titter"!)

Spinning

Debbie Blue

The angel of the Lord also said to her, "I will so greatly multiply your descendants that they cannot be numbered for multitude." And the angel of the Lord said to her, "Behold, you are with child, and shall bear a son; you shall call his name Ishmael..."
—Genesis 16:10–11 RSV

Poet David Milch has said that a good poem, a good human being, or a good story "spins against the way it drives." There's a story the Bible wants to tell, but it keeps interrupting itself, blurting out irreverences; it spins against the way it drives. The Bible keeps undermining its own plot. It's as though some joker, or prophet, or joker-prophet followed the official storytellers around yelling out obfuscations and banging on drums to distract them. Or maybe there was a subversive scribe who just quietly planted these seeds. Or maybe it was some insurgent woman who snuck in at night replacing pages in the manuscript with her own texts to undermine the patriarchy.

Anyway, it's brilliant.

15

It's these moments that keep me coming back. It's this tendency the Bible has to unsettle itself that makes me love it.

If there's some chance (and I doubt this is very realistic, but you know we're free to imagine) that there was a woman behind some of these little anarchies, she might have something to do with this story: the story of Hagar.

I mean, why is Hagar in this book at all? There are two long, detailed stories given over to her, even though these narratives undermine, really, what the rest to the story is trying to say. This is Hebrew Scripture, after all; it's about Israel and how that particular nation came into being and where it will go. It's about Abraham's heirs through Isaac—God's blessing to the Jews. Hagar's story, however, thrusts out in an entirely different direction. It's about Abraham's other son and the other woman in his life.

Hagar's name means "other," "outsider." Who let *her* in?

For as small a role as it *seems* she should have, she's quite tremendous. To review the biblical story: Sarah, Abraham's wife, can't get pregnant. She knows there needs to be an heir, so she tells Abraham to have sex with her Egyptian maid, Hagar. Hagar gets pregnant. Mission accomplished. Sarah, theoretically, should be happy, but she's not.

Some translations say that once Hagar got pregnant, she looked at Sarah with *contempt*, but the Hebrew is actually much softer than that. It's more along the lines of "Hagar looked at Sarah with *less esteem*." This could have been because Sarah had forced Hagar to have sex with her eighty-five-year-old husband. Maybe it was because Sarah was asking her to bear a child that she'd have to give away. Maybe they'd been friends before, and now *this*. I don't know, but there seems like there could have been plenty of reasons for Hagar to look at Sarah with "less esteem."

In any case, Sarah tells Abraham that she didn't like the way Hagar looked at her. Perhaps Sarah is being a tad oversensitive and possibly paranoid. Sarah is menopausal; maybe she was prone to irritable misinterpretation.

Whatever Hagar was thinking when she looked at Sarah, Abraham allows Sarah to do what she wants with her, so Sarah "deals harshly with her." Maybe she yelled at her. Maybe she beat her. Seems like it must have been something fairly awful, because it makes Hagar flee. She goes out into the wilderness, where the angel of the Lord finds her and tells her to go back home, because "Behold, you are with child, and shall bear a son; you shall call his name Ishmael..."

This will not be the last time you will hear this line in the Bible, but it *is* the first. An angel. A pregnant woman. Remind you of anyone? Maybe the Virgin Mary? This interaction between Hagar and the angel is the first annunciation!

"Behold, you are with child, and shall bear a son; you shall call his name..."

And then God gives Hagar (a slave, a woman) the same promise God gave the patriarch Abraham. God says, "I will so greatly multiply your descendants that they cannot be numbered for multitude."

Hagar then gives this God, the God who had promised to make a great nation of her, a name. She's the first person in the Scriptures to call God by name, and it's a name she seemingly has made up on the spot. What thrilling audacity! She names God "the God who sees." (That's a pretty good name, if you ask me.)

Hagar *does* go back, and she has her son at home instead of in the wilderness—a good survival strategy. The story continues, and then Sarah (miraculously) gets pregnant and gives birth to her son, Isaac. The true heir. At the festival of Isaac's weaning (A festival of weaning? We should carry on this tradition today!), Sarah goes after Hagar again. It's a big party. Sarah's probably been drinking—after all, she's been nursing for a long time, and her son is finally weaned. Maybe she's a mean drunk. I don't know, but she sees Ishmael playing with Isaac at this party, and she gets very upset. She decides that Hagar and Ishmael should be sent to the wilderness to die.

This text invites a lot of questions.

Sarah wants to send a very little boy and his mother to their deaths? Really? Why? Some rabbinic writers defend Sarah here. They say she was a very incisive judge of humanity and knew that the two sons of Abraham could never live peacefully together. Whereas Abraham tended to be so clouded by his sense of the multifaceted quality of, well, everything and was emotionally entangled, Sarah was smart. Decisive.

Abraham, the father of faith, is so open to life that adhering to only one thing, one path, one way of seeing is impossible. But Sarah has laser-beam vision and says, "The slave woman's son will not share in the inheritance with my son." Abraham, though, being the sort of guy he is, is deeply troubled by Sarah's pronouncement. But God tells him to do what his wife says.

Some interpreters rush to say, "See! The voice of God and Sarah are *one*."

But I doubt it.

Then there's the wrenching scene in which Hagar is sent away into the desert. Abraham puts their little son on her back and gives her a small amount of water and bread. Later, when the water is gone, Hagar puts her dying boy under a bush and sits down and cries, "Please, don't make me watch my baby die!"

Can you imagine? I can.

She weeps, the child weeps, and that God she's named— the God who sees—sees! God says, "Hagar, don't be afraid. Lift up the lad and hold him fast with your hand for I will make of him a great nation."

This is definitely a story that spins against the way it drives.

The voice of Sarah and the voice of God are clearly *not* one. I'm not even sure if God has one very easily discernible voice. At any rate, God is not yielding to the official, canonical, patriarchal Hebrew plot here. It's as though the story knows what it wants to tell. Isaac is the chosen one, and the Israelites are the chosen people.

But then this intense other narrative is dropped in. Hagar and Ishmael not only survive in the wilderness, they thrive.

There's a small line at the end of the story. You might not even notice it's there, but it's startling. It's fantastic. Hagar finds a wife for her son. This is actually the only place in the entire Bible where a woman finds a wife for her son. Men find wives for their boys. It's a patriarchy: you don't let a woman mess with the bloodlines. But Hagar does. (Sometimes we accept the patriarchal nature of our Scripture as a sort of unfortunate but immovable fact, but actually there are holes in the fences.)

Hagar's story parallels Abraham's to a stunning degree. She takes Abraham's first son, Ishmael, into the wilderness, where his death seems imminent—until an angel speaks and shows her a way to survive. Abraham takes his second son, Isaac, up to Mount Moriah, where his death seems imminent—until an angel speaks and shows him a way to save his son's life. The language in the stories of the two incidents is parallel; it sometimes even uses *exactly* the same words.

Abraham is the central character in the Isaac story.

Hagar is the central character in the Ishmael story.

It's almost like: here is a matriarch on a par with a patriarch.

I love it, and I want that narrative to spin on. And you know what? It actually does. But what is so heartbreaking, so surprising, really, is that there is this great, lush, creative possibility, but it turns out to be so fraught. The story of Ishmael and Hagar creates a tension in the narrative, but as it spins on, it's not just some cool, interesting literary tension. The children of Abraham's two sons become enemies (as in violent, bombing, oppressive, tanks-driving-over-little-boys enemies).

From Isaac come the Jewish people; from Ishmael—Islam.

There aren't any more stories in the Hebrew Scripture about Hagar and Ishmael, but there are *many* stories in the Islamic tradition. Whereas Christians don't pay much attention to Hagar, in Islam she is the matriarch of monotheism, and Ishmael is Muhammad's forefather.

God-Who-Sees led Hagar into the wilderness so that, through her, a new faith might be born.

The story of Hagar in the Islamic tradition is similar to the story in the Hebrew Scripture. She's sent to the wilderness with Ishmael. She runs out of water. In a complete panic, she starts running back and forth between two hills, desperately looking for water. After her seventh run, Ishmael kicks the ground with his heel and causes a miraculous well to spring out of the ground. It's called the Zamzam Well. When Muslims make their pilgrimage to Mecca, they visit the Zamzam Well. As part of their pilgrimage, they reenact Hagar's grief by running seven times between the hills. Then they drink from the Zamzam, and they take some of the water back home in memory of Hagar.

The Kaaba is the holiest shrine in Islam, at Mecca. According to tradition it was first built by Adam and then rebuilt later by Abraham and Ishmael when Abraham came to visit his son. In the Hebrew Scripture, Abraham seems to abandon Ishmael. In the Islamic stories he keeps coming to visit him.

There's something heartbreaking and beautiful about these stories. One son is in one place, and one is in the other. Abraham trudges back and forth, the father of not one faith but two. Abraham loves both his sons. The tension created by these different narratives hasn't always turned out to be creative (it's been dreadfully destructive, of course), but couldn't it be?

I think there's often something wrong with the way we read, something that has devastating consequences.

We can't "stand alone on the Word of God," as the familiar song says: it should knock us off our feet.

Some readers say, "See? Sarah was so smart. Sarah was right. It would have been better if Hagar and Ishmael's story had just died with them in the desert. Sarah saw that Ishmael was the wild man whose progeny would oppress the chosen people forever." Clearly a Muslim reading this narrative might have something very different to say about who goes on to oppress whom.

Surely there are about a million other ways to read this, but trying to simplify the story, following only the dominant theme and ignoring the destabilizing narratives within it, seems not only less interesting but also dangerous. We need to listen for the joker's drum. We need to hear the tune that undermines. We need to do so not because it's clever to read this way but because the life of the world depends on it.

And if Scripture hardens our hearts against *anyone*, I'm pretty sure we're reading it wrong.

I like this odd, beautifully undermining little detail that pops up in the story of Joseph. When Joseph, an important figure in the official Hebrew narrative, is abandoned in the wilderness by his family (sound familiar?) and dying of thirst in a pit, a passing caravan of *Ishmaelites* saves him.

Ishmaelites save a Hebrew patriarch.

This detail in the text doesn't really fit into the history the narrative is trying to tell. There is no way that the descendants of Ishmael could really appear so soon in the story, because Ishmael wasn't much older than Joseph's grandfather, Isaac. It seems like it is just a very lovely little plant. The Hebrew is saved by the outcast.

And then there's this: after the bit about Hagar, Sarah disappears from the narrative until her death. She isn't mentioned regarding the near-sacrifice of Isaac, her beloved son. Some midrash says she dies because she couldn't face that her husband nearly sacrifices her only son. Author Avivah Zornberg suggests that it is Sarah's "laser beam vision that disentangles complexity and cuts to the quick"—the characteristic some Midrashim admire—that kills her. It makes her life unlivable when "structures and certainties are undermined."

Abraham comes across very differently from Sarah in the narrative of Hagar. He gets up early to see Hagar off, gives her food and water—his "tendrils of concern" (Zornberg's expression) don't allow him to cut "the other" off. He's greatly distressed when Sarah sends the woman and the boy away. Abraham is entangled in a complex world, and clarity is not his thing. His "thing" is something more like love. He can't simply cut off Hagar and Ishmael. God tells him to go ahead and do it, so he does. But if there are more stories to tell, and there always are, I like the ones in which he trudges back and forth between both of his beloved sons. It would be like him to do so.

Sarah, suggests Zornberg, dies because of the way she lived. She can't meet the challenge of later life, "which demands reversals, the confrontation with counter possibilities: 'What was true in the morning, will at evening have become a lie.'" Sarah can't live in the tension, can't allow counter narrative. She doesn't listen for it, but she sends it to the wilderness to die.

There are ways of practicing religion—ways of reading and living and believing—that are like this, and I'm afraid they lead to death and "deathiness," not to a flourishing life everlasting.

Near the end of Abraham's life, after Sarah has died, he marries Keturah. According to midrashic tradition, Keturah is actually Hagar's real name. Hagar was just a descriptive name, meaning "other," but Keturah was her real name. Far from cutting off the counter narrative, Abraham embraces it. Takes it into his heart. Lies in bed with it. Makes love with it. And Abraham and Hagar have many more children.

In this reading, Hagar and Abraham embrace in their old age.

The world is not hopelessly divided.

There isn't one side or the other.

May this somehow be so.

The Bible: It's Full of Crap

Karen Swallow Prior

You shall have a place outside the camp, and you shall go out
to it. And you shall have a trowel with your tools, and when
you sit down outside, you shall dig a hole with it and turn
back and cover up your excrement.
> —Deuteronomy 23:12–13 ESV

I think about crap a lot.

I mean actual crap. After all, I have horses, teach literature, and love God. Horses make me think about crap a lot
because I have to clean it up every day. Teaching literature
makes me think about crap because of my area of specializa-
tion, British literature of the eighteenth century, a very scatological age. And God? Well, my love of him and his word leads
me to think about crap, too.

Because the Bible is full of it.

I don't mean "full of it" in the sense of "baloney." On the
contrary, I believe the Bible is the inerrant, authoritative,
and inspired word of God, every jot and tittle. No, I'm talking about the scatological references dropped throughout the
Bible like fertilizer on a field. (Which, by the way, is exactly

what the Bible says in 2 Kings 9:36–37 (KJV) was the fate of the corpse of that ne'er-do-well Jezebel: "In the portion of Jezreel shall dogs eat the flesh of Jezebel: And the carcase of Jezebel shall be as dung upon the face of the field." In fact, a fair number of scatological passages in the Bible are similar warnings to those who will be destroyed and become "dung for the ground.")

Admittedly, one does have to hunt for the scatology in the Bible, since it doesn't show up in the typical Bible drill or Sunday school lesson. It can also be obscured because many English-language versions choose to employ delicate translations of the original terms. *Dung* is about as coarse as it gets in English-language Bibles, and believe it or not, we find that word most often in the poetic King James Version. (One can always count on the Elizabethans for earthiness. Just think Shakespeare.) Other translations dance around the idea with euphemisms such as *intestines, refuse, rubbish, trash, ash piles,* and even *other parts*. Nevertheless, the Bible has piles (sorry, couldn't resist!) of scatological references. The word *dung,* for example, appears more than forty times in the King James Version, according to the tally done by BibleGateway.com.

You can't really blame the ancient Israelites—or their God—for a bit of a preoccupation with waste in those pre–indoor plumbing days. Then as now, it had to be dealt with, flush or no flush. Hence the instructions in Deuteronomy 23:12–14 (ESV):

> You shall have a place outside the camp, and you shall go out to it. And you shall have a trowel with your tools, and when you sit down outside, you shall dig a hole with it and turn back and cover up your excrement. Because the LORD your God walks in the midst of your camp, to deliver you and to

give up your enemies before you, therefore your camp must be holy, so that he may not see anything indecent among you and turn away from you.

As it turns out, what's good enough for God is good for his people, too. These instructions ensure a level of sanitation that had yet to be supported by modern science, and they put the chosen people ahead of their times.

Of course, in an agrarian society, concern with waste disposal naturally extended beyond human waste. And because this was an age of ritual sacrifice, in which many of those sacrifices were animals, God supplied directions about the proper handling of their waste, too, as we see in Exodus 29:12–14 (KJV):

> And thou shalt take of the blood of the bullock, and put it upon the horns of the altar with thy finger, and pour all the blood beside the bottom of the altar. And thou shalt take all the fat that covereth the inwards, and the caul that is above the liver, and the two kidneys, and the fat that is upon them, and burn them upon the altar. But the flesh of the bullock, and his skin, and his dung, shalt thou burn with fire without the camp: it is a sin offering.

Similar commands are found in Leviticus 8:17 and 16:27 and Numbers 19:5.

But the Bible's scatological references go beyond mere sanitation engineering. One oft-cited passage is the Old Testament's graphic description of the killing of the Moabite king by the Israelite judge Ehud in Judges 3:21–22, the passage here rendered in the English Standard Version:

And Ehud reached with his left hand, took the sword from his right thigh, and thrust it into his belly. And the hilt also went in after the blade, and the fat closed over the blade, for he did not pull the sword out of his belly; and the dung came out.

But this appearance of dung is nowhere near as shocking to modern sensibilities as the rank object lesson God offered his people when he commanded the prophet Ezekiel to make and eat wheat cakes cooked on human dung within sight of the people. This prophetic act was meant as a symbol of the unclean food the Israelites would be eating in the pagan lands to which they would soon be exiled.

There's not much worse than eating food cooked on your own dung. Unless, of course, it's eating your dung. That is exactly the curse used many times in prophetic biblical texts to foretell the coming suffering of those about to endure defeat:

But Rabshakeh said, Hath my master sent me to thy master and to thee to speak these words? Hath he not sent me to the men that sit upon the wall, that they may eat their own dung, and drink their own piss with you? (Isaiah 36:12 KJV)

And as if eating one's own waste isn't bad enough, those who rebel against God were warned that they would live in their squalor, too, as stated in Ezra 6:11 (KJV):

Also I have made a decree, that whosoever shall alter this word, let timber be pulled down from his house, and being set up, let him be hanged thereon; and let his house be made a dunghill for this.

Of course, scatology proper covers all forms of excretion, and the Bible references these, too. Many Levitical laws were aimed at purification of men and women whose bodies had been made ceremonially unclean because of various bodily secretions. Such proscriptions, based as they seem to be on a view of the body as dirty, grate against modern views. Yet once again, such laws also promoted a level of sanitation that was uncommon in the ancient world.

Modern science, handy inventions, and the fulfillment of the Old Covenant with the New through the redeeming work of Christ have done away with a much of this preoccupation with our own waste. (It's important, of course, to note that the majority of people around the globe still eat, sleep, and live dangerously—often fatally—close to waste.) Even those of us with access to good soap, flushable toilets, and pristine porcelain bowls can't really remove ourselves much farther from the reality of dung, no matter how hard we try. Our illusion of being separated from it is, perhaps, what makes us shy away from the Bible's scatological passages.

That's a shame.

Sometimes we use passages from the New Testament, such as Ephesians 4:29, Ephesians 5:4, and Colossians 3:8–10, which caution us against the use of coarse language, to try to avoid the matter. But we must keep in mind that the Bible itself uses what some of us today would consider coarse language. Despite varied and culturally determined definitions of manners, distaste for dung is a constant. Let's face it: excretion of waste is an unpleasant but undeniable and unchanging aspect of the human condition.

But is there a sweet side to dung?

Well, besides making good fuel and fertilizer, it also serves as a regular reminder of the death and decay that are part of the human condition. And just as our bodies need to be rid of the waste that would otherwise be poison, so, too, must we rid ourselves of spiritual and emotional waste that would otherwise erode our souls.

Our need to eliminate also serves as a constant check on human pride. It is a humbling act, which is why we both hide these functions and flagrantly joke about them, too.

No wonder the brilliant eighteenth-century English writer Jonathan Swift employs shocking scatology in satirizing human vanity. Consider his wicked but insightful poem "The Lady's Dressing Room." Here Swift uses the discovery by a foolish lover that his angelic sweetheart actually excretes to explode all romantic illusions about the human condition.

The glory of the human condition is that we are made in the image of God. And yet in his ingenious and bewildering design, God saw fit to place the regions for creation and excreting together. As Saint Augustine famously put it, "We are born between feces and urine." By placing the most attractive and repellent parts of the human body side by side, God places our pride and our shame in wondrous tension.

The poet William Butler Yeats concludes his poem "Crazy Jane Talks with the Bishop" with these famous, startling lines:

> *But Love has pitched his mansion in*
> *The place of excrement;*
> *For nothing can be sole or whole*
> *That has not been rent.*

The verse echoes a Biblical depiction of our salvation expressed in scatological terms:

He raiseth up the poor out of the dust, and lifteth the needy
out of the dunghill. (Psalms 113:7 KJV)

We are all poor and needy, mired in dung, and in need of
salvation. Thus the apostle Paul conveyed the joy of his salvation in terms that most scholars suggest in the original Greek
are far coarser than those found in any English translation:

Yea doubtless, and I count all things but loss for the excel-
lency of the knowledge of Christ Jesus my Lord: for whom
I have suffered the loss of all things, and do count them but
dung, that I may win Christ. (Philippians 3:8 KJV)

Yes, it is a truth of the universal human condition that—as
one bumper sticker delicately puts it—excrement befalls.
But Christ lifts us up and washes us clean.
And that's no bull.

Wherever Two or Three Are Gathered

Ian Morgan Cron

When Mary came where Jesus was and saw him, she knelt
at his feet and said to him, "Lord, if you had been here, my
brother would not have died." When Jesus saw her weeping, and the Jews who came with her also weeping, he
was greatly disturbed in spirit and deeply moved. He said,
"Where have you laid him?" They said to him, "Lord, come
and see." Jesus began to weep. So the Jews said, "See how
he loved him!" But some of them said, "Could not he who
opened the eyes of the blind man have kept this man from
dying?" Then Jesus, again greatly disturbed, came to the
tomb. It was a cave, and a stone was lying against it. Jesus
said, "Take away the stone." Martha, the sister of the dead
man, said to him, "Lord, already there is a stench because
he has been dead four days." Jesus said to her, "Did I not tell
you that if you believed, you would see the glory of God?"
So they took away the stone. And Jesus looked upward and
said, "Father, I thank you for having heard me. I knew that
you always hear me, but I have said this for the sake of the
crowd standing here, so that they may believe that you

sent me." When he had said this, he cried with a loud voice, "Lazarus, come out!" The dead man came out, his hands and feet bound with strips of cloth, and his face wrapped in a cloth. Jesus said to them, "Unbind him, and let him go."

—John 11:32–44 NRSV

In May of 1999, my wife, Anne, and I received a phone call from a fellow named Steve asking whether we might be interested in starting a church in Greenwich, Connecticut. I told him that attempting to summit Everest in a T-shirt and flip-flops would be easier.

See, I grew up in Greenwich. I know the lay of the land. Thirty-five miles north of New York City, Greenwich is an idyllic New England town. With its leafy lanes, undisturbed views of Long Island Sound, and proximity to Wall Street, Greenwich is home to some of the most successful investment bankers and hedge fund managers in the world.

If Greenwich sounds like a cushy place to start a church, think again. Affluent New Englanders classify religious enthusiasm as a social disease. They'd rather be trapped in a corner at a cocktail party with someone who wants to talk about their battle with involuntary flatulence than in the same room with a Christian talking about Jesus. In other words, these camels couldn't squeeze through the eye of the Holland Tunnel, never mind the eye of a needle.

But alas, Steve talked me into coming to meet with him and his team and, regrettably, they were wonderful and persuasive people. Two trips from Denver to Greenwich and countless phone calls later, Steve and his friends offered me the position. Rather than popping open the Champagne and celebrating, I became emotionally incontinent. Throughout the interview process I managed to suppress a deep-seated insecurity about both my Bible knowledge and my preaching abilities.

Most pastors in Greenwich receive their master of divinity degrees from prestigious schools such as Yale and Princeton. On graduation day they're handed Latin-inscribed diplomas the size of movie posters. I, on the other hand, graduated from a no-name evangelical seminary with my master's degree in counseling psychology and a diploma that resembled the certificate I was given when I passed driver's ed.

As a student on an MA counseling track, I was required to take only one class in biblical studies. One might want more than "Introduction to the New and Old Testaments" under one's belt before starting a church for people who believe the word of God flows from the pages of the *Wall Street Journal*.

To complicate matters further, I'd had a confidence-killing experience in an expository preaching class I took as an elective. As an artist who was raised and educated by Roman Catholics, I viewed the Scriptures more *sacramentally* than *dialogically*. For me, the Bible was the story that explained the way the world is, not the "manufacturer's operating instructions for living," as my classmates called it.

In my mind, Scripture was a suggestive and evocative painting, not a black-and-white photograph a defense attorney could present to a jury during closing arguments as irrefutable evidence that their case rested on facts and was therefore true. I realized there would be little room for my perspective in the evangelical world when on the first day of class the professor handed out a five-hundred-question multiple-choice exam to test our knowledge of the Bible. Or, in my case, our lack thereof.

My classmates grew up attending Ivy League Sunday schools, and several were five-time Bible Jeopardy champions. They blew through the test, then went outside to drink coffee and celebrate inerrancy while I was still at my desk trying to answer the question "How long was King Og's bed?"

Over the course of the semester, each student was required to preach three expository sermons in front of the class. The professor swooned as my classmates dissected and explained assigned texts with surgical precision. He brushed away tears and blew his nose when they closed their discourses with anecdotes like the one about the blind kid who scores the game-winning touchdown while his recently deceased father proudly looks on from heaven. (Who knew responsible adults let little blind kids play football?)

I, on the other hand, blasphemed the Holy Spirit because I preached "topical" sermons that didn't "plainly, accurately, relevantly, and without addition, subtraction, or falsification" let the Bible speak for itself, and concluded them by reading lines from Mary Oliver's poetry. I received a D in expository preaching, the lowest grade in the class and in my seminary career.

My wife, Anne, listened patiently as I rehearsed my history and confessed how scared I was about taking a position in which I would be expected to do things I wasn't good at, such as knowing and explaining the Bible. The next morning I awoke and found a note left on my bedside table saying, "Mother Teresa doesn't read the Bible in the original Greek."

With fear and trembling I took the job.

———

My first years as founding pastor of Greenwich Community Church were hard. Because we didn't have a building, my Subaru Outback served as the church office. I began a Saturday morning men's Bible study in the bar of a local country club. The guys were smart, and they took perverse pleasure in playing Stump the Pastor. I had to read countless books and commentaries so we didn't end up spending sixty minutes trading ignorance in a saloon with mahogany walls that reeked of expensive cigars and single-malt Scotch.

We held our Sunday services in a dreary middle school auditorium that one of our high school kids said "smelled like ass." There were Sunday mornings when I arrived to set up for church only to find that a school musical had been performed on the stage the night before. "Real" ministers in town wore robes and expounded the word of God from behind ornately carved pulpits while I sweated through sermons in front of the garishly painted sets of *Grease* and *Oklahoma!*.

Curious visitors peeked their heads through the doors, but when they saw our five-piece worship band playing contemporary music and video loops of floating votive candles projected onto two giant screens, they hightailed it back to their Lexuses and sped out of the parking lot. Still, I was determined. Day after day, week after week, I put my head down and trudged forward like a mule in a snowstorm.

It took what seemed like forever, but we began to grow. Couples were married, babies were baptized, we held on to each other when several of our members died on 9/11, and while in our company, more than one or two souls fell in love with Jesus.

But after nine years, my gut told me I was gathering someone else's crop. God made me a planter, not a harvester, so one January I announced I would be departing in June. As my farewell Sunday approached, I began thinking about my successes and failures as a pastor. Most of the fears that dogged me when the church began turned out to be no more than scarecrows, but what I feared most when we set out on our journey proved to be true: I really was a sad-ass expository preacher, and my people suffered for it.

Throughout my pastorate I tortured myself by comparing myself to master expository preachers whose messages I downloaded and listened to in my car. Some church members measured me against them as well. Every Monday morning I received four or five e-mails from folks complaining that they were tired of "milky sermons" when they needed "solid food."

You'd think after nine years I would've gotten over my insecurity and told people like them not to let the door hit them in the ass on the way out, but I didn't. Like them, I felt I was failing to give my flock an accurate, relevant, and clear understanding of the Bible (without addition, subtraction, or falsification, of course).

That's when God sent us a twenty-eight-year-old Jamaican man named James Ellis.

A church member named Bill brought James to church. The two of them had become fast friends while working on a grounds crew for a local landscaping company. James was in his late twenties and had migrated to the United States from Jamaica only a year earlier.

James was shy when he first arrived, but that didn't last. Soon he was coaxing sockless men in Gucci loafers and women clad in pink-and-lime-green floral dresses to dance with him during the music portion of our worship services. It was like watching a group of Mitt Romney and Nancy Reagan impersonators Hula-hooping. James's laugh was throaty and cocoa-sweet. He shouted, "Glad you're here, mon," to newcomers, and he taught people who typically embraced each other sideways how wonderful it was to receive a full-body hug. James was deeply loved.

A few months before I announced my decision to leave,

James approached me after church one day to ask if I had a few minutes to talk. It was a fine autumn day, so we grabbed what was left of the fellowship-hour coffee and sat on a bench near the school playground. James filled me in about the woman he was dating. He told me about his struggle to send money home to his family in Jamaica and pay his own bills at the same time.

"Pastor, I'd like to become a plumber," he said, abruptly changing the subject.

"James, that sounds great," I said. "How does one do that?"

James smiled at my lack of knowledge about the world of plumbing. "First you have to be an apprentice, then take an exam. I've been working nights and weekends with a master plumber, but now I have to take the test."

I smiled. "You're almost done, right?" I said.

A shadow passed over James's face, and he grew quiet. He bowed his head and gazed down at the pavement.

"Is something wrong, James?" I asked, leaning forward.

James sat up and stared into the distance at a stand of maples whose leaves had survived the previous night's rainstorm.

"I can't take the exam, Pastor," he said, pinching the bridge of his nose to prevent tears from breaching the banks of his eyelids.

I frowned. "Why not?"

James took a deep breath and exhaled like a swimmer mustering the courage to jump off the high dive.

"I don't know how to read," he whispered.

If I've learned one thing as a pastor, it's that there is a room in every heart behind whose door a sorrow is hidden from view like an unmade bed. I am silenced whenever I'm invited into such a room.

With James's permission, I pulled together a small group

of folks from church to hear him tell his story and to ask if or how they could help. Looking back, I'm glad I wasn't able to be there for the occasion. It made what followed all the more beautiful to witness.

A few days after this meeting took place, I learned that a fund had been set up for James. Contributions would go to an adult literacy specialist who would work with him. A family in the church invited James to live in their home rent-free so he could afford to work fewer hours and dedicate more time to his reading homework and studying for his plumber's license.

Soon after that, an easel appeared beside the honey-colored oak doors that led into the auditorium where we worshipped, along with a sign-up sheet. Members of the congregation would sign up for one-hour sessions so that they could listen to James practice reading each week. By the time services were over that Sunday, every time slot had been filled.

The more the community grew in its love and commitment to James, the more we sensed God's love and commitment to us. During the Prayers of the People, folks seated near James laid their hands on him and asked God to shower favor on his work. One night I found our high school youth group sitting in a circle on beanbags listening to James read from his workbook. Every time he successfully completed a page, they snapped their fingers like beatniks expressing appreciation for a poet reading from a new chapbook.

Our annual church picnic was always held on the third Sunday after Pentecost. The previous year we were rained out, but not this time: it was a bright June morning, the cherry and dogwood trees were bursting, and the flower beds on either side of the walkway that led to the entrance of the school were teeming with daffodils and marigolds.

I'd like to believe church was packed that day because I

was leaving two weeks later, but I think the elders' decision to allow people to bring wine and beer to the picnic jacked up the numbers more than anything else. One wry saint suggested the church adopt the motto "Wherever two or three are gathered, there's always a fifth."

On a typical Sunday, our order of worship began with singing, followed by community prayers and announcements, after which someone came forward to read the Scripture. I always sat in the front row and looked at my notes as the lector broke open the word.

On this Sunday, however, I didn't hear the reader's footsteps coming down the aisle. For a moment I wondered if the person who volunteered had forgotten to mark it on his calendar. I was about to get up and read it myself when I heard the sound of six hundred people turn around and rise to their feet. Not sure what was going on, I stood up and looked back.

It was James.

He was processing down the aisle wearing a dark brown suit and a yellow-and-red striped necktie, and he was carrying a Bible.

James walked across the stage, took his place at the microphone, and tugged the red ribbon marking his page. His Bible was so new you could hear the binding crack through the microphone as he opened it. He waited for the congregation to take their seats, but no one seemed to think that sitting was the right posture to take at that moment. So James cleared his throat and began.

"There was a man named Lazarus who was sick..."

With those nine words, all of us were filled with awe, like those who once watched the apostles perform their many signs and wonders. Our eyes were opened as James read to us the story of an illness that didn't end in death but instead brought glory to God. Many of us had heard or read this passage a thousand times, but this was a strange and beautiful translation. How had we missed the oceanic depth of Jesus' love for Lazarus, the way he wept for him, the import of his claim "I am the Resurrection"? We were as stunned as the people who were actually present when Jesus commanded his friend to come out from the tomb—and he did.

When James was finished, he walked back to his seat while hundreds of softened and beaming faces followed him the way sunflowers follow the sun. I'm not sure how long we stood there feeling God's joy pressing down on us, but it was long enough for me to realize that the entire Bible could be reduced to one idea: God is in the resurrection business.

It's fine if folks want to know the length of Og's bed, how many chariots and horsemen the Philistines had when they fought the Israelites, or what color socks Goliath was wearing when David slew him, but if you don't know that we live in a multichance universe created by a God who loves us, who weeps for us, and who uses his people to call each other out from their tombs, then you don't know anything about the Bible.

I may have never excelled at expository preaching, but over the years—mysteriously, imperceptibly, and in spite of all my insecurities and shortcomings—the Bible had found its way into the bones and blood of my people.

There was no sermon, no collection, no Eucharist, and no benediction that Sunday. We'd heard with our own ears, and seen with our own eyes, someone whom we had touched with our own hands speak the word. Our joy was complete.

From the back of the auditorium, some fool cried out, "The word of the Lord," and we all responded with a resounding "Thanks be to God!" before racing outside to break bread together beneath an umbrella of crystalline blue sky.

The Gentle Fatalism of Ecclesiastes

LaVonne Neff

> Go thy way, eat thy bread with joy, and drink thy wine with
> a merry heart.
>> —Ecclesiastes 9:7 KJV

Some people have biblical life texts. My father had a life *book*,
and so do I.

Dad's life book was the book of Job. I don't know why:
he did not have a victim's mind-set, and his life was no more
troubled than most. Maybe it had something to do with an
uncle he'd never met. According to family lore, this uncle was
nameless until he turned twenty-one, whereupon he named
himself Job. I learned more about Great Uncle Job when I was
researching relatives online. He died the day after his sixty-
sixth birthday in a psychiatric hospital in Kalamazoo, Michigan. His occupation was listed as "sweeper."

By contrast, my father was a respected college professor
with lots of friends, a well-deserved reputation for kindness,

and a capacity to make the best of any situation, including, eventually, Alzheimer's disease and life in a nursing home. ("I have a wonderful view from my window," he repeatedly told me.) And yet he loved Job and even wrote a book about him. When Dad died, that book—*Saint Under Stress*—was lying on a chair near the bookcase, as if he had taken it out to read it once more before departing.

I like Job, but I'm a baby boomer, and we boomers don't get suffering the way people who lived through two world wars and the Great Depression did. My generation grew up listening to Pete Seeger's "Turn! Turn! Turn!" as performed first by Judy Collins and then the Byrds; my life book is Ecclesiastes.

How weary of the world we adolescents were (when we weren't proclaiming the dawning of the Age of Aquarius). "What has been is what will be, and what has been done is what will be done; there is nothing new under the sun" (NRSV). Pleasure is pointless. Money disappoints. Labor is vain. Everything is a chasing after wind, which is where, my friend, the answers are blowin'.

Ecclesiastes was my kind of book.

Granted, chapter 12 could be annoying, and it was the only chapter anyone ever quoted at youth group meetings (and always in the King James Version):

> Remember now thy Creator in the days of thy youth, while the evil days come not, nor the years draw nigh, when thou shalt say, I have no pleasure in them... Fear God, and keep his commandments: for this is the whole duty of man. For God shall bring every work into judgment, with every secret thing, whether it be good, or whether it be evil. (v. 1, 13–14)

Oh, be careful, little hands, what you do!

But even chapter 12—which was probably an add-on, anyway, written by scribes who didn't like the gentle fatalism of the rest of the book—had its redeeming parts. The description of old age, I thought then, was a hoot. (It is not quite as funny now that I have a Medicare card.) And even though I have always loved to read and indeed ended up with a career in publishing, I still appreciated the observation that "of making many books there is no end; and much study is a weariness of the flesh" (v. 12).

And yet Ecclesiastes' famous bits aren't the reason I fell in love with the book. The parts that grabbed my attention were 2:24:

There is nothing better for a man, than that he should eat and drink, and that he should make his soul enjoy good in his labour.

And 3:13:

And also that every man should eat and drink, and enjoy the good of all his labour, it is the gift of God.

And 5:18:

[I]t is good and comely for one to eat and to drink, and to enjoy the good of all his labour that he taketh under the sun all the days of his life, which God giveth him: for it is his portion.

And 8:15:

Then I commended mirth, because a man hath no better thing under the sun, than to eat, and to drink, and to be

merry: for that shall abide with him of his labour the days of
his life, which God giveth him under the sun.

And especially 9:7–9:

Go thy way, eat thy bread with joy, and drink thy wine with
a merry heart; for God now accepteth thy works.

Let thy garments be always white; and let thy head lack
no ointment.

Live joyfully with the wife whom thou lovest all the
days of the life of thy vanity, which he hath given thee under
the sun, all the days of thy vanity: for that is thy portion in
this life, and in thy labour which thou takest under the sun.

When I first discovered those verses, they shocked me.

Like many Christians, I suffer from a mildly ascetic con-
science, though my problem isn't as serious as that of whoever
changed the words of "All People That on Earth Do Dwell"
(a paraphrase of Psalm 100) from "him serve with *mirth*" to
"him serve with *fear*."

There is apparently something very scary about mirth.

Wait, I thought—you mean "Eat, drink, and be merry, for
tomorrow we die" isn't a warning?

Is the Preacher saying that work should make us happy?

Is he actually advising us to *party*?

Well, Jesus had a reputation for being a glutton and a
winebibber, didn't he? And though admittedly his life was
short, his early death does not seem to have resulted from the
fact that he loved his job and enjoyed good meals with friends.

In fact, Scripture consistently teaches that *created things are
good*. It commands God's people to keep feasts. It observes that
wine "maketh glad the heart of man" (Ps. 104:15 KJV). It tells

us that bread and wine are Christ's very body, just as Christ's gathered people are his body. It makes sense of the little ditty ascribed to satirist Hilaire Belloc, a concise description of why I eventually became a Catholic in spite of a Seventh-day Adventist upbringing:

Wherever the Catholic sun doth shine
There's music and laughter and good red wine.
At least I've always found it so:
Benedicamus Domino.

I don't know why my father loved Job.

I'm thinking it might have been because of Job's unswerving loyalty to God, no matter what. Or maybe it was God's commitment to Job that comforted my dad. At my father's funeral in 1995, we read Job 19:25–26: "For I know that my redeemer liveth, and that he shall stand at the latter day upon the earth: And though after my skin worms destroy this body, yet in my flesh shall I see God" (KJV).

I think Dad would have liked that.

There are many reasons why I love Ecclesiastes. It's jam-packed with pithy quotations, clever book titles, catchy song lyrics, and wry observations. All that helps. It includes that wonderful advice to eat, drink, and be merry. But I'm not attracted to happy-clappy Christians, those people who fixate on silver linings and really don't know clouds at all.

(Maybe there's more Job in my DNA than I realize.)

I think what I love most about Ecclesiastes is its realism.

The world sucks, says the Preacher. You can't control it: in the long run, what you do doesn't matter a whole lot. You're going to die. So given that, what should you do in the meantime? How about enjoying what you've got? Work, friends, family, food, wine, raindrops on roses, and whiskers on kittens.

This was helpful advice when I was a teenager.

It's even more helpful now, as I approach old age. I may be close, as Shakespeare put it in Sonnet 73, to "That time of year... / When yellow leaves, or none, or few, do hang / Upon those boughs which shake against the cold, / Bare ruined choirs, where late the sweet birds sang." The appropriate response, however, is neither despair nor forced piety but, as Shakespeare says, "to love that well which thou must leave ere long."

But I confess that the bit of Ecclesiastes wisdom I most treasure—and certainly the one I quote most often—is this great advice from 7:16 (KJV):

> Be not righteous over much; neither make thyself over wise: why shouldest thou destroy thyself?

One, Single Life

Ina Albert

Therefore was man created singly, to teach you that whoever destroys a single life from Israel is considered by Scripture as if he had destroyed an entire world and that whoever
preserves a single life from Israel is considered by Scripture
as if he had preserved an entire world.

—Talmud Bavli, Art Scroll Series, Tractate Sanhedrin, folio 37a

An American couple looked sorrowfully at the tarpaper
shacks of Lusaka, Zambia's capital. To them the city was a
contradiction in terms. It boasted of being the most successful commercial center in the country, but many of its people
were among the nation's poorest and lived in the most over-
crowded conditions.

The trip to Zambia that day was made even more unpleasant
by their guide, Charles, who, resenting his clients' imagined
wealth and comfort, stopped to make a phone call (and smoke
a cigarette) on the outskirts of one of the city's most dilapidated
compounds.

The day was hot and unusually humid for this area of the
country, so the woman opened the door and stepped out of

the Jeep to cool herself and look for a store where she could buy something to drink. As she scanned the dusty street, her eyes fell upon a child sitting on the side of the road. He had the largest and most haunting eyes she had ever seen, and she was inescapably drawn to him.

"I must speak to that child," she told her husband, and she walked over to the boy and sat down on a bench beside him.

"What is your name?" she asked, not knowing if he spoke English.

"Matemwe," he whispered.

"Come sit with me," she said.

The boy smiled up at her and surprised her by sitting on her lap. As his body collapsed against hers, she felt his heart pounding rapidly against her breast in an uneven, sickly rhythm. He was a small boy, reed-thin, dirty, and exhausted. His clothes smelled of grime and sweat, and the flesh of his arms and legs was drawn tight over his bones. Yet his haunting eyes and bright smile were open and welcoming. Her fingers stroked his cheek, brushing perspiration and street soot away.

In the distance, an old man wearing a long robe and carrying a walking stick stood watching her. She called to him.

"What's wrong with this child?" she asked.

"Oh, he has a bad heart," the man said.

"Where are his parents?" the woman asked.

"His parents died last year. He is alone. He has no home; he begs for food and sleeps in doorways. Because the villagers believe he will die soon, none of them wants to waste what little they have on helping him."

"Arthur," she called to her husband. "See if Charles will take you to a store and get something for him to eat. And water, please."

Ten minutes later, Arthur returned with a few fresh rolls

of bread, a mango, and bottled water while the woman held Matemwe close, unable to let him go. His young eyes held her in their spell, and his optimistic smile and stumbling English enchanted her.

"It's time to leave, madame," said their guide, impatient with her involvement in what he believed was none of her business, wanting to cut it short. "Now!"

As they left, the woman reached into her bag, found a New York Mets T-shirt, and handed it to Matemwe, tears tumbling down her cheeks. She told him she loved him and that she'd see him again. Then she climbed into the Jeep and headed down the road to catch a plane to Tanzania.

"I want to help that boy," she said, weeping, as Arthur listened, frozen, not knowing what to do or say to console her. "I know there are thousands of street children, but my rabbi told me that the Talmud says if you save just one person, you save the whole world. I pray that this boy will be our one."

After Tanzania, the couple returned to their home in New England. Back at work, she dedicated her next newspaper column to telling Matemwe's story and asking readers to join in an effort to save this one child, who would surely die on the streets of Lusaka if something were not done.

"Let this boy be our one," she wrote.

In the days that followed, doctors and hospitals in the city promised to treat Matemwe without charge if the husband and wife could bring him to the United States. Newspaper readers sent thousands of dollars to pay for his transportation, and eighteen months later, Matemwe finally arrived. They arranged for several Zambian women who spoke the child's native dialect to be with them and instructed the hospital's admitting department to be ready for his arrival.

As the boy came through the doorway and entered the

arrivals lounge at the airport, he looked even smaller than the woman remembered, and his eyes, which had haunted her through the months of waiting for permission to bring him to America, were anxious and fearful.

As the couple rushed forward to comfort the boy, Matemwe smiled in recognition and snuggled up to the woman as he had on the dusty bench in Zambia.

The hospital staff was waiting for him, and after examinations, tests, and treatment for malaria, an operation was scheduled. His faulty heart valve was replaced, and he was on the road to health.

As the couple watched at his bedside through weeks of recovery, they became more and more attached to the child. One day as they hovered over Matemwe's sleeping body, their eyes met, and, without needing words, they nodded to each other. They would adopt him as their own.

He would be their one.

As they left the hospital to take Matemwe to their suburban home, the husband noticed an old man in a long robe standing on the corner, watching them.

"That man looks familiar," Arthur said to his wife.

But when she turned to look, the old man was gone.

The couple moved from New England to Southern California to live among old friends in a climate more similar to that of Matemwe's homeland. They enrolled him in school, took him to church, coached him in English, taught him how to run, how to swim, and how to play soccer, and they watched his smile broaden each day. His undernourished, thirty-five-pound body was replaced by the fullness of a healthy nine-year-old who could ride his bike, run on the soccer pitch, and surf the ocean.

Several years later, the woman returned to Zambia on a work trip. She brought her son with her, along with gifts for his half brother and extended family and a pledge that the boy, when he became a man, would not forget them.

"I'll return to you when I have learned enough to help you," he promised.

That fall, Matemwe planned to be baptized in the Pacific Ocean, which he surfed and swam in almost daily. The ritual took place on the beach in the presence of the entire community. The day was warm, the sky clear and bright, and the smell of salt air rode on the warm breeze.

The woman asked her rabbi and his wife, Matemwe's "Jewish grandparents," to give him a Hebrew name, because if it were not for the Talmudic quotation, Matemwe might never have become their son.

The boy bowed his head prayerfully as his adoptive grandparents wrapped him in a prayer shawl.

"We bless you in love and name you David, which means 'beloved' in Hebrew. Your light grows in love and is nurtured in beauty as was the biblical David—a poet, psalmist, musician, and king," the rabbi and his wife said together.

With that, Matemwe punched the air triumphantly, ran to the water, and dove into the waves.

Sitting alone on the sand, watching the ceremony, was an old man. His robe draped around him. His walking stick rested on the sand.

He held out his hands in blessing as Matemwe walked out of the ocean. The boy paused for a moment to acknowledge the stranger. They did not speak.

One evening years later, as Matemwe walked along that same beach, he reached the spot where he had been baptized and noticed the same old man sitting by the water's edge. This time the man spoke to him.

"When you came to us, your light was dim, your energy weak," he said. "Though your body needed healing, your spirit never wavered. In your eyes, we all saw a bright future born of pain, solitude, and great courage. At a young age you survived against all odds and did so with grace.

"And so your mother, Grace, found you. Grace healed you. Grace brought you back to life. Grace gave you love," he said. "Your light is strong now. It is time for you to share your power. You've grown in love with people of wisdom and courage around you. It is time to help others share the light of love as well. Therefore, Love will be your guide."

The old man raised his hands in blessing: "May the Creator bless you and keep you. May Spirit cause light to shine upon you. And may Spirit bring you and those you touch love and peace. Amen."

The old man looked into Matemwe's eyes and knew that he understood.

Then he watched Matemwe walk away, knowing that the young man's light would bless his loved ones, his community, and the entire family of beings.

And that saving one of us is indeed the salvation of all of us.

The Inerrant [comma] Inspired [comma] Infallible Word of God

Dale Hanson Bourke

All scripture is given by inspiration of God, and is profitable for doctrine, for reproof, for correction, for instruction in righteousness: That the man of God may be perfect, thoroughly furnished unto all good works.

—2 Timothy 3:16–17 KJV

I was not a disrespectful child, but I had an active imagination. I was inquisitive, a trait often mistaken for impertinence by my conservative religious community. It was perhaps inevitable, then, that my imagination combined with my never-ending questions would lead to a Sunday school class showdown and a crisis of faith.

It all started one Sunday with a fiery sermon by our Baptist pastor, who was preaching against those liberals who threatened our very way of life by reinterpreting the word of God. Rumor had it that a group of apostates ("a *so-called* group of biblical scholars") was creating a new translation of the Bible. My pastor held up his well-worn Scofield Reference Bible and declared, "*This* is the only inerrant, inspired, infallible word of God, and no one can tell me any different."

He then quoted 2 Timothy 3:16–17: "All scripture is given by inspiration of God, and is profitable for doctrine, for reproof, for correction, for instruction in righteousness: That the man of God may be perfect, thoroughly furnished unto all good works" (KJV). The sermon centered on that first phrase, and the pastor was, as my father observed, "on a roll." This particular pastor was a yeller, a preaching style that involved choosing a single word and giving it repeated emphasis. This Sunday the word was *all*.

"*All* Scripture...*ALL. ALL. ALL.*" (At this point his voice was so loud that I sank down into the pew and plugged my ears until I felt a jab from each of my parents.) "*ALL!* That means every single last word. Every syllable. Every comma, every period. *ALL!* It's *ALL* right here," he said, holding up his Bible again. "*ALL* inerrant. *ALL* inspired. *ALL* infallible. And if anyone changes one word or one comma, he or she is sinning against God." The sermon continued for nearly an hour, and at first I amused myself by counting the number of times the pastor yelled "all." But eventually I grew bored, and my imagination took over.

I thought of a popular television show in which the boss dictated letters to his secretary.

Was that how God did it?

Did he dictate the Bible to the apostles?

But what if God talked too fast, and one of the apostles missed a word?

What if God forgot to say "comma," and the apostle just wrote the sentence without a comma?

Was the apostle allowed to add one in? Would that be a sin? Could an apostle go to hell because he added a comma?

In the television show, the boss's dictation and the misunderstandings of his secretary were often fodder for humor. But this was serious business. How could we know for sure that every single punctuation mark was directed by God?

I took my questions to my long-suffering Sunday school teacher, who had planned a lesson on some much safer topic.

I simply couldn't contain myself.

"But what if..."

She tried to explain divine inspiration, but she took a slightly less dramatic stand than the pastor. For some reason, it was the notion of a misplaced comma that really had me concerned. We were learning punctuation in school, and commas were eluding me. They seemed so arbitrary until the pastor equated them with sinning. I really needed to have more answers, so I kept raising my hand until my Sunday school teacher finally had enough.

She told me I had to stop questioning and have faith. Then she pulled out all the stops and told me I was sinning by asking so many questions about commas. That stopped me cold. I did not want to go to hell because of commas. Or question marks, for that matter.

From that day on, I took extra care with commas. But mostly I tried to avoid discussions about "the inerrant, inspired, infallible word of God." I knew it was a basic tenet of evangelical belief, but I was never sure how literally I should take it. I tried to stuff down all my concerns and confusion and just believe. Truth be told, however, I still wondered if it really applied to every comma.

Eventually I went off to a Christian college with my own Scofield Reference Bible, only to discover students and professors there with other versions of the Bible. They didn't *seem* like sinners. Many seemed deeply faithful. Maybe, just maybe, it was okay to read another version of God's word. One day at the student bookstore, I bought a copy of the Living Bible. It was a paperback with pictures of young people on the cover, so different from my staid, leather-bound Bible.

I felt as if I was buying something illicit.

Then I began to read it, and I couldn't put it down. I read it instead of doing my homework. I skipped outings with friends so I could keep reading. I began to highlight and underline and make notes in the margins. I fell in love with the words and never once wondered about the commas.

In 2 Timothy I found the passage quoted by my pastor so many years before; the words that had stopped me in my tracks and in some ways stunted my growth as a Christian. "All scripture is inspired by God and is useful to teach us what is true and to make us realize what is wrong in our lives. It corrects us where we are."

All was still there.

But there was so much more.

It wasn't just about commas. It was about *inspiration*. The word of God had come alive to me, and I began to read it to tell me how to live my life, to show me what was true, to correct me where I was. Even more amazingly, verses I had read before had new meaning to me. It was as if God were speaking directly to me, knowing exactly the situation I faced.

I had even more questions, which I took to my kind theology professor. I began to ask him about inerrancy and inspiration, and he smiled patiently and listened. Then he did something surprising. He asked me questions. He asked what I thought about inerrancy, and I spilled out my story about commas. He chuckled. Then he asked me what I thought about inspiration. And I began to tell him about my recent experience of reading the Bible and not being able to stop. I told him how I felt God was speaking just to me, that even though the words had been written so many centuries before, they seemed so perfect.

The professor smiled and then said something surprising. "You know God cares about something even more specific than commas," he said.

I panicked for a minute, thinking he was dooming me to more nightmares about punctuation.

Then he continued: "He cares about every hair on your head. He cares about every question you have. He cares about *you.*"

I left his office feeling better but wishing he had simply given me the answers. I was still struggling with the idea that God had time to care about *me.* I had learned all about God's rules, but I'd heard less about God's love. Day after day, I read my Bible and asked God to help me understand.

Later that week, my writing professor announced that, having read some of our early papers, he felt we needed a grammar review.

"Today, commas," he announced.

I dissolved into laughter.

"Do you think commas are funny?" the professor asked.

Trying to suppress my amusement, I said, "No, sir. I think they are very, very serious."

The End of the World as We Know It

Katherine Willis Pershey

> Therefore keep watch because you do not know when the
> owner of the house will come back—whether in the eve-
> ning, or at midnight, or when the rooster crows, or at dawn.
> If he comes suddenly, do not let him find you sleeping. What
> I say to you, I say to everyone: "Watch!"
> —Mark 13:35–37 NIV

Sometimes Jesus sounds far too much like a character from
the apocalyptic Christian novel *Left Behind* for my personal
comfort. In the thirteenth chapter of Mark, gentle Jesus (meek
and mild?) describes a whole host of terrifying events, from the
fall of the Second Temple to the shaking of the earth's crust.
He claims that this is but the beginning of the "birth pains."

The chapter is bombastic, an apocalyptic crescendo of
despair and hope. Every sort of warning bell clangs: watch
out for the false prophets, and while you're at it, keep watch
for "the Son of Man coming in clouds with great power and

glory" (v. 26). There are visions of darkened moons and fallen stars and prophecies of betrayal and suffering. It all culminates with the foreboding cry: "If he comes suddenly, do not let him find you sleeping" (v. 36).

Batten down the hatches, folks; it's the end of the world as we know it.

Or not.

When I was a kid growing up near Cleveland, Ohio, a new alternative radio station—107.9, the End—announced its inception by playing the same song for twenty-four hours straight. Up to that point, the station—previously known as WPHR, Power 108—had been my preteen favorite for mainstream pop music, so the song the new management chose to repeat was a perfect reflection of my adolescent despair: "It's the End of the World as We Know It" by R.E.M.

In the refrain, Michael Stipe sings the title, over and over (and over) again. Apparently some people got nervous that the apocalypse was actually upon us and called the station in a panic. (At least, that's how the story goes. Maybe they were really just panicked that there would be no more New Kids on the Block.)

The marketers for the movie *2012* certainly tapped into the collective fear that lurks beneath the surface and stoked it for all it was worth in order to draw attention and ticket buyers to the apocalyptic blockbuster. The seed for that particular hysteria came from the overcooked rumor that the ancient Mayan calendar ended in 2012. No matter that the simpler explanation is that the calendar is a cycle that repeats itself every few millennia or so; it's more exciting to imagine all the horrible things that might happen as time skids to a halt. One of the promotional posters for the anything-but-timeless *2012* pictured a Buddhist monk standing on a mountain in the Himalayas as the water level rose to the top.

Personally, I am far more concerned with the incremental rising of the ocean level caused by climate change than with the off chance that the seas might suddenly overtake Mount Everest in an apocalyptic hurricane. I am also much more concerned with the words of Jesus than with the ways in which countless Christians have twisted them into something they are not. Despite the fact that Jesus warns against the deceivers who will make arrogant claims, there is a vivid and storied history of Christian doomsayers claiming to have cracked the code revealing when Christ will come again in glory. Invariably, the story they tell is a gory one, littered with bad news for all but the few who are chosen and/or saved.

I hate picking on other people's theology. I really do. As a pastor in a liberal Christian denomination, I'm all about theological diversity and religious tolerance. But I am downright *allergic* to certain strains of Christian end-times prophecies.

Perhaps it's because I had a particularly scary childhood experience: one of my elementary school friends told me in great detail about how the end of the world was coming. A beast was going to mark people's foreheads with the number 666, and if my family and I didn't get saved we were all going to suffer a horrible tribulation and go to hell.

I was like, "Um, I'm Methodist. Does that mean I'm covered?"

But in truth, it scared the bejesus out of me, and it made me scared of Jesus.

I followed her instructions to invite him into my heart roughly seventeen times. I didn't know how to make sure he was there, and I didn't want to risk the flames of hell if he wasn't. I didn't pray the Sinner's Prayer because I was a contrite and sincere believer moved by the love of God. I prayed it because if I didn't, God would come and get me. It breaks my heart that my first Christology was not that Jesus is fully human and fully divine, but that Jesus is the sacred boogeyman.

That being said, I can totally see how easy it is to take some of these confounding messages and run with them. At one point in his speech, Jesus' words are absolutely chilling: "When you see 'the abomination that causes desolation' standing where it does not belong—let the reader understand—then let those who are in Judea flee to the mountains. Let no one on the housetop go down or enter the house to take anything out. Let no one in the field go back to get their cloak. How dreadful it will be in those days for pregnant women and nursing mothers! Pray that this will not take place in winter, because those will be days of distress unequaled from the beginning, when God created the world, until now—and never to be equaled again" (v. 14–19).

These words are taken literally and interpreted wildly, and that's a dangerous combination. But it is equally dangerous to ignore them completely.

So here goes: What on earth does this all mean?

For the love of God, *let the reader understand* (Mark 13:14, NIV).

I know what makes the most sense to me. I believe—or at least try to believe—that these apocalyptic visions are ultimately about hope. Not destruction, not fear, not doom, not death. Hope.

The fact of the matter is this: things *are* bad. Here is where I could insert any number of statistics demonstrating the cold, hard numbers of how bad things are—the rates of poverty and violent crime and the prevalence of HIV and AIDS in sub-Saharan Africa. Or I could tell any number of heartbreaking stories illustrating the breadth and depth of suffering in the world today. But you don't need statistics or stories to believe this one. Like the monkeys who hear no evil, see no evil, and speak no evil, we often try to block out the atrocities that fill every newspaper. But the evil is there. And I mean *evil*. There is no doubt in my mind that there is evil. The only reason I'm not so keen on the idea of the devil is because I think it only minimizes the enormity of the powers and principalities holding the earth in thrall.

So things are bad. And apocalyptic visions flourish in times and places where such evil is most acutely felt. John's book of Revelation was written in the midst of excruciating oppression. Indeed, John was imprisoned when his visions came to him. Christians were experiencing vicious persecution at the hands of the Roman Empire. In that hopeless context, John cast a vision of vindication, of hope. The evil would be trounced by God, Christ would claim a glorious victory, and the people of God would enjoy an eternity of pleasure in the presence of their Lord.

It's about hope. It is always about hope, always about good news. But Jesus does not offer us false hope. Jesus does not make himself a liar by murmuring, "Everything is going to be okay; you're never going to suffer, and there's nothing to be afraid of."

I think this may be what I love the very most about Jesus— his refusal to mince words. We are not fed cheap comfort. The message is brutally honest. It may get worse before it gets better. But it is going to get better—better beyond imagining. Christ will come again in glory. Wrongs will be made right, broken relationships will be healed, despair will be transformed into rejoicing. The kingdom of God will be established, and while its doors are always open to sinners who long to come home, they will be impenetrable to the forces of evil. It will be the end of the world as we know it, and the beginning of the world as God intended it.

This is not bad news.

Jesus likens the suffering of the world to the suffering of a woman in labor: "These are the beginning of birth pains" (v. 8). That's a tricky metaphor. Labor pains are necessary to bring forth new life, but are wars and earthquakes and famines really necessary to deliver the kingdom of God? I'm willing to go out on a limb and say no. I don't think that's what this means. Consider this: once that baby is in the arms of the mother, the minutes of god-awful, searing pain, the hours of on-and-off misery, the months of discomfort—all that dissolves into the past. It happened, but it is *so* not the point when the baby is there, bloody and screaming and full of life. I think that this might be what Jesus means here. The evil doesn't make the good happen—that's ridiculous. We know that it is God from whom all blessings flow. But once God restores the heavens and the earth, once time is fulfilled into eternal blessing, well, the pain of the past can be released. To quote another apocalyptic pop song, we ourselves shall be released.

The refrain of "The End of the World as We Know It" ends with a phrase that used to seem utterly inexplicable to me: "and I feel fine." But now I know a frightening world and the Jesus who is anything but frightening.

No wonder Michael Stipe felt so fine.

"Piece" Be with You

Greg Fromholz

That's my parting gift to you. Peace. I don't leave you the way you're used to being left—feeling abandoned, bereft. So don't be upset. Don't be distraught...Get up. Let's go. It's time to leave here.

—John 14: 25–27, 31 MSG

Slow Dance

Reading the Bible is like the slow dance I had at age eleven with my third stepmother at a family reunion. Awkward. Foreign. Slow. And it wasn't until I was older that I could move more gracefully when I read the Scriptures—that they began to have meaning.

Through my childhood years, my experience of the Bible was punctuated by two distinct associations: victory and defeat. On the victory side of things, there was the celebrated Sunday school game of the ages: Bible Sword Drill. God's word is the "sword of the Spirit," you know (Eph. 6:17 KJV). In Sword Drills, we kids sat in a row, massive "genuine leather" King James Versions in hand—*our swords*—and our bodies poised for the hunt. The Sunday school teacher shouted out the reference for a verse, and with reputations on the line, we raced to find it. Sword Drills served to establish the obvious and inseparable connection in my mind between God, weapons, and winning.

Standing next to me in the only church service he and I ever attended together, my first dad said to me, "I don't get it. I thought Jesus was a *pacifist*."

I was a kick-ass Bible Sword Driller and won numerous medals at my church. This helped me to overdevelop a sense of reward-driven spirituality. I won! So this means Jesus loves me even more, right? What a prize!

My understanding of the Bible as an agent of defeat came when my mother, exhausted by annoying children, shouted: "Gregory, go to your room and read the third chapter of James... now!" I still shudder when the book of James pops up in the liturgy.

This, in fairness, was usually because I had driven my mother to distraction through my own cheek and provocation, and she felt that some solid biblical truth would get me back on track. (That and making me literally chew on some Irish Spring soap. Oh, the irony that I now live in Ireland!) Victory and defeat: they sing such a strange disharmony, leaving me without peace. You can imagine my recent surprise when, a few decades after my stunningly awkward slow dance, I opened the Bible and found Saint John and Saint Eugene (Peterson) metaphorically tapping the stethoscope on my bare chest, telling me to breathe deeply. I paused. I took a breath, and the verses I inhaled spoke of "peace" and "don't be distraught."

John 14: 25–27, 31:

That's my parting gift to you. Peace. I don't leave you the way you're used to being left—feeling abandoned, bereft. So

don't be upset. Don't be distraught…Get up. Let's go. It's
time to leave here. (MSG)

These words grabbed me and shook my bones.

They first hit me in that unavoidable and frustratingly self-
centered way. I felt the words vibrate from within my own
story. But more than that, I felt those words ricochet throughout *our* story; not just the church as the body of Christ but
throughout the global soul. This is Our Story. The story of a
tangible, God-given peace that is found both in bright dawn
and in the dark storms of life.

Craving

To know me is to know my dysfunction.

My soul has a scar, and its name is Forgotten. The feeling that I don't belong has been a resounding, peace-barren
echo in my guts since childhood. This scar gets fainter as I get
older, but it's audible all the same.

My scar *whispers* (and sometimes shouts) about my broken
family. It *speaks* of the brokenness of some of the churches I've
attended. My scar *aches* with the confusion of attending multiple schools, living in many homes, having fragmented friendships, and having a battered faith in God.

And all these fragments are as scattered across the globe as
I have been—a person who has lived abroad for most of my life.

I grew up knowing that there was beauty in these fragments, these broken things. I may wish to trade a few parts of
my childhood, but I would never trade the distinct whole; the
broken spectrum of my childhood, which still refracts light.
My story has given me many a wonder, but lumped in with it
was the accelerant of feeling abandoned and forgotten amid
myriad broken promises.

Broken promises are like weak tree branches; you can't trust them, and there's no peace in the climbing. So when the book of John has the audacity to tell me not to feel upset or distraught but to be at peace, it rattles me to the core in unexpected ways. Anger and hope are now on the dance floor in that awkward slow dance.

I want this peace. I crave it. But peace is elusive.

In a ballsy move, Jesus makes a promise: "That's my parting gift to you. Peace. I don't leave you the way you're used to being left—feeling abandoned, bereft. So don't be upset. Don't be distraught... Get up. Let's go. It's time to leave here."

Together.

Together.

Flesh and Blood

What I'm constantly amazed at is that even those closest to the very Jesus struggled with knowing peace even though they had felt his calloused hands on their shoulders, his breath on their faces, the stench of his sweat in their noses, and they knew the sound of his laughter. He was present with them. Peace had a name: *Jesus.*

Presence precedes peace.

The Word became flesh and blood,
    and moved into the neighborhood.
We saw the glory with our own eyes,
    the one-of-a-kind glory,
    like Father, like Son,
Generous inside and out,
    true from start to finish. (John 1:14 MSG)

His peace was not—*is* not—a whisper from the dead. It

is not a postcard sent from the road, a support check slipped under the door in silence. It is physical. It is tangible. This is the very Jesus saying: I'm here, and I get it. My immortal *physicality* impacts your mortal *fragility*. I'm not a leaver and I'm not a hand-holder, so here is a parting gift, "a comforter" (KJV): "You know him already because he has been staying with you, and will even be *in* you!" (John 14:15–17 MSG).

Here is peace. Peace be with you. A piece of myself I give to you. Only this kind of peace can penetrate the skin and the soul and can touch the loneliness in the human condition. A piece of you enables a peace in me.

A Problem with Steeples

Here's my problem: I love, and am a part of the body of Christ, but the peace I find in it today seems evasive, elusive, and exclusive, not like the Jesus I've read about and experienced.

Steeples, which could serve as lighthouses to guide us home, now rise up like jagged middle fingers to a society that needs beacons of peace. The actual presence of peace has eroded in the tides of entitlement. Peace is not exclusive.

Do you remember this childhood rhyme?

Here is the church
Here is the steeple
Open the door . . . but where are the people?

Obviously, I've changed the ending, but it's closer to the truth now, so what's going on? Surely more than those who enter a church are in need of peace, right? My daughter once said, "Church can't just be for the people who can find it."

This peace that Jesus left behind, having affected individuals and nations, has now breathed a collective sigh, seemingly giving up, now failing to penetrate the fear, the distrust, the hurt that we have caused in our exclusivity. Peace has become a plastic sword on dragon skin—blunt, ineffective. A punch line in an ill-timed gag.

It is far cry from "Peace. I don't leave you the way you're used to being left—feeling abandoned, bereft."

Am I avoiding the places that are in need of peace?

Enchiladas

Reportedly, Woody Allen once said something along the lines of, "Eighty percent of living is just showing up." Recently in our family, we have been feeling rattled. It was family stuff, work stuff, life stuff. A sudden family illness. A violent burglary. A confusing transition in work. The old demons of abandonment reared their familiar heads in my mind.

Then a friend showed up at our door with freshly made enchiladas. It was simple: simple enough to change our posture that day and that week.

It's all about the enchiladas. Sometimes, it's just that simple. Peace follows presence. A piece of you always precedes a peace in me.

Why are the seemingly simple things—like accepting comfort or giving hope—so difficult?

The Abnormality of Beauty

Globally, the phrase "Peace be with you" resonates with us. In traditional churches in Ireland we used to cross the aisles to reach out and sometimes even embrace one another, saying, "Peace be with you" in every mass. Lately, though, it feels like we are increasingly concerned with personal space, cleanliness, and not too much contact. We keep the holy water beside the hand sanitizer and stay on our side of the aisle.

But when we let it, peace can be wonderfully disruptive.

I went to mass on a Tuesday in the Wicklow Mountains, and it changed everything for me. It was there, in a battered church, with its scar-faced priest, that verses about peace moved beyond syntax and began to shape me. The normally mundane became abnormally beautiful.

At the sign of peace, the priest walked up and down the church, pew by pew, shaking the hand of everyone in the building. Even the hard-to-reach ones. Especially the hard-to-reach ones. A mother who had lost a son in a car accident, looking grief-worn, possibly questioning the cruelty of sovereignty. Two men who chose not to receive the Eucharist. A silent Protestant at the back. And all the other outsiders, muddied by the day and its rain. All were welcomed and offered peace by this abnormal priest in a battered church. This priest found his destiny in being a restorer of trust between God and us. A restorer of trust between us and us.

This priest's authentic faith began to restore dignity and care to a broken church and broken people. I pray that abnormality like this continues to cross aisles and walk out of the buildings, offering restoration to all. The priest could have retreated and entrenched himself in the safety of the altar, but by understanding his own brokenness, he was able to break through, reaching out to embrace the brokenness in the room.

I want to be that guy.

I want mine to be that church.

What if, in those moments of giving the sign of peace, we choose to move beyond words and into action? What if we say that peace is, effectively, me giving a piece of myself to you? That is Jesus' way: I'll be there for you beyond words and with my whole being. Here's my money, my time, my car, my home, my all. And not just when it's convenient.

Love is not convenient. Whenever we actively choose to give ourselves away, we create life. Where we are indifferent, atrophy prevails. A piece of my life I give to you, that you may know true peace.

Dirty Church

You and I can be the restorers of peace.

Peace can be found when we get stuck with our hands deep in the soil, muddied in the beautiful muck of life. Maybe there we can become a dirty church of peace shaped by God incarnate, Jesus, whose hands were in the sand, who spit in the mud, who was cut and bruised by the weight of the cross.

Jesus cried at his friend's tomb. It is his blanket that covers the homeless. It is his hoarse voice that calls for peace. It is his heart that breaks over a father's abuse of a child. His body is hunched over a child ripped apart by a land mine. His arms are wrapped around the mother who cries alone. His front door is thrown wide open to the lonely. His love and peace are offered unconditionally, to everyone.

Jesus became human, was blessed, broken, and was given for us.

And so I desperately pray:

Take me.
Bless me.
Break me.
Give me to others.

My awkward dance with Scripture continues. This time, I'm a little more sure-footed with the knowledge that I no longer dance alone, that Jesus has left me his extraordinary and tangible partner in peace.

The Scandal of *Imago Dei*

Caryn Rivadeneira

So God created human beings in his own image, in the image of God he created them; male and female he created them.

—Genesis 1:27 NIV

What horrible luck!" Tom said. "My dad has four kids. Three Christian. And he ends up with me! The agnostic! He gets his gay, agnostic son at his deathbed!"

I laughed out loud, quickly turning to make sure none of the black-frocked folks around us heard my impropriety.

We stood huddled together—Tom, Tom's boyfriend, and me—whispering secrets and stifling giggles off in the alcove while people in the parlor next to us murmured and held back tears.

(I don't know how it happens, but even at wakes I manage to find folks to laugh with; it's just not usually the dead person's *son*.)

Tom kept going. "I mean: I tried. I held his hand and stroked his face and said, 'Dad, *maybe* there's something. Maybe Grandma *is* waiting there for you. If you see her—or

72

a light or Jesus or whatever—go toward it. I don't think that there is, but *maybe...'"*

I laughed once again, though this time my laugh was lighter, offered to be polite. The mood had shifted. As Tom told the story and offered the image of his "bad luck" father—this poor man, long suffering from cancer, long sunk into a coma, with his a-shrug-for-religion son at his side, talking him sweetly into death—what I saw was no longer funny as much as it was lovely, humbling, and take-my-breath-away moving.

What I saw in the story of gay, agnostic Tom at his father's deathbed was Jesus, tenderly caring for a man on the brink of heaven.

Made in the image of God, the *Imago Dei*, Tom was Jesus for his father in that moment.

———

Reflecting God's image. Seeing God in you. *Being* Jesus to one another.

These are all things we Christian folk proclaim and cling to when our skin tingles with the presence of the divine working in, through, and around our lowly selves. It's one of my most favorite things about being a God-fearing human, actually. It's amazing. But if we're honest, it's also kind of troubling.

Because, I mean, it's all good and lovely to believe that God made all of us in his image when we're clucking and cooing into our precious newborns' faces, when we're lost in the blushes and fires of fresh love, when we're deep in wine-fueled conversation with good friends.

Yes!

We see God, his lovely face, his strong arms. And sure, it's easy enough to hear and see God when we read a rolling lyric, when a melody moves us to dance, when the brushstrokes leave us woozy with delight.

Our creator! Right there! In human form! Still creating in us!

When a friend drops off that meal, when your mother loans you that money, when your husband forgives the way you snapped.

Father, Son, and Holy Spirit!

But what about the other times? What about when the image of God, the likeness of Jesus, isn't a silver-haired pastor in a three-piece suit? Can we believe that someone we perceive as "outside the fold"—perhaps someone like my friend Tom—reveals the image of God?

Or what happens when the person who has been created in God's image is truly a total jerk?

———

Mother Teresa famously followed a call, built a life, formed a ministry, saved a zillion lives, and changed the world based on one of the Bible's great definitions of how we can know when we're looking at the image of God, into the very being of Jesus.

> Then the righteous will answer him, "Lord, when did we see you hungry and feed you, or thirsty and give you something to drink? When did we see you a stranger and invite you in, or needing clothes and clothe you? When did we see you sick or in prison and go to visit you?"
>
> The King will reply, "Truly I tell you, whatever you did for one of the least of these brothers and sisters of mine, you did for me." (Matthew 25:37–40 NIV)

Again, this is rough. Because sometimes the "least" are awesome, grateful, and endear themselves to us. Sometimes halos appear, and we're pretty sure we see stigmata forming. Sometimes it's so easy to see Immanuel. But then there are the *others*. And this passage from Matthew doesn't seem to separate them at all—not any more than Genesis 1:27 does. And it turns out that we're *all* made in the image of God. Not just the people we like. Not just the nice or cute or funny or "like-us" ones. And sometimes the "least" of us are total jerks.

Mother Teresa must've figured this out fairly quickly. I'm slower on the uptake. I only realized this the day I stooped to drop some money into a coffee can held out by a man who was sprawled on a blanket by the train station. Maybe it was hearing coins clatter instead of the soft sink of bills; maybe it was that I didn't say anything more than "Morning!" to him. Frankly, I'm not really sure what made him scowl at me and growl, "Fucking cunt."

Although these are two of the ugliest (and most potent) words in the English language, it wasn't the words themselves that stopped me in my tracks along the sidewalk. (I'm a writer with strong and often off-the-wall opinions. It wasn't the first time I'd been called something in that vein, nor would it be the last.) What stopped me—made me turn back to look once again at the mouth that spouted them—was just *who* they were coming from. Not an angry Internet troll, not an author at the other end of my less-than-flattering review, but according to the B-I-B-L-E, those words came from *Jesus.*

Et tu, Jesu?

Of course, the Bible itself is full of examples of total jerks glowing with God's grace and *being* Jesus (even if, in earthly terms, they predate him). David comes to mind. As do Peter and Paul and John's descriptions of himself as the "loved one."

I'd guess troublesome Mary of Bethany came across as jerky (at least to her sister and the disciples) more than once. As did the Samaritan woman (does she not know her place?!?!). Certainly Sarah was no peach. At least not to Hagar.

But my favorite of the Jerky Jesuses is Esau, the guy who sold his birthright for some soup and had the nerve to get murderously angry at his brother for his own stupid mistake.

But still, I think and write about Esau a lot lately. Because, well, I've made plenty of stupid mistakes myself, done enough dumb things to last a lifetime. Certainly I've shaken my fist at God just as Esau shook his fist at his father and demanded that God "bless me, too!"

And I love that this man Esau—this red-faced, hairy, smelly dim bulb who made a mistake and paid a steep price—became none other than the "very face of God" by the end of his story. If you haven't read it, do. It's pure magic. And strange comfort.

Because what troubles me so much about these passages that say we bear the very "image of God" is what they ultimately say about me and about you and about all of us. Whether I'm duking it out with my demons—and winning—or whether I'm indulging them; whether I'm behaving or performing horribly or wonderfully; whether the words flow like a faucet or if they drop barely at a drip, not enough to fill out the bucket of my thoughts; whether I'm riding high on the waves of life or sinking into one of its dark holes, I am created in God's image. I am capable of *being* Jesus to another, of reflecting some angle of God. So are you. And so is everybody else.

Rush Limbaugh, Barack Obama; Adolf Hitler, Julian of Norwich; your sweet grandmother, your abusive father; Virginia Woolf, Stephenie Meyer; my funny neighbor, our neighborhood prowler; the pastor, the prisoner; the painter, the garbage collector; Greta Garbo, Jack Black; that lady who just cut you off in traffic, the guy who let you merge; those who take lives, those who save them.

God's image, all. Capable of communicating his grace, his truth, his beauty, his love, his all.

Sometimes—face it—that stinks. Depending on just whom we're talking about. But in truth, it's grand. Because in every moment of human kindness and human wretchedness is the grace of God, who marked each of us with a measure of himself.

———

At my church, where I'm now on staff, the curtain—and whether it's open during the service or closed—is just about as big an issue as there is. As one particular elbow in the body of Christ, we can agree on all sorts of things, but the curtain? No.

At issue are the folks who love to look out the huge side windows that overlook our labyrinth, our garden, and the bit of woods just beyond. It is quite a view. But the trouble is the sun. When it's out—especially in midwinter, when it lurks low beyond that window—it likes to blind the organist and the choir members and render the screens useless.

So we close it. Amid much complaining.

"We want to see God's creation!" we hear. "God *lurks* there. *Speaks to us* from there." And of course God does.

But one colleague has cracked: "Right. We want to see God's creation. We don't want to have to look at *each other*. What could these fools have to show us about God?"

It's just less trouble to see God in the trees and in the blinding sunshine and to feel him in the spook and mystery of the labyrinth than it is to see him in the worn and weary, made-up and ghoulish, fresh and old faces all around.

And yet: there it is.

There we are.

Images of God.

Imago Dei.

Sometimes troubling proof, difficult reminders that God is with us and all around us and so much more than we think or hope or know.

Probably Less Holy Than Thou

Karen Walrond

For the grace of God has appeared, bringing salvation for all
people.
—Titus 2:11 ESV

I am, apparently, not really a Christian.

I learned this several years ago, when a family friend
invited me to an event at her church. My friend (whom I'll call
Dee, although that's not her real name) is extremely active in
her spiritual community and was thrilled to give me a tour,
introducing me to the clergy and the elders and describing all
the aspects of her religion that she held incredibly dear. It was
fun to see her light up as she linked her arm in mine, leading
me all over the church grounds.

The tour lasted about an hour, and while we walked, she
animatedly talked. At one point, however, her voice dropped
to a whisper. "Karen," she began in confidence, "I know you
weren't raised Christian, but..."

I interrupted. "Wait—what?" My voice was louder than
I intended. "You know I grew up Catholic, right?" In fact, I
grew up aggressively so. My mother was devout, making it

her vocal duty to ensure that my sister and I attended mass and catechism classes every week without fail. We never once missed a holy day of obligation. We ate fish on Fridays. I made my sacraments at all the appropriate ages: first communion at six, first confession at ten, confirmation at thirteen. I attended a girls-only Catholic high school located in a convent and run by some of the strictest nuns in the land. In fact, my *aunt* is a nun, for heaven's sake. It would be hard to find anyone with a childhood more Catholic than mine.

Dee smiled, with not a small amount of pity. "Well," she said, patting my arm, shaking her head. "Catholic isn't *really* Christian, now, is it?"

I stared at her, stunned, but she didn't even notice my astonishment.

"Now, then. If you look over here . . ." she continued, walking and gently guiding me forward.

I followed along in silence, but truthfully, I was troubled by her statement, her implication that somehow my Christianness wasn't up to snuff—that on the list of things that make one a Christian (and I'm assuming she had quite a list), very few of my boxes were checked. I was dismayed because I believed that in her mind, on some level, I was failing in what it takes to "make the Christian grade."

I was upset because I suspected she might be right.

It has been several years since that day with Dee, and with the benefit of hindsight, I've gotten over my discomfort, realizing that Dee's opinion, frankly, need not carry a whole lot of weight. After all, Dee isn't the only person who has ever questioned the state of someone's Christianity or spirituality—in fact, the issue of how faithful we all are is discussed all the time. Think about it: our friends bring it up, if only by implication, that the way they practice (or don't practice) is the one right way. Politicians of all stripes talk about it constantly: they tell us that if we vote this way or the other, we're not "Christian" enough. Even some preachers and ministers can't help themselves: they tell us that if we don't tithe enough, or volunteer enough, or simply be "good enough," we ought not to claim that we are "Christian." And this isn't just in the realm of Christianity—people debate which religions are "better" than others *all the time*.

The ranking and rating of faith is *constant*. Ultimately, though, I don't think it really matters.

For one thing, I've come to believe that there are as many definitions of faith as there are people in the world, because I believe that all faith is a deeply personal experience: one that is multilayered, formed by many characteristics, including but not limited to religious instruction (if any) and the cultivation of a personal relationship (if any) with a higher power. And I believe this to be true across *all* religious practices.

In my own story, while I have had years of religious instruction, the formation of my own faith is also deeply influenced by personal experiences outside of the church, including meditation and other faith practices that I have developed. I am a Christian because I am an admittedly imperfect follower of the teachings of Christ, and my formative religious education took place in the Catholic Church; however, had I been born to a Jewish or Muslim or Hindu family, I believe that my relationship with God, although likely very different, would nonetheless remain just as valid and true. I am a Christian, but I've studied and read texts of other faiths and incorporated a few of their teachings into my own personal spiritual practice. I am a regular churchgoer, but I now attend an Episcopal church instead of a Catholic one, if for no other reason than I enjoy its particular church community—and as long as I'm being honest here, I appreciate the added benefit of its proximity to my home.

In addition, my beliefs about God are similarly fluid in that I believe my relationship is an ongoing one; moreover, I believe that this relationship is *meant* to be so, requiring constant care and cultivation. My practice of my Christianity has always been more of a journey than a destination, a continuing quest to know the God within and without me. I'm not concerned about ticking all my virtues off of some predetermined list and comparing that list against the lists of others. In fact, I've always identified with the parable in the Bible about the prodigal son: living a blemish-free life (like that of the prodigal son's perfect brother) is far less important than the process of self-evaluation and reflection on my own authenticity and God's light within me; continuing to return, like the prodigal son, to what I know within my soul to be my true self and to the source of limitless love and kindness is far more important.

Furthermore, I believe that God encourages my humanness, and that he (or she?) doesn't expect perfection and purity but understands that I will occasionally behave in ways that stray from what I know to be rooted in love. However, as long as I remain mindful of the purpose of my life's journey, and am therefore diligent in following my spirit back to my true self, I believe God is okay with that. In other words, I believe the fact that I am human means *it's okay for me to behave like a human*. That faith, in essence, is a process of evolution far more than it is a competition for the title of Most Immaculate. And besides, as another friend of mine reminded me recently, if I'm ever wondering what Jesus would do in any particular situation, I can cut myself some slack and remember there's a passage in the Bible indicating that he once viewed freaking out and flipping tables over as a viable option.

The point, I think, is to keep returning to your path.

Finally, and most important, I believe in the possibility that all my beliefs—including every one of the ones I've shared here—might be completely off base. That despite all my reading and practicing and churchgoing, I could very well be wrong. That there is the possibility that believing any of these things, coupled with my own spiritual practices, might make me decidedly un-Christian, whether by Dee's definition or anyone else's. But I also believe that this might be okay—in fact, it might be perfect. Because each of our spiritual journeys, no matter what faith (or lack thereof) we hold dear, is going to be different from those of others, creating distinctions as numerous as there are people in the universe.

And I believe that this diversity, a tapestry made of millions of people on their own individual paths trying to just *Be Better*, is a beautiful thing—*especially* in the eyes of God.

The Vulnerable God

Kenneth Tanner

And the Word became flesh and dwelt among us, and we have seen his glory, glory as of the only Son from the Father, full of grace and truth.

 —John 1:14 ESV

Therefore he had to be made like his brothers in every respect, so that he might become a merciful and faithful high priest in the service of God, to make propitiation for the sins of the people.

 —Hebrews 2:17 ESV

On a wall in the chapel of the Saint Catherine's Monastery, a remote wilderness abbey at the base of Mount Sinai in Egypt, hangs an icon.

It's not a poster of Brad Pitt or a reproduction of the Apple or Microsoft logo. This is a religious icon, perhaps the oldest in the world—a special painting the first Christians called a window into heaven.

This figure of Christ Pantocrator, or Christ the Ruler of All (see page 85), is no ordinary icon. No surviving icon of its era looks anything like it. It seems fresh, as if painted yesterday.

Believed to have been given to the desert monastery in the mid-sixth century by the Byzantine emperor Justinian, it survived a period when icons were destroyed in many urban churches, was preserved against deterioration in the arid climate, and was secured from invaders by an order of protection the prophet Muhammad himself granted after the monks of Saint Catherine's gave him shelter and hospitality.

The icon shares sixty-three points of precise alignment with the image of Jesus "burned" into the Shroud of Turin, five times the number of alignments needed to match fingerprints.

For many, this is the closest thing we have to a photograph of God.

Note the difference between the left side of the face (in which some see evidence of Christ's torture and passion) and the right side (in which some discern his transfigured, resurrected radiance). The icon tells the story of Good Friday and Easter.

The eyes stand out. Something about them is not quite right. For some, they have an unsettling quality.

One of my childhood friends had a lazy eye. He was wonderfully unconscious of his difference, but I often was distracted by it. More frequently than I'd like to admit, I caught myself staring.

The more time I spent in prayer looking at this unique image of Jesus—the Pantocrator—the more the asymmetry of the eyes troubled me. I pondered why the artist would paint Jesus with a physical "imperfection."

Eventually I realized this was not a problem with the artist or the image but rather a limitation of my imagination, a failure to see everything there is to see in Christ. After all, the word became flesh in Jesus (John 1:4) and was made like us in every respect (Hebrews 2:17).

Jesus took on everything it means to be human. One early Christian pastor taught that "what has not been assumed has not been redeemed." Jesus grew tired, donned a cloak against the piercing cold and burning sun, could catch a virus or suffer a wasting disease, and if all that is true, he might also have borne some physical "defects." Isaiah's prophecy of the suffering servant warned us that Jesus had "nothing beautiful or majestic about his appearance, nothing to attract us to him" (53:2b NLT).

Still, I discovered it wasn't just a matter of accepting that Jesus might have had physical imperfections. I had never absorbed into my heart the reality that the divine became one with matter in Jesus. Real flesh, real bones, real heart.

My encounter with the Sinai Pantocrator helped end my

inherited mental image of Jesus as a stick figure in a Bible story—a Sunday school flannelgraph character—and experience the full-blooded actuality of how things are in Jesus Christ; even the possibility that the sinless one's participation in our nature involved bearing physical infirmities, just as daily he grew thirsty, hungry, and weary.

Icons of Christ help us consider that Jesus is no abstraction—no mere thought, no matter how beautiful; no protagonist in a children's story told to make us feel better—but the express image of the unseen all-holy God made vulnerable (Col. 1:15), made like us "in every way."

We see in Jesus the sacred reality of our humanity as God intended it from the beginning; his was the first human life to fulfill that intention. The Sinai icon helps us comprehend that we become most truly human when we embrace the humanity of God in Jesus Christ.

Embracing the humanity of God, icons help us visualize such an incredible possibility; that we might, by grace, become transfigured partakers of the divine nature in clay (2 Peter 1:4).

I have a sort of odd pastoral practice. I keep small wood-mounted reproductions of this Sinai icon in my backpack to give to strangers and friends. I started this about ten years ago on Chicago's trains, subways, and buses. My commute was four hours round trip. Eventually folks figured out I was an undercover man of the cloth, commuting and working just as they did every day—someone imperfect enough that they eventually came to share with me their questions about God.

The icon gave me a way to show them the gospel and allowed me to use fewer words when I did so.

Fifteen hundred years after its creation, the icon still hangs in the shadows of the mountain on which God forbade the worship of idols.

The reason this isn't ironic is that icons are not idols. Idols are objects that *we* make and worship in place of the living God. In Jesus Christ, *God* has acted to make a perfect image of himself (Heb. 1:3).

God has made Jesus the "visible image of the invisible God." When iconographers depict Christ in the icons they write—in their parlance, icons are "written," not painted—the writers are not fashioning a god for themselves but rendering an image of what the Father, Son, and Spirit have already done in the incarnation of the one God in Jesus Christ.

It is not idolatry that God became flesh in Jesus, and it is not idolatry to depict what God has done and hang these depictions in our homes and houses of worship just like we hang family photos or images of contemporary leaders. We would never think to tear such images up or deface them, because these pictures represent the people we love.

Almost no one worships these depictions. Christians do, however, worship a God who clothed himself in clay, in the same material stuff with which he made our ancestors in his image in the Garden of Eden.

Women and men are made in the image of God, female and male *together* bearing all that is in God, and so it shouldn't surprise us when our incarnate Lord looks like us. The Sinai icon reminds us that we are one with him and he is one with us.

Ponder with me for a moment the mystery that we've entered when we encounter Christ in the Gospels ...

When Jesus is on the Sea of Galilee with the disciples, and storm winds and waves frighten even seasoned fishermen, we find the God who made the waves, the wind, and the wood the boat is crafted from—who made everything and holds everything together—tired and asleep in the hold of the ship.

God is asleep on a boat, even though our first thought as

readers is that, of course, Jesus, a mere human, is napping (and that is true, too).

When the disciples awaken Jesus and he surveys the situation (and their hearts), he rebukes their fear, and then a mere man stands up on two feet in a vessel sloshing with lake water and speaks: "Peace, be still."

Someone just like the rest of the disciples—with breathing lungs and a beating heart, sleepy and finding his sea legs— makes the wind stop gusting and turns the waves to glass with his words. As readers, we think Jesus is God and this awe-inspiring ability fits his divinity, but Jesus is also merely human, no more special in his biochemistry than anyone else in that boat on a sea gone wild.

When we read every story about Jesus with the sort of contemplation that icons allow—realizing this protagonist is in every moment God "all-in" and human "all-in"—we begin to discern that something has happened forever in God and something has happened forever in us, because the Son who breathed the stars into fiery existence and set their courses in the sky, who made the orchid and the hummingbird, humbled himself and was made like us in every way: weary, thirsty, hungry, aching, longing, striving, rejected, fallen, marvelous clay that we are, that we might be as he is, as God from all eternity. World without end.

The Sinai icon reminds us that in Jesus Christ, God leaves fingerprints, leaves DNA, wherever he goes (Jesus is human without measure); that Jesus breathes the spirit of the Father's loving-kindness on all things (Jesus is divine without qualification). His blood, his touch, his stops of breath reconcile the creator and the clay that as female and male alone in all creation bears the image of God.

Jesus walks with us, walks *as* us now, and we participate

by our prayers, by our touch, by our faith and compassion—sometimes even by our blood—in the renewal of all things.

We see the likeness of Jesus in every human. Would that they might behold in our faces the icon of his vulnerability, self-sacrificial love, and resurrection in this wild, wonderful world he became human to restore to life without end.

Wrestling with Hovering Spirits

David Vanderveen

And the spirit of God was hovering over the waters.
　　—Genesis 1:2 NIV

Years ago, when my wife and I lived in Northern California
and we surfed from Monterey Bay to the Mendocino coast,
I occasionally wrote a "People Who Surf" column for *Surfer*
magazine. One person I wrote about was Dave Schmidt.

Dave, or Birdman, as he is known, is one of three surfing
Schmidt brothers, two of whom surf huge and dangerous
waves. Richard Schmidt is the most famous of the brothers,
but I interviewed Birdman because he was one of the first
people to surf Mavericks, a deadly and colossal wave outside the Half Moon Bay harbor, between Santa Cruz and San
Francisco.

The Schmidts' father was a Presbyterian minister, and
the way he raised his sons on Monterey Bay reminded me of
Norman Maclean's father and fly-fishing Montana's rivers—
the family freely integrated their spirituality and outdoor-
adventure lifestyle. They believed in surfing as much as
they believed in the Westminster Confession. Their ideas

were applied in the heavy waves of the Northern California coast. Debates about heaven and hell, three fins or four, and where the waves were hitting the best were won in the water through experience.

Dave gave me a quote about riding big waves in our interview that I've never forgotten. He said, "Power doesn't come from having power everywhere, but from knowing where to put it on." True power comes from grace through elegance. You can't stop a big wave from breaking, and you can't really even harness the massive energy it generates, but you can ride it, survive, and be exhilarated by the energy. Tapping that energy will change you. Surfing offers a crucible where man and board fit, where time seems to slow, and the experience is so powerful that people who've tasted it and survived will risk it all again for another sip of that elixir.

Søren Kierkegaard found something similar after the death of his parents. From the shore on the Danish coast, he observed a violent storm and the seabirds that flew in it. Watching the scene, the philosopher described feeling alone and forsaken in the midst of that battle between the sea and the elements, but he also observed the confidence of the birds that flew amid the chaos. He remembered Christ's words about sparrows being included in God's design, and the pride Kierkegaard felt in being part of God's plan while still feeling lost in the cosmos came to define the way he understood his place with God.

What I read into Kierkegaard's existential insight is that the happy tension of pride and humility creates a point of leverage like Archimedes' lever, which can move anything, even the world. But moving the world should never be the goal. Being in that special place requires trusting in—and surrendering to—the creator of the universe, embracing the grace that is available to us all despite ourselves, and stepping away from our own power. The power of grace doesn't accept demands. It isn't about what we want; it is about how we fit into a relationship that flows with the spirit of God. Real power doesn't come from inside ourselves but from tapping into the power of a sovereign God, finding the plan she created for us, dwelling in it, and knowing where to "put it on" in faith. That is the energy we should be surfing instead of trying to make our own waves.

I believe that the creator of this universe is closer to us than our own skin—"hovering" over the water is not a real separation; rather, it reflects our inability to experience anything beyond the observable dimensions of length, width, depth, and time. Our constantly expanding universe requires extra dimensions to exist. Among other things, the Large Hadron Collider near Geneva, Switzerland, is attempting to watch gravitons—gravity particles—escaping our known dimensions into the dimensions that are wrapped tightly around the ones we inhabit. And those dimensions are where she waits. They are where God lives with us, knows us, and interacts with us.

If only we had eyes to see.

My experiences, not my theology, brought me to these ideas, and those experiences shape my beliefs today. I cannot imagine truth apart from experience. Existence itself—my personal interactions with the trauma and beauty of life, not abstract rational constructs—is what has primarily shaped the movement of my beliefs, which are fluid truths that acknowledge the author of our universe and the elegance that speaks to us and awaits response.

Beliefs, for me, are less about God writing impossible-to-keep commandments on stone tablets than they are about the person with whom Jacob wrestled on the banks of the Jabbok, as was recorded in the epically true mythic poem that is Genesis. The Jabbok struggle transformed Jacob into Israel and fulfilled with skin, blood, and bones the undefined covenant of Yahweh with Abraham. God created a new relationship with Jacob, changed his name, and put new meaning and definition into the understanding that his parents had held. Jacob's wrestling with his family's customs, traditions, and covenants, through his wrestling with God, created new channels for the spirit of God to carry him into a new future.

The power of the fluids in our life and our interaction with them are not about how we can contain them but about how we can embrace the waves of energy transmitted by the storms of life through the various dimensions of the universe. It is about finding a place to wrestle and dance with that power, much as surfers do.

My own father is a surgeon and a sailor. He raised our family, especially my brothers and me, to become real sailors. We were raised on an inland lake that feeds into Lake Michigan, and we were expected to race scows: fast, sleek boats with far too much sail area for zero keel weight. Scows are called hot rods. The whole point is to go fast. Speed in a scow comes from finely tuned, efficient sailing and applying the right strategies and tactics, which in turn come from knowing where the wind bends and blows. A boat wins the race because it rides the wind with the most elegance. Being one with the wind and water makes a boat the fastest through the buoys. Elegance equals speed; extra movement or misapplied surface area causes drag. And drag is the antithesis of the truths of scow racing.

My Dutch American life started in Michigan. Now I live on the Southern California coast. My collective DNA and my environment, my nature and nurture, have both been about a relationship with hydrodynamics—fluids and flow.

The traditions and theology of the Dutch Reformed Church—the knowledge, the catechisms, the history, and the questions and answers—served as a good foundation for me, much as geometry did. You just don't realize what is valuable and what isn't until you have to paint a house and figure out how much paint to buy. Of course, the laws of geometry are very different from opinions about theology. They are harder to test objectively. Most of us come to authentic (i.e., not inherited) theological beliefs because they ring true for us based on our subjective experiences. The phenomena that I have interacted with define the filters that let truth shine through.

The beliefs of my youth, which were taught by loving people with the best of intentions, were mostly valuable because they informed me about belief in general. Ultimately, I adopted and adapted many of them, but it was the deep and powerful experiences of life that transformed me. The application of theories to experience, and vice versa, have created what I believe is true.

Throughout the summer months, a scow racer accumulates points based on the positions in which he finishes each race. Missing races means falling out of contention. In the Dutch Reformed tradition, Sundays are sacred. That meant that my father, brothers, and I could not race in half the required races in the biggest weekend series. Instead we went to church, attended catechism classes, had a large Sunday meal at midday, and watched *Meet the Press* or sports on television. God, apparently, did not find scow racing as sacred as my father, brothers, and I did. My older brother, Tim, and I lost much of our interest in the sacredness of scow racing because of our religious handicap.

Sailboarding became popular right about the time that Tim and I were losing interest in sailing boats. The boards were faster, and their ability to surf storms on Lake Michigan was more exciting, so we switched gears. During big storms on the Great Lakes, Tim and I would lose sight of each other's masts in offshore swells. We would see waterspouts and lightning strikes. At times the violent wind and waves would shred sails and break universal joints or masts, destroying critical pieces of equipment far from shore, making for long paddles home with broken gear.

The demands of elegance and the desire to progress in our aquatic pursuits pushed us into surfing. We wanted to simplify our pursuit of storm surf: if we had less gear, there was less that could break.

———

Between the sand dunes and beach grass of the Big Mitten— also known as the state of Michigan—and the flat coastline of Wisconsin is Lake Michigan. It is an inland sea, hundreds of miles long and more than ninety miles across. The prevailing westerly winds and storms that blow across the Great Plains can create surf capable of sinking seven-hundred-foot freighters. The furies pop up quickly, violently, and, for surfers, create short periods of high-impact waves that often last only hours. Serious surfers on the Great Lakes have to seize the days and hours when swells appear.

I lost interest in church during my adolescent years because it encroached on my surfing. Concepts of truth interfered with my experience of the sport. My mother did not like us surfing on Sundays because she thought the other surfers were not an "edifying influence" on us. Sunday was a day dedicated to God and worship. Surfing, like sailing, was verboten. Forbidden. So my brother and I would scheme about how to break our Dutch Sabbath in the interest of aquatic pursuits.

Like prisoners making half-baked escape plans, we were often busted for breaking our family's blue laws. One time we claimed we were going to attend a special youth group meeting and neglected to inform our parents that it was a group of two and that the meeting took place in some of the best summer waves that year. Our damp hair gave us away, and we were grounded.

One Sunday, however, my mother was taking our younger sister to band camp, and the surf was enormous. My dad looked at my brother and me and said, "There's not much that I can do to keep you from surfing, is there?"

"Probably not," we said. With a wink from Dad, we were off.

Waves break as their energy cycles find the sea floor and slow from that friction. The speed of the crest causes the peak to spill kinetic energy, which explodes from blue water into white foam with dramatic power. When the waves get large on the Great Lakes, they find mysterious sandbars that we didn't know existed before. The distance between waves—the travel, as it's called—is determined by the distance the waves of energy have to move through water to get to you. The farther they go, the greater the travel. In Southern California, where we receive swells from New Zealand in the summer, the travel can be measured in twenty-to-thirty-minute intervals. Lake Michigan doesn't provide much distance—maybe one hundred to two hundred miles. The waves are very close together, and when they are big, you look for piers and points that provide easy access and protection from the wind, and that focus the confusion into a more consistent shape.

The Sunday of our surf-ban reprieve, my brother and I ended up on the north shore of Grand Haven, on a small, concrete pier that defines the northern border of our town's harbor entrance. The waves were washing over the pier, and most of our friends were surfing the second sandbar, which was shallower than usual and producing fast-breaking hollow barrels—or tubes, as surfers call them.

I was only fifteen that summer and riding a salvaged and yellowed eleven-foot Royal Hawaiian longboard—a board that big doesn't fit into tubes very well unless you get in early and can angle the board along the wave face. An angle keeps the nose from auguring into the wave's trough, or "nose-diving." A nosedive will catapult the rider and board into the air, suck you up the wave face from where you land and over the falls, and then slam a person to the bottom.

So as Tim and I stood at the pier and looked at the waves, I noticed bigger, almost mountain-like waves breaking way out on a distant, third sandbar that rarely broke except on the biggest swells.

"Hey, Tim. Check that mysto spot," I said. "I'm gonna head out the back and see if I can get into one of those sets."

"I don't know," Tim said. "Seems like a long paddle, and there aren't that many breaking all the way through. I came out here to surf today, not swim. You don't even have a leash on that turd," he added, pointing at my sun-bronzed board.

"I'll take my chances and see if I can get into something fun. See you on the inside!"

We dodged sets roaring down the pier, washing over the concrete. Tim jumped off about seventy-five to a hundred yards from the beach and joined our aquatic brethren bobbing in and out of breaking waves, taking beatings, and occasionally getting into some overhead bombs that pitched and hollowed out as the green water hit the shallow sand and sucked liquid silicon up and out into a tan foam. It was about as good as it got.

The wind was blowing more than twenty knots, and watching a fifteen-year-old maneuvering an eleven-foot-long board along the pier was like seeing a seagull flapping down the beach. The board wanted to take flight, but the pilot was barely anchoring its wing to earth.

Waves smashed into the end of the pier, shooting spray over my head, easily fifteen to twenty feet in the air. I waited patiently, timing a large set as it slammed into the pier and wrapped around the concrete. Then I launched onto the back side of the breaking wave and paddled farther out, to the place where I had seen the rogue sets of combined wind swells.

When you get offshore during storms, the swells become less mixed up and violent and also appear larger, like rolling mountains under your board or boat. Near the sandbar, I sat on my board and looked back toward shore. I was a quarter mile or more out to sea. The deep water was darker blue than the shallow green-and-tan water on the inside. Losing my board would mean a long swim through Lake Michigan's infamous riptides and undertows. But I couldn't resist those waves. Something inside me pulled against my fears, like the riptide that pushes against wind-driven water along the pier and back out to sea. That sandbar had me in its tractor beam.

Eventually, three of the biggest waves I had seen that day appeared on the horizon, and I started paddling out toward them. I barely scraped over the first wave and accelerated my paddling, pushing through the capping white water on the second wave. The third wave was the largest, and I hustled an extra ten yards to get into position. Then I sat up, leaned back quickly, and spun the nose of my board around.

As I started paddling back toward shore, the wave caught up to me and started lifting me up the face as it pushed me toward the beach. The biggest waves I had surfed up until that point were probably head high or a few feet overhead. This wave was at least two or three times that size. It was a mountain, but it was a moving mountain, alive with energy that was about to become kinetic.

Waves are impersonal. They don't care about you. Surf, swim, or drown—it's all the same to the waves. This wave was clearly agnostic about my presence—my job was to find a point of leverage where my board and I could fit into its path and the curl, the place where the wave transforms from a blue wall of caged energy into an explosion of foam and power. If you misjudge that point of change, the wave either passes under you and you miss it or you get too far in front of it and wipe out. When you fall on a big wave, it takes you and your board deep underwater, in what we call spin cycles of subaquatic somersaults, until the energy passes by and you're released to resurface.

To make it on a big wave, you have to commit. You have to put everything you have into catching the wave and dropping into what feels like a vertical wall of fast-moving water. A half-baked attempt means you'll either miss it or get caught too late on your drop.

I was determined, and I paddled as hard and fast as I could into the peaking lip, dropping in just ahead of the breaking wave. As I got to my feet and stood in a wide, stinkbug stance a couple feet from the tail, I noticed that a section of the board about eight or ten feet long was totally out of the water. My slight, tanned, barely pubescent teenage body was just heavy enough to keep the last few feet of tail in the water. It was just my checkerboard Quiksilver trunks, my longboard, and me.

I bounced along with the board, hitting chop, crouching, and holding on with my toes. As I neared the second sandbar, I could see my brother and friends waving as the wave re-formed and I was able to angle the board along the face of the wave, sliding farther forward and forcing the nose back down the face just before it stood up and pitched over the much shallower bottom. My board and I made a small airdrop into the pocket as I crouched on the inside rail.

The lip of the wave, which was now green and tan, sucked up, out, and over me, forming a ceiling and then a narrowing tunnel that at first scared me—there was no way out of the barrel except to hold on and hope to make it out the opening at the end. But then, as I embraced my situation and fit my frame to the shape of the tube, it seemed like time slowed down. I can still see the green ceiling and walls and feel the sense of helplessness, elegance, speed, and power. All I could do was trust my positioning, my board speed, and that the wave would stay open. I was beholden to the sovereignty of the lake.

When I popped out, my brother and friends were hooting and cheering for me.

Afterward, Tim said, "Holy shit! That had to be the biggest wave and tube I've seen anyone ride out here. Look at you! Your face is glowing. You look like Moses coming down the mountain."

A few years later, Tim would contract leukemia. He died in his early twenties. My brother and I shared something special, spawned by our father's love of sailing. We had a baptism of water and spirit in those waves, a communion of saints, in which we truly felt that we touched the power of the universe. We came to know the addiction of being watermen. It was by the grace of our positioning and the predestined surf from storms we could not see that we were able to experience the real power of God, whomever you may or may not think she is, in a way that gave us tremendous hope.

Riding a wave fueled by an energy you cannot see, except for its effects, can be compared to Saint Peter stepping out of the boat and walking across the water to Jesus. You know it should drown you, as it does so many, but if you put your faith in the power of the universe and align yourself with its demands, miracles happen as tangibly as if Christ were standing next to you in human form, making the blind see and the lame walk.

———

As we connect to the dynamic energy of nature in one of the most intimate and playful embraces possible, time seems to take on a different dimension. The separation that I discovered in surfing helped me understand the difference between religion—the model of a spiritual experience with God—and God herself. It was understanding that a culture's expression of truth is not truth itself and that, ultimately, when that model and culture become irrelevant to a person's life, it is okay to find or create better models and expressions in which to contain the living water that flows through us all.

The stars tell me that I am an Aquarius, a water sign. My soul has a correspondingly deep and unexplainable longing for full immersion. There is mystery and deep magic in the sea. It is where I escape the life on land. It is where I not only observe but also wrestle and clumsily dance with God as elegantly as I can.

There are reasons why I must keep my gills wet. I have to get into the water—water feeds a mystical connection between how I experience the power and grace of God and how I feel the life force that pulses through the universe. It is where I feel connected to my brother, now departed almost twenty years from this plane of life. It is where I renew my covenant with my God, how I mark myself as Christ's own and seal myself by water with the spirit. I believe that the spirit of God continues to hover over the water, showing off with surf and sunsets, demanding to be noticed and waiting for our response.

And all this brings me back to the spirit hovering over the water in Genesis, the same spirit that hovered over Christ as he rose from the Jordan. She waits for our wrestling so that the Father can name us and we can begin a mysterious future full of great promise and beauty beyond our wildest imaginations.

In the beginning was the word, and the word was God. Nothing was birthed except through this word that walked among us. There is great power in finding true words from our experiences that allow us to abide in the energy of the universe through the spirit that waits for our acceptance of the gift of that word.

And when we finally see and embrace this spirit, this energy that is in all things, the Father who created us says, "This is my child, in whom I am well pleased." God expresses profound and inalienable love for us.

I am haunted by this spirit who hovers.

Why Isn't the Link to the Divine Salvific Download Working?

Margot Starbuck

But we all, with unveiled face, beholding as in a mirror
the glory of the Lord, are being transformed into the same
image from glory to glory, just as by the Spirit of the Lord.
—2 Corinthians 3:18 NKJV

You know how high-rise hotels will sometimes have no
thirteenth floor? The elevator button just above 12 is 14. The
thirteenth floor—the one that creeps out the very supersti-
tious—simply does not exist. Though it's hard to imagine,
apparently these hotel designers must be fooling *someone.*

More and more I've found myself wanting to apply that
whole disappearing "thirteenth floor" rule to the thirteenth
chapter of the Westminster Confession. Written in 1646,
still esteemed by many Reformed bodies today, including
the denomination in which I'm ordained, this gem of orthodoxy has certainly stood the test of time. And its thirteenth
chapter deals with *sanctification.* (Picture me here with a

sour-lemon face.) *Sanctification* means that those of us who've received grace, who've been redeemed by God, are now being renewed. Regenerated.

We're becoming a little better than we used to be.

Specifically, the Confession boasts,

The dominion of the whole body of sin is destroyed, and the several lusts thereof are more and more weakened and mortified; and they more and more quickened and strengthened in all saving graces, to the practice of true holiness, without which no man shall see the Lord.

That last line is yet one more situation in which I want the presumably inclusive "man" to specify the exclusive "man," the penis-owning man. (In that case, as a woman, I'd be off the hook for practicing true holiness. Good idea, right?)

Please hear me. In my deep places, I long to be transformed. I'd like to sin less and love more. I'd even welcome a heavenly infusion of grace that would cause me to want these things more than I already do. But cognizant of my own dirty heart and painfully aware of the sin and brokenness of those around me, I am having a difficult time recognizing a predictable upward curve that suggests that any sort of measurable sanctification was ever standard issue.

I embrace gluttony.

I am regularly wildly envious. (Damn your books, you bestselling authors!)

I enjoy finding fault with others—especially slow and incompetent drivers.

I resist forgiving—both the anonymous snail's-pace drivers and those closest to me.

Were someone to graph my sanctification curve, it wouldn't be upward so much as…squiggly…in a somewhat downward fashion.

Different groups of Christians understand the contours of sanctification differently. The Christian doctrine of perfectionism means that moral and religious perfection can be experienced here on earth. Sure, sure, we're all very quick to say that we can't be perfect perfect (like God or Jesus or Superman), but our doctrine clearly announces that after we're saved, this thing—being transformed and renewed—is what the shape of discipleship looks like. And whether you interpret it rigidly, to mean "sinless," or loosely, to mean "maturity," the gist is that we're getting *better*.

Except that I'm not.

And a lot of people I love aren't.

The ones I hate certainly aren't. They're a complete mess.

With all my heart I want to believe that Christians—by virtue of divine salvific download—have some leg up on the rest of the slobs on this planet when it comes to being a little less sinful. I just have such a difficult time putting my hands on the evidence.

Our divorce rate matches the national average. Far too often we're wildly racist and homophobic, even using God's name to justify our bad behavior. We drink and cheat and use and lie and overeat and covet and steal like everyone else. (I don't do *all* those things, but I do enjoy a few of them quite a bit.) *We* do these things. *Christians* do these things. And to make matters worse, an *atheist* friend of mine has the gall to behave, quite consistently, like frickin' Mother Teresa.

So I guess I'd have to say that the main thing that keeps me from recognizing and embracing the reality of ongoing sanctification is…all the *evidence*.

All the while, the Westminster Confession and all its confession "friends" belligerently insist that sin's dominion has been destroyed. Sinful lusts are mortified. And we're quickened and enlivened and vivified to be more righteous and holy and pure than we once were.

Yet while orthodoxy seems to describe an upward trajectory of holiness across time, I feel certain that, years ago, I was a wee bit holier than I am now. So, battered with the insistent voice of the Confession, I beat myself up not only for *not* being better than I once was but also for maybe being a teeny bit worse.

The burden of this unholiness I carry is why—if nobody orthodox were looking—I'd carefully rip chapter 13 out of the Westminster Confession, wad it up in a ball, and toss it into the fireplace. And if I couldn't physically remove it, I'd be happy enough to write off renewal and transformation and regeneration as having been applicable to those earnest seventeenth-century Christians but not to us. I want this— the Christian doctrine that God's people are becoming better in a measurable way that others are not—to be one of those ancient "cultural context" situations, like a law that's been overturned in the courts or the once-timely admonition against wearing cotton-poly blends or giving your goat's beard a trim on Wednesdays.

Of course all the desperate wanting to lower the bar is probably just an attempt to ameliorate my shame...for being...so...unsanctified.

What consistently throws a real wrench in my bar-lowering imaginings is...*Scripture.* The Bible. Despite my layers and layers of sinful resistance, I'm mostly a Bible believer. And when I'm honest, the earnest, fervent Calvinists in 1646 didn't make this stuff up. The pattern is actually woven into the natural rhythm of God's design. The template I recognize in Scripture flows: creation, fall, redemption, *sanctification*.

> I will give them an undivided heart and put a new spirit in them; I will remove from them their heart of stone and give them a heart of flesh. (Ezekiel 11:19 NIV)

> Be holy because I, the LORD your God, am holy. (Leviticus 19:2 NIV)

> Be perfect, therefore, as your heavenly Father is perfect. (Matthew 5:48 NIV)

> And we all, who with unveiled faces contemplate the Lord's glory, are being transformed into his image. (2 Corinthians 3:18 NIV)

The first-century and second-century Christians, along with the seventeenth-century and eighteenth-century Pietists, believed something I'm having trouble believing right now: that the God who *forgives* human beings was, and is, powerful enough to transform broken human lives.

Like mine.

One Disgusting Mess

Tracey Bianchi

When one of the Pharisees invited Jesus to have dinner with him, he went to the Pharisee's house and reclined at the table. A woman in that town who lived a sinful life learned that Jesus was eating at the Pharisee's house, so she came there with an alabaster jar of perfume. As she stood behind him at his feet weeping, she began to wet his feet with her tears. Then she wiped them with her hair, kissed them and poured perfume on them. When the Pharisee who had invited him saw this, he said to himself, "If this man were a prophet, he would know who is touching him and what kind of woman she is—that she is a sinner."

—Luke 7:36–39 NIV

I pulled myself out of her embrace, lifted my head up off her shoulder, and wiped my tears once again, this time with a sigh of resolution. My breath was still shaky, but I could now inhale fully. A string of snot dragged between my nose and her blouse, where I'd left two tear-soaked mascara bull's-eyes and a long smudge of Dusty Rose blush, which she'd definitely need to get dry-cleaned.

"I think I'm okay now," I whispered through slowly lengthening gasps, as the meaty part of my thumb sopped up the remaining ooze from my nose. "Crap, I didn't think I needed to cry this much. Who the hell thought I'd still be crying about this?!"

I jammed a wad of soaked tissues deep into my purse and began erasing my eyeliner with both middle fingers. Deep breaths. Deep breaths.

"I'm such a mess," I finally said with a laugh.

She assured me that yes, indeed, I was a mess, but added, "This is what people do. We cry. Sometimes life affords us the luxury to giggle until we pee, but mostly we just try to survive the day."

She's right.

I like to watch the maroon paint peel off my front porch. Sometimes it reveals a smooth, beautiful slice of virgin wood that's been preserved from the elements, but usually I pick away at the flakes to discover the rot and jagged splinters lurking below.

She's right.

People get sick and die. Heck, sometimes they don't even get sick first and gift you with a warning. They get cancer and crash cars, their kids piss them off, they lose their jobs, they cheat on their spouses, they drink too much.

My best friend. She's so right and she feels everything and I hate her for that, because she makes me feel it, too. She is one of the few people who give me permission to feel all my fear, doubt, and misplaced longings, and I don't like to inhabit that space. And yet I'm always more me after being with her.

There's a story about Jesus and a woman all muddled up at his feet in a pile of snot and tears. Jesus receives a dinner invitation to the home of a well-educated, high-profile, wealthy, and utterly arrogant man named Simon. Simon loathes Jesus. Simon will never possess the sort of fame and camaraderie that come easily to Jesus. When Jesus arrives for dinner at Simon's home, half the town is camped out in the courtyard, TMZ-style, hoping to catch a glimpse of the famous rabbi and other distinguished guests. It's the perfect scenario if you are Simon and planning to show up Jesus. Even the town whore stopped by to catch a sound bite. An added bonus, in Simon's view. Someone else to help show this man the error of his ways.

The scene is dark and brooding. Simon stands off in the shadows, waiting for his moment to trip up Jesus. He and the other guests, smug and contemptuous, say, "Let's show this little runt of an upstart how things really work in our town."

Jesus walks in and is immediately snubbed. No one offers him the customary foot washing or dab of perfumed oil to remove the stink of travel. No one offers him the courtesy of a kiss or a warm gesture of any sort. The commoners and the paparazzi outside are aghast as they peer through the courtyard at the scene unfolding.

"Did that really just happen?"

"Did they really just snub Jesus?"

Suddenly there's pushing and crying, commotion and sobbing, bursting forth from the crowd. The famously scandal-ridden town prostitute, of all people, tumbles from the throngs of people to the inner rooms of Simon's home and throws herself at the feet of Jesus. Washing his dirty feet with her tears, sopping up the snotty mess with her signature long hair, and eventually breaking open the vial of perfume she carries in a necklace. Taking what was left of her miserable life to make right what was overlooked.

A pile of scandal, pain, and tears.

A moment of raw, splintered worship.

I have cried like this. I have felt her shock and horror. I have felt pain and, deep in sorrow, wished myself into a ball at the feet of Jesus. I, too, have been filled with a bizarre blend of worship, confusion, and wonder. Moments like this are what I believe God wants us to bring to life. The moment when we cannot stand the audacity of life for one more moment and throw ourselves and all the raw wonder we have at the feet of Jesus so that he can do something beautiful with it.

Moments like these mostly never happen in church.

I am a pastor. I spend half my professional life planning Sunday worship experiences for people and the other half serving as a receptacle for their snot and tears.

My weeks involve meetings about set and stage design, lighting, and the right bread for communion, mixed with a few jeers at the skinny, jeans-clad worship leaders. Hours and hours are spent trying to orchestrate a way for people to "meet God" on a Sunday, and despite these efforts, rarely are the gaping emotional holes in our lives met on a Sunday morning. We plan songs, we pray. There are the routine mike checks, sermon preps, and mediocre videos. We drink the required justice-oriented coffee from savvy, compostable cups.

Then people go home and ache.

Maybe we sort of met them, but probably not so much.

I go home and ache.

During that hour, we were not about to crash the party and lament the injustice we did to Jesus.

At our best, I and most pastors I know want church to be the most real part of a person's week. I daresay we desperately want the reality of God to meet our parishioners; it's our life's work. We say weird things like, "We want them to encounter the living God" and "We want them to know God's love and holiness." We divide the spheres of life into the "world out there, where those bad things happen" and "the world in here, where we tend to deny all those things and feign peace." We think that perhaps the right combination of hymnody paired with prayer and a drive-by from the Holy Spirit just might bring people to a place where they say, "Hey, I'm a mess. You are, too. Let's get some help."

Some even have the audacity to say that "the real world is what happens in here, in this building, in this gathering of God's people." But if you press most of us, we will confess that we try hard—heck, many of us have four-year graduate degrees aimed in this direction—but rarely do moments like I had with my friend or the prostitute had at Simon's house happen at church. And by "moments" I don't mean snot-filled emotional sabotage. I mean moments when the most raw parts of our soul meet with love and grace.

The grit and dirt of life are rarely exposed in church, even though Jesus mostly dealt in life's grime and residue. Rarely do the experiences we have outside the holy spaces compare to those inside. Ask even the holiest of rollers to compare her favorite concert experience to a Sunday morning. Ask a thirteen-year-old girl to compare her passion for One Direction with that for Sunday school. Compare Mumford & Sons' lyrics with those of popular worship tunes and ask yourself which sum up the human experience more honestly. Bono is the most effective preacher of my generation. He has rallied more masses for his sermons and spurred more people to action than anyone in recent history by far. He is raw and in your face.

As I pastor and fumble my way along, I hope that the people of God meet God. Worshippers say they want to "know Christ" or that they want to "live for Jesus," but when we consider the mess this actually makes, we lurk in the shadows like Simon or we hide behind a choir and hymnal. It is easier than facing the splinter and rot beneath the floorboards.

The most authentic, honest worship of God happens in that moment when you reach the end of yourself and someone else meets you there. Maybe it is God who meets you, as he meets the woman in Luke. Or maybe it is another person who senses your soul and serves your need, as if God nudged him or her to do that very thing. It may not happen in a sanctuary or during a song; it will happen when you look up from the tears and the mess and find yourself at the feet of hope. It will happen at a stadium when you sing along with twenty thousand people or it will happen in your garden when you stop to marvel at growth and abundance. It happens when you flop down and hook up the IV for chemo and a friend wraps her blanket around you. It happens when you see pain and grief and you cannot help but crash into the scene and make it stop.

I remember the day my friend comforted me. It felt like worship. I felt loved and known, and as I sat and devoured her embrace a small part of me was already yearning to return the favor. I was so needy, and all that the actual moment required of me was to absorb and receive. But I also did not consume myself entirely that day. And as the pain and hurt of that moment later reorganized themselves into bits that were tolerable, the desire to be that same salve for someone else grew.

That was transformation. That was a worship experience.

As was that moment when love and grace abruptly crashed into the dark demeanor of Simon's soiree. The least likely observer barely recognizing the moment before her but moving to act anyway. A chance to set right that which was neglected. A prostitute who literally stumbled into true worship. Neither moment happened in a setting we might describe as church. Both recognized fully the limits of humanity and the breadth of God.

Transformation in worship. The honest life change that church folk so desperately discuss abounds in a million ways every day. Just not a lot on Sunday mornings. Lord willing, church types like myself will find a way to foster real worship in the pew.

Evangelical Blues, Genograms, and the Sins of the Fathers, or, The Stories We Tell Ourselves

Jennifer Grant

The LORD, the LORD,
a God merciful and gracious,
slow to anger,
and abounding in steadfast love and faithfulness,
keeping steadfast love for the thousandth generation,
forgiving iniquity and transgression and sin,
yet by no means clearing the guilty,
but visiting the iniquity of the parents
upon the children
and the children's children,
to the third and the fourth generation.
    —Exodus 34:6–7 NRSV

I used to believe that if I could travel back in time and prevent my eleven-year-old self from hearing those verses read, I would. I imagined pointing a magic wand and conjuring a coughing fit in someone in a nearby pew. Better yet, an ambulance could race by outside just at the moment when those words were pronounced, and the siren's wail would drown them out. But alas, all was quiet that morning as I sat beside my mother in a sanctuary painted in that lethargic, dusty blue so often favored by conservative Protestant churches. Evangelical blue, I've heard it called.

The beginning of the passage from Exodus is as comforting and poetic as one of the Psalms. God is merciful and gracious. God is slow to anger. God forgives. God's is a "steadfast" love, a point so important that it is repeated. The second half of the passage, however, and the sermon that followed took sinister turns, upending my confidence in God's love for me. (I don't remember much about the sermon, except for the gleaming bald head of the man who delivered it, the thick, brown plastic frames of his glasses, and a tone that seemed to congratulate most of the people in attendance for having the good sense to be born into fine, upstanding Christian families.)

That Sunday morning, I decided I'd been terribly mistaken—not about who God was but about the nature of the relationship the two of us shared. I remained certain that God was loving and good and, as we sang in Sunday school, "worthy to be praised." But I went from thinking I was a cherished member of the family to feeling like the neighborhood kid who's always dropping by and whose presence is tolerated but who is never asked to stay for dinner. "Okay, time to run along now . . ."

In the months after my parents' divorce, I was ravenous for signs from God, signs that somehow everything was going to be all right. Marking promises of love and comfort, I dragged a yellow highlighter across the tissue-thin pages of my Children's Living Bible. Its cover depicted Jesus, the shepherd, navigating a rocky cliff, cradling a little lamb. As a child,

I had been confident that what had been written for and about other people thousands of years ago was somehow, mystically, also written *very specifically* for me. *I was* that lamb, resting in Christ's loving arms. That morning, however, the message that I heard was disturbing: I learned I was spiritually contaminated and even cursed because of the family into which I had been born.

I was all too cognizant of the sins of my own particular father. Adultery, drunkenness—these and others were well known around town, and a number of the clean-cut suburban saints I knew seemed to derive a sort of twisted pleasure from mentioning them to me.

One afternoon, stepping out onto the driveway, I leaned into the car to thank my friend's father for driving me home. His face stern, the man looked me directly in the eyes and said, "What choice did I have? It's not like your dad's ever been around. Anyway, the Bible tells us to care for widows and orphans." *Widows and orphans?* As far as I could tell, I was neither, but his reproachful tone was one I'd get accustomed to over the next few years. I felt ashamed and singled out for my family's brokenness, and my faith slipped farther and farther out of reach.

On that day in church the puzzle pieces of those verses from Exodus, the *tsk-tsk* comments from people who knew about my family situation, and the new questioning and spiritual loneliness I had been experiencing came together to form an ugly picture. The abundant and steadfast love of God, I determined, was reserved for others, those who had worthy spiritual lineages. As for me, I was a second-class citizen, not good enough to rest in God's love. I would spend years taking that puzzle apart, sorting the mismatched pieces into their appropriate boxes.

As a child, I didn't have to look far to see the kinds of people who were worthy of God's blessings. In the first pew on that Communion Sunday sat our church's elders. These twelve white men, dressed in almost identical navy-blue suits, somehow moved in precise unison as they made their way from the front of the congregation to the back, passing trays holding wafers and tiny plastic glasses of grape juice.

After church every week, these same men greeted the congregation as we exited the church. Their haircuts were impeccable, their faces were shaved close, and they had voices as smooth as the Muzak that played over the sound system at the grocery store. They had intact marriages and "quiversful" of children who—as I learned that fateful Sunday—would be the recipients (*for generations!*) of God's favor. As for me, well, my family tree seemed over-pruned and misshapen. I would need to be content with the leftovers of God's goodness, mindful that I didn't quite belong.

Even then, however, I knew that the idea that I was spiritually cursed was at odds with many other parts of Scripture. *Consider the lilies! He counts the number of hairs on your head! He knows when a sparrow falls!* And Saint Paul promised that nothing—not angels, demons, height, depth, nor anything else in all creation—could separate us from God's love.

But somehow—maybe as a result of my age, my bruised heart, or my propensity for gathering loose moments together and trying to weave them into cohesive story—the "sins of the fathers" narrative had gotten under my skin and become part of my own personal myth. When it rose to the surface, it would make me feel "less than"—unworthy.

Even though, over the following few years, I'd begun to distance myself from those damning words and again identify as a valued child of God, doing an intricate genogram project in a high school psychology class again made the floor drop out of my trust.

The teacher at my Christian school, after asking us to fill in a family tree and to note instances of eating disorders, mental illness, substance abuse, divorce, suicide, adultery, and so on, commented that genograms caused him to reflect on God's words concerning the "sins of the fathers."

"As we read in Exodus, and many other parts of the Bible, God says that the sins of the fathers will be visited on the children for *generations*," he said. "By making a genogram, we can see patterns of dysfunction and brokenness in families, illustrating the truth of Scripture." Glancing around at my classmates' papers, I saw that mine was the most colorful chart. I'd drawn my father's first two marriages in black and then had slashed through the lines in red pencil. My sister's substance abuse was annotated in a jarring orange. The names of family members with depression were circled in blue. And on it went. There it was in black and white (and a rainbow of colors): the sins of the fathers had indeed been "visited" on my family. My chest tightened, and old, familiar thoughts filled my mind. *You're not worthy. You're not good enough. You were defective from the start.*

Decades later, I have learned to head off those damaging thoughts at the pass by acknowledging them and putting into play the aggregate wisdom I've gleaned from sources as varied as self-help guru Byron Katie, Zen Buddhism, and the Bible— particularly Saint Paul's advice to "forget what lies behind." I've visualized myself in that Sunday service and extended kindness and grace to the confused, hurt little girl I was. I've prayed to be mindful and strengthened by what is true. I've done all I can to let it go.

But, alas, my armor isn't without its chinks.

Once in a while, it's someone else's uncomplicated faith that throws me. Not long ago, a friend told me the harrowing events of her day: her baby was colicky, a pipe burst in her basement, and she left a meal too long in the oven, where it nearly caught fire. But then her story changed direction. Her voice warmed, and she told me how good God had been to her. On rushing out to the store to replace the burned dinner, she prayed for a good parking spot, and just as she arrived at the market someone pulled out, leaving the spot closest to the door open. *Thank you, Jesus,* she prayed.

I longed—for what felt like the millionth time—to have faith like that. I wished I could truly believe that God loves me enough to finagle a great parking spot for me when I'm having a bad day. I rolled questions around in my mind. Is God really *that* present for her? Am I doing something wrong in not believing that God does these things for me? Is my faith just too small to see what he does? Am I somehow disabled spiritually? Is the old "sins of the fathers" thing a kind of curse that blinds me to God's acts of kindness?

I've also found myself beginning to unravel spiritually after being hurt. A few years ago, after receiving the last of a few "breakup" e-mails from a particular (then soon-to-be-former) friend, the "sins of the fathers" verses and their best pals, Discouragement, Anxiety, and Self-Doubt, entered my mind out of nowhere, flopped down on the couch, and made themselves at home. In her messages, my erstwhile friend told me that she wanted nothing more to do with me. She put such little value on knowing me, she said, that it wasn't even worth her time telling me why she was ending the friendship.

It was late at night when I read her last message, and my husband was out of town. I stood staring at my reflection in the dark window above the kitchen sink. I looked haggard, almost haunted. Hateful, hissing messages pummeled me. *You're not worth knowing. She is tossing you out like garbage. People have always wanted to be rid of you.*

Finally, I texted a friend and told her what I was feeling: *Unwelcome. Unwanted. Unworthy.*

"It's bringing up old scars," I texted. "Stuff I thought I was done with. I feel like garbage. Discarded, tossed out."

"You're not garbage. You've got to stop listening to those lies. They're not from God," she wrote. "You are deeply loved. I love you." My friend's kind words were enough to evict those unwelcome visitors from my mind, to help me acknowledge that rejection echoes old wounds, and to begin to let it go. I was standing before a real mirror again, the mirror of a true friend's love, reflecting the divine to me.

Like so many people I know, I make sense of life through story. And although parts of my own story can sometimes push me into dark places of insecurity and doubt, I don't think I would obliterate these tricky bits even if I could. If I expunged all that has hurt or confounded me, who would I be?

And despite what I often think of as my mustard seed–size faith, I have been gifted with moments of lucidity when I've been aware of God's presence, a presence as irrefutable as the reading glasses that sit on the desk beside me, the car horn that just blasted outside my window, or a chilly draft that makes me shiver and draw my sweater closer around me. These include the words that settled into my mind before the birth of my third child, words that calmed my anxiety and assured me that everything was going to be all right. They include the experience of sensing a hand holding my own when I walked alone into my sister's hospital room in the oncology ward only days before she died. I had to look down to see whether there was a real, physical hand; I couldn't see it, but there was the sensation, comforting and strong. I knew God was with me. And years ago, I received a message—one as unambiguous as a telegram—that I was going to adopt a child.

But still, I am usually more at home with the doubters and the skeptics than with those people who march through life with unblinking certainty, whatever their faith practices, convictions, or ideology may be. I like the stories each one of my motley crew of friends tells and the ways we tell them. I see that our own failures and weaknesses often result in stunning acts of generosity and a posture of openness that isn't always found among the ones who are so very sure that they are right or who privately lick their wounds and keep their own brokenness hidden from sight.

And even though we don't usually ask God for prime parking spaces, we skeptics tend to be thankful people, ever grateful for what is true: real friends, real beauty, and real wrangling with faith, our stories, and our broken world.

A High Tolerance for Ambiguity

Steve Brown

For my thoughts are not your thoughts,
neither are your ways my ways, declares the LORD.
For as the heavens are higher than the earth,
so are my ways higher than your ways
and my thoughts than your thoughts.

—Isaiah 55:8–9 ESV

It's said that when Moses was first given the commandment to be circumcised, his initial reaction was, "What? Wait! Let me make sure that I've got this straight. You want me to do *what* with *what*?"

All my life, I've struggled with knowing what God wants from me, and on those occasions when I found out what he wanted, I've struggled even more to do it. In both of those cases (the knowing and the doing), my record isn't altogether that good. In fact, if God is keeping count, I'm in serious trouble. Now I'm an old, cynical preacher who thought he would be clearer on God's will and better at doing it than he is.

I teach at a theological seminary, and I love theological students. They wash out my soul and sometimes make me

124

less cynical. But still, I'm amazed by the passion (it sometimes smells like arrogance) of seminary students. I often find myself wishing that I knew as much as they know and that I could be as sure as they are. When the frustration level gets unbearable, I often say to the students, "You guys aren't old enough, and you haven't sinned big enough, to even have an opinion on that subject."

Well, I'm old enough. And God knows, I've sinned big enough. So listen up: *I'm not your mother, and I don't know.*

If you've stood before God and haven't been confused, you're probably not worshipping God. You're worshipping an idol. Not only that, but God's ways are circuitous, and whatever you think God is doing, he probably isn't. If you want to make God laugh, someone has said, tell him your plans. But even more relevant, if you want to make God *really* laugh, tell him what you think he told you.

Steve, are you leaving and becoming a Buddhist or something?

I've thought about it. Buddhists don't seem to care about diets, and they're always smiling; but frankly, I've gone too far here to get out. Besides, I hate change, and I wonder who will forgive me and love me the way Jesus does. So I'm probably going to stay—bloodied and wounded sometimes, afraid and angry sometimes, sinful and rebellious sometimes, confused and lost sometimes...and always needy—because I don't have any other place to go.

I'm just not as sure as my students. And I'm not as sure about God's ways as I once was, either. Saint Paul asked a rhetorical question in Romans 11:34: "Who has known the mind of the Lord, or who has been his counselor?" (ESV). The obvious answer is that I certainly don't, and nobody else here does, either. The eternal verities of my faith are perhaps more sure now than ever. But what I once thought was important isn't so much anymore, and the list of those things for which I would "die on a hill" is much shorter than it used to be.

There is an interesting comment in the book of Acts related to Saint Paul's plans for ministry. Saints Paul and Barnabas had separated (they had a major fight . . . so much for returning to the pristine days of the New Testament church!). Saint Paul had some big plans to preach in Bithynia, perhaps even to start a church there.

Luke wrote: "They attempted to go into Bithynia, but the Spirit of Jesus did not allow them. So, passing by Mysia, they went down to Troas. And a vision appeared to Paul in the night: a man of Macedonia was standing there, urging him and saying, 'Come over to Macedonia and help us'" (Acts 16:7–9 ESV).

Interrupted plans. Shattered dreams. Truncated ministries. It goes with the turf of doing traffic with God. If we can't deal with that and somehow process it, we should spend our time doing something far more productive and conducive to control—like, say, vinyl repair. But if there is a God (and there is), if he calls us to define ourselves by him (and he does), and if we are somehow to represent him and his love in the world (and that's what he calls us to do), then a high tolerance for ambiguity is the essence of godly maturity.

Henri Nouwen wrote in his book *In the Name of Jesus: Reflections on Christian Leadership,* "I am deeply convinced that the Christian leader of the future is called to be completely irrelevant and to stand in this world with nothing to offer but his or her own vulnerable self . . . The leaders of the future will be those who dare to claim their irrelevance in the contemporary world as a divine vocation."

I'm not altogether happy with that, but it rings true to all I know about the Bible . . . and I know a lot. It's all over the place in those passages that I didn't underline when I was younger.

I just read what I wrote, and it sounds so bleak. The truth is that there is an incredible release and freedom when we finally come to the realization that God is God and we don't have to be. At first, not having a vote seems unfair and somewhat less than empowering. But when we deal with the fact that God really doesn't need us or our help, and that he was doing fine before we came along, we can do all we can with the little we know and it will be enough. God's power really is made perfect in weakness.

And then there's the love. It's true that if you haven't stood before God and been confused, you're probably not standing before the real God. But it is also true—and far more important—to realize that if you haven't stood before God and been loved unconditionally and without reservation, you're not standing before the real God, either.

Women and Children First

Linda Midgett

An excellent wife who can find?
    She is far more precious than jewels.
The heart of her husband trusts in her,
    and he will have no lack of gain.
She does him good, and not harm,
    all the days of her life.
She seeks wool and flax,
    and works with willing hands.
She is like the ships of the merchant;
    she brings her food from afar.
She rises while it is yet night
    and provides food for her household
    and portions for her maidens.
She considers a field and buys it;
    with the fruit of her hands she plants a vineyard.
She dresses herself with strength
    and makes her arms strong.
She perceives that her merchandise is profitable.
    Her lamp does not go out at night.
She puts her hands to the distaff,
    and her hands hold the spindle.

She opens her hand to the poor
    and reaches out her hands to the needy.
She is not afraid of snow for her household,
    for all her household are clothed in scarlet.
She makes bed coverings for herself;
    her clothing is fine linen and purple.
Her husband is known in the gates
    when he sits among the elders of the land.
She makes linen garments and sells them;
    she delivers sashes to the merchant.
Strength and dignity are her clothing,
    and she laughs at the time to come.
She opens her mouth with wisdom,
    and the teaching of kindness is on her tongue.
She looks well to the ways of her household
    and does not eat the bread of idleness.
Her children rise up and call her blessed;
    her husband also, and he praises her:
"Many women have done excellently,
    but you surpass them all."
Charm is deceitful, and beauty is vain,
    but a woman who fears the LORD *is to be praised.*
Give her of the fruit of her hands,
    and let her works praise her in the gates.
    —Proverbs 31:10–31 ESV

I was thirty-four and working temporarily in Los Angeles when the concept of biology as destiny became very personal. It was an awesome time in my career as a TV producer. I was senior management on a reality series that would go on to win multiple Daytime Emmys. Every day I would drive from my rental apartment to the multimillion-dollar house in the Hollywood Hills where we filmed.

As my little car climbed up the steep mountains, I would look over the sprawling view of LA and want to pinch myself. Though the hours were brutal, I loved what I was doing, and my husband and I were seriously considering a permanent move to the West Coast. He was just finishing up his doctorate in psychology in Chicago. We were ready to relocate; we just didn't know exactly where we'd go.

And then I got pregnant.

(SCREEEEECH!)

We continued to look at housing, trying to find an apartment or home we could afford. Yet at some point, between searching for elastic-waist pants, crying at ridiculous commercials, and trying not to hurl on everyone around me, I came to the realization that LA wasn't where I wanted to raise a family. Both our families were in the South, and we couldn't imagine our baby not having its grandparents, cousins, aunts, and uncles at least within driving distance.

So we made a decision that once my show ended, we would move back to my home state of North Carolina, where I would eventually start my own production company. John would start a private practice as a psychologist. It was a risky move, but we were excited. I had long wanted to develop shows of my own, and I was confident that I had the credentials and experience to succeed.

The plan seemed even more viable when my agent, who had just signed me a few months earlier, called with some big news. He had accepted a job with one of Hollywood's most prestigious agencies...and he wanted to take me with him. We set up a meeting in Beverly Hills.

Maybe the fact that I didn't order a drink tipped him off. I'm not sure. But by the time I had revealed my "baby news" and my big plan to open a company in North Carolina, it was clear that something was off. He was lukewarm, almost... resistant. Finally he revealed what was on his mind.

"When you become a mom, you aren't going to be interested in doing this anymore," he said. "You're going to be interested in mommy things. Going to the park with the kids, meeting other moms, that kind of thing. You're going to hang out with other moms. You aren't going to want to do this."

And then he dropped me.

Crying in the car on my way home, I wasn't sure which was more humiliating: what he said or my fear that he was right. Was I going to lose interest in my work when I became a mother? Were all my friendships going to change? Was my biology really going to override my creativity, drive, and ambition?

There was no way for me to know. Plenty of women do dramatically modify or drop their careers once they become mothers. I'd never had a baby before, and it was clear that lots of other things were changing. My stomach was getting round. I suddenly couldn't bear the texture or taste of chicken. And I was moving to the other side of the country based on my unborn child's well-being. I was in uncharted territory. And it was confusing.

Eight years into motherhood and another child later, it still is. Because if there's one thing all mothers experience in our society, it's guilt. There are so many ways to be a "bad mom."

You only breast-fed two years? *Your child is going to be a sociopath!*

You aren't buying organic? *You're giving your baby cancer!*

You put your child in day care? *Complete strangers (who might be wolves) are raising your child!*

And if you don't feel bad enough about those things, look in the mirror: *You haven't even lost the baby weight yet!*

Christian women are not immune to these messages. On the contrary, from what I've observed, being in a church community can sometimes intensify the pressure on mothers. Because in addition to the guilt and confusion women absorb from popular culture, there is a special guilt reserved specifically for women who deeply care about Scripture: you aren't being the Proverbs 31 woman.

Ah—the Proverbs 31 woman. She is part Martha Stewart—she selects wool and flax and works with eager hands. She's part Mother Teresa—she opens her arms to the poor. And there's some Betty Crocker in there, as she gets up while it is still night to provide food for her family. Oh, and she's also part Oprah Winfrey, because she speaks with wisdom and faithful instruction is on her tongue. She does all this while laughing at the days to come, mocking the rest of us with her Mona-Lisa, I am-perfect-therefore-my-husband-praises-me smile.

No wonder I run in the other direction when someone suggests studying Proverbs 31. Thanks, but I'll just stick my hand in a wood chipper. It sounds less painful and exhausting.

To be honest, though, there are plenty of things that I actually admire about the Proverbs 31 woman. For one thing, she should be on the cover of *Entrepreneur* magazine. She is buying fields, trading, planting vineyards with her excess money, and helping provide food for her family and servants. (Hooray! Servants!) She and her children are well dressed (they apparently have nice winter coats). She even has a great bedspread. When you look at all she's doing, the Proverbs 31 woman is actually an amazing working mom who manages to juggle meaningful employment while caring deeply and effectively for her family. (And she has a good relationship with her husband to boot.)

So why am I not more drawn to her?

For one thing, in evangelical Christian culture, I never, ever hear her presented as an example of a working mother. For the most part, her legacy has been domesticated thoroughly, focusing only on what she does *inside* the home as opposed to *outside* of it. She is simultaneously idealized and minimized. Idolized yet marginalized. Her full range of achievements and accomplishments is eclipsed by her status as a mother and a married woman, as though those are the only two roles that a biblical woman can fulfill. In essence, the evangelical church has told the Proverbs 31 woman to just go watch her kids play at the park.

This, as you can tell, strikes a nerve with me. You see, my agent was wrong. Not only did I continue to work after my son was born, I continue to love it. I love writing scripts and producing documentaries, and I love the nuts and bolts of all that entails.

At the same time, I really, truly love my children beyond imagination. That love does not, however, make me want to go to the park. I get bored at the park. I sit there thinking of projects I'd like to be working on instead of swatting bugs. I don't have a lot of friendships based on being "mommies," either. I prefer to talk to girlfriends about other things. Like work. Or books. Or politics.

There are women who absolutely love being stay-at-home moms, and in no way am I putting them down. I truly believe we all have different callings and that our families need different kinds of care. For some of us, it's full-time work because of financial need. For others, it's part-time work. For many, it's a combination that changes over the years based on complicated and shifting realities. Yet in many circles, the full-time, at-home mother is the only "godly" mother. And Proverbs 31 is used to support that.

That's not who God created me to be. I'm tired of feeling slightly defensive about not fitting into the cookie-cutter shape that evangelical Christianity has created out of this part of Scripture. Because I believe that the church, of all places in the world, should be a sanctuary where women are encouraged to be who God made them to be: people who have been freed by the grace of Jesus to create lives that contribute to the kingdom.

Yet when you Google "Proverbs 31 woman," there is little mention of God's kingdom and quite a bit of emphasis on our own earthly kingdoms. You know—the ones within the walls of our homes. It all borders on the comical. For example, there is a Proverbs 31 Ministries that has a list of "Friday craft ideas" on one of its blogs. I have rarely had free time on a Friday. But I would quite seriously organize my closets (it's on my perennial to-do list) before I would "craft."

A Google search also pulls up a list called "10 Virtues of the Proverbs 31 Woman." One of her virtues is being a "homemaker." The other is that she "seeks her husband's approval before making purchases." To be clear, I work hard at creating a loving, warm home for my family. And I think talking to your husband before making major purchases is wise advice.

What bothers me is that:

- there is more in Proverbs 31 about this woman being an entrepreneur than there is about her housekeeping skills;

• there is nothing in Proverbs 31 to suggest that this woman consulted *anyone* before buying her fields; and

• the unspoken "virtue" that underlies this entire passage of Scripture is, of course, that the woman is married.

I guess that's just bad luck for the intelligent, fascinating women I know who are single or divorced. That the ideal Christian woman is so often presented as a married, homemaking mother leaves out many of us who are just, well, not that. As one of my friends, whose spouse recently left their marriage and three kids, says, "My husband is never going to 'rise up and praise me.' Maybe we need to redefine what a husband is."

Indeed. And maybe we as Christians need to redefine who the Proverbs 31 woman really is. Because for those of us who love God's word, there is true liberation in the support of our brothers and sisters in Christ. Even when someone tells you to go to the park.

A few years after my agent dumped me, I found myself in the North Carolina mountains with my senior and associate pastors. They had a vision for using my documentary skills on the mission field and had brought me to their denomination's headquarters to meet with a bigwig. They were young, church-planting pastors—excited and a little nervous to present their idea. I was their star: the Emmy Award–winning producer, the ace in the hole for their concept.

We arrived during a rainstorm. The bigwig was just finishing up his lunch and prepared to lead us outside to his office. He had a problem, though. He was halfway through eating an apple and couldn't easily manage the fruit plate with his umbrella.

He needed help and glanced first at my senior pastor, who is African American. You could almost see his thoughts in a cartoon bubble: "Hmm—handing the apple to the only black man. That's a great way to get sued." Then he looked at my associate pastor, a white guy with red hair. "Hmm—can't give it to a white guy...he's a peer." Then he looked at me. "The only woman. Descendant of Eve. Bingo!"

He handed me his plate with the half-eaten apple resting on it. He didn't appear to notice my jaw on the ground as he proceeded to walk out in front of us, the umbrella effectively protecting him from the rain. The three of us walked behind him, getting drenched.

Did I want to laugh? Cry? I wasn't entirely sure. I knew I was indignant that I wasn't under the umbrella. After all, this was the *South*. There are codes of conduct, such as: *women and children under the umbrellas first!*

Still, I dutifully followed, carrying his half-eaten, browning apple. As my hair began to frizz, I glanced out of the corner of my eye at my pastors. They were looking at their feet, walking in embarrassed silence. Did they realize how ludicrous this was? Was I overreacting? I couldn't be sure.

After the long, awkward meeting, we all got in the car, and my pastors began to vent. To my delight, they were incensed by the man's actions. Outraged! They even cussed. And I started laughing, because it was so freeing to have permission from my church leaders to say, "That is just jacked-up!" We snickered all the way home, and they called their wives to tell them the appalling thing that had just happened. (Their wives cussed a little, too.) On the trip home, the three of us stopped at a restaurant—and ordered apple martinis.

What could have been the second half of my disillusioning agent story became the point where the narrative turned. It was a moment of redemption. Of liberation. Because my pastors saw me as the Proverbs 31 woman *should* be seen. I'm someone who works hard and deserves accolades for what she does. I'm a mother whose biology in no way diminishes her dignity or worth. I'm someone who can't be minimized by being sent to the park or being expected to carry someone's half-eaten apple.

They rose up and praised me.

And it felt good.

The Necessity of Solitude

Christopher L. Heuertz

Finally one day Paul lost his temper...
—Acts 16:18 TIB

A few hundred prominent leaders of evangelical missions had gathered together in South Asia. Folks from close to seventy countries—mostly white, male, from the so-called "Developed World"—came together to consider some of the most urgent and pressing issues in global evangelism.

I was seated at a round table in a typical conference room in a nice hotel. The luxury of the hotel stood in stark contrast to the poverty surrounding it. The insulated walls and the absence of windows in the posh, comfortable, but otherwise nondescript conference room isolated us from the sights and sounds of urban squalor outside as we concentrated on our very important theological work.

This particular group absolutely loves the inductive Bible study method. The conference organizers added space on each morning's schedule to dig into the book of Acts. One morning we were given a copy of Acts 16:11–24 and encouraged to observe, interpret, and apply it.

So I did.

The story recounts Saint Paul's and Silas's visit to Philippi, a business hub in the first-century Roman world. Paul and Silas were on a long trip and were making several key stops. Because it appears there was no synagogue in Philippi, on this particular Sabbath the guys left the city to go outside the gate. They were looking for a quiet place to pray where they wouldn't be bothered; it's plausible they were simply in search of what must have been some long-overdue solitude, silence, and stillness.

Maybe they were there to pray as well. Regardless, a little crowd of ladies distracted Paul and Silas from their quest. One of the women in the group (other than Paul and Silas, she is the only person named in this passage) was Lydia, a cloth merchant in the purple-dye business—extremely subversive herself, as Philippi was one of the first places in the Roman world where women were allowed to run their own businesses. Her specialized industry indicated that Lydia was wealthy—she had a stack of change.

Now, from one perspective it might look as though Paul, by chatting up these ladies, was making a bold and courageous attempt at breaking down gender walls. Outside the gates of Philippi was where outcasts and those who were marginalized often gathered to avoid transmitting disease; it was also where they would sometimes sift through garbage heaps in search of something to eat. That these women were outside the gates suggests a kind of gender marginalization—one that still persists in many religious circles today. Regardless, here we see Paul and Silas go outside the city to pray to a marginal God. But that's just one angle: from another angle it could seem as if Paul was setting his patriarchy aside for a quick minute to hustle some money from a wealthy lady and her friends for his travels. In any case, Lydia responds favorably to the message Paul and Silas were peddling. She starts following these guys around the city.

Enter another businesswoman, but of a completely different kind.

On another afternoon, again while the guys are on their way to pray, a young enslaved woman (overwhelmingly referred to as a "slave girl" in most English translations) shows up. The passage indicates that she was possessed by a spirit that could tell the future. The general consensus among Bible scholars is that these mystic powers were attributed to the Pythian spirit of the god Apollo. Apollo's temple in Delphi was erected to commemorate his defeat over Python, a dragon or huge serpent. The exploited woman's owners were making serious cash off her fortunetelling skills.

The enslaved woman also follows Saint Paul and Silas around, but rather than accepting their message, she heckles them—for days. One day Saint Paul finally has had enough. Out of frustration he commands the spirit out of her.

Ta-da! She was freed.

But her owners were pissed.

Although I don't want to diminish the possibility that her possession was traumatic in and of itself, one can only imagine the torment this young woman must have endured on the other side of her so-called liberation.

This enslaved girl's owners very likely took her to the temple and subjected her to all sorts of rituals to stuff that spirit back into her. She might have been draped with snakes or made to endure other horrific practices to *un-exorcise* her. That this woman may have been tortured physically, psychologically, and spiritually is troubling. That Paul seems calloused and unconcerned about her life postexorcism is of further concern. The text tells us that Saint Paul was annoyed. He lost his temper. The exorcism was not performed out of compassion or love. If anything, his actions appear self-centered—an abuse of his spiritual power.

Unlike wealthy Lydia, this woman is not named in the story. We actually learn more about her *owner's* response to the exorcism than we do about her. These folks have lost a significant source of income; if they can't be compensated, they want justice. Her handlers seize Paul and Silas and drag them into the marketplace to face authorities for judgment.

Putting your hand in someone's pocket and stealing cash is serious. So serious that Paul and Silas have their clothes ripped off and are beaten up with canes and rods. As if that's not bad enough, they're thrown in jail. Apparently these guys are such a threat to the economy that they're locked down in maximum security. The passage says that they were placed in the inner cell and that their feet were fastened in the stocks.

That's a messed-up story.

There's a lot of ego and a lot of malformed notions of power being played out in this little passage. But I found out pretty quickly that the conference organizers who put this narrative in front of us had a different take on it. They broke us up into small groups of seven or eight people to discuss a series of reflection questions. We were given questions about the strategic value of Philippi to Paul's and Silas's mission and asked to think of today's equivalents as locations on which to focus our evangelistic efforts. We were asked to consider how crucial the missional role of successful businesspersons such as Lydia is and how people such as Lydia could be used to train folks for transformation in the workplace. We were asked to consider the positive impact of the gospel on the slave girl's social, economic, and spiritual life. Finally, we were challenged to consider the implications of Christians presenting the gospel in the workplace and in the market.

I was struggling to make sense of the whole thing.

From the thirteen verses we were given, I saw lots and lots of problems. First, I was troubled by the disparity between the two women highlighted in the story. Wealthy Lydia was identified by name; the young girl who was enslaved and possessed remained anonymous—actually, even worse, she was overidentified with the ways in which she was exploited. This is pretty typical, actually; we usually know the names of those we perceive to be valuable in our own communities. For example, in Omaha, where I live, lots of people don't know the names of their neighbors, but most folks know exactly who our richest Omahan is: Warren Buffett. Many of us could even take you to his house.

I find hope in another part of the Scriptures, where this disproportionate ascribing of power and dignity is subverted in the life of Christ. In all the parables Jesus tells, he only gives one person a name: Lazarus, a poor man who begs outside the house of a wealthy neighbor. In this example (Luke 16:19–31) Jesus highlights a reversal of the power dynamic: when fueled by our egotistical need for esteem, he finds the name of those pushed to the margins—in Paul's case, the one reduced to the dehumanizing term "slave girl"—and ascribes dignity to her by celebrating her identity. It's also telling that Jesus' naming of Lazarus takes place in the Gospel of Luke, whereas in the passage from Acts Luke fails to mention the enslaved woman's name . . . possibly a nuanced nod to Paul's ego.

Second, I know some folks who fail to recognize the gift of Saint Paul's humanity and deconstruct him as this cranky, old, dogmatic sexist; we must not forget that he was human, tragically flawed, like each of us. Though he clearly possessed profoundly developed natural gifts, and of course blessed talents, Saint Paul had an ego, a shadow, and frequently confessed his personal struggles with his false self. In this little story his dark side is exposed. His response to the girl who was trapped in slavery comes from his *frustration* with her. Where's the compassion for her subjugation? Where's the concern for her welfare? Where's his sense of justice for her oppression?

Third, the marketplace in this tale is a background of reductionism, one that allows for humanity to be bought and sold into slavery and one that protects the interests of the slave owners over the interests of those yearning for freedom. The market commodifies humanity into products that can be purchased or traded. The market puts itself first and uses humanity to generate an illusion of power—one that when threatened invites stern consequences. In fact, when confronted on justice issues, the market becomes a place of judgment, a kangaroo court that is the antithesis of fairness and compassion.

It seems in that meeting room at the conference in South Asia we were all a little guilty of this commodification. Some of the conference organizers and attendees seemed blind to the disparity between the wealthy and the poor, the chauvinism of Paul and his myopic sense of mission, and the reductive power of idolatrous economics.

After all, it's the idolatry of the marketplace that leads us to celebrate people like Lydia, like Buffett, while simultaneously sacrificing others, such as persons in slavery; it's the idolatry of the marketplace that leads Paul to prioritize the abstraction of his mission over the particular pain of the oppressed woman.

Fourth, a final sign of hope I find in the passage is the consequence of Paul and Silas abusing their power: they are incarcerated. Certainly I don't think the punishment fits the crime, but I find the language used to describe their incarceration quite provocative. They are thrown in the *inner cell*, and their feet are *fastened* in the stocks. Contemplative mystics use the language of the *inner cell* as the quiet place, that deep place in our souls we can access only through inner solitude, silence, and stillness.

My sense is that God so cared for the young girl and the consequences of Paul abusing his power that Paul was forced into solitude by being thrown in prison. Being locked up, away from the crowd, obviously silenced him. Having his feet shackled imposed stillness. If we don't make time for contemplation, often the circumstances of life will force us into it. By being put in prison—forced into solitude, silence, and stillness—Paul had the opportunity to reflect on his unconscious motivations for social engagement.

I've come to learn that unless our social engagement is grounded in a deep, contemplative spirituality, it will perpetuate unintended harm, and the consequences are most acutely felt by the vulnerable. The contemplative stance is supported by solitude, silence, and stillness. Solitude cultivates our ability to be present. Silence helps us listen. Stillness allows for effective impact.

The story here begins on the Sabbath, with Paul and Silas looking for a place to pray, and continues days later, when they were on their way to pray and first met the girl who was exploited because of her magic powers—but in both scenarios we *don't* hear that Paul and Silas actually did stop and make time to pray.

The interruptions to both occasions for Paul's and Silas's withdrawal are opportunities for social engagement. One with words that can liberate, another with actions that can lead to freedom. But in sacrificing their prayer practice for service, their motivations for serving go unchecked and unsurrendered—leading to unintended consequences that diminish the humanity of everyone involved.

Because of the prospects for witness—an audience made up of a little crowd of ladies, and then a person possessed by a spirit of divination—it appears they forgo their prayer practice and jump right back into ministry.

Certainly they would have had good reasons to engage the crowds and confront supernatural abilities they perceived as evil, but perhaps in those moments, the most important thing was to get grounded and centered in God.

Silence was wasted on them while they filled the air with their words, working to persuade the wealthy to follow them while growing frustrated at the oppressed woman following them.

When mission is focused on preaching, it often overlooks God's mission among those on the margins. And who suffers? Those who are poor—for example, a girl sold into slavery, who needed all kinds of liberation and freedom.

The consequences? The girl who longs for freedom is cast aside, and Paul loses his freedom while incarcerated. Maybe it's an ironic imposition of divine intervention.

The unintended consequences of Paul's seemingly good act, and the spiritual connection to his imprisonment in the wake of it, illuminate a simple yet difficult reality a lot of us know so well: unless we deliberately make room for solitude, silence, and stillness, we will be taken to solitude, silence, and stillness *against our will*.

Some of us will burn out, others may simply give up, a few of us may keep plugging away for good until we have nothing left to give, and many of us will genuinely attempt to help the world while missing the quiet voice of God that beckons us to the undramatic contemplative practices that ground us—that awaken us to our unconscious and subconscious motivations to serve.

I sat in that conference room stunned.

As I looked around I saw some modern s/heroes of the faith—all those folks sincerely believed they were making the world a better place with their efforts and their strategies and through their organizations. From the platform, the presentations delivered were loaded with chest-pounding triumphalism and self-congratulatory affirmations of the excellent work done by by those gathered in that room. But all the words drowned out the real invitation. An invitation to reflect deeply on the reductionist violence, the unintended harm perpetuated in the name of Christ and the subsequent cost vulnerable folks have had to pay for that.

Had we only made room for a little solitude, silence, and stillness, then perhaps the questions given to us as interpretive guides for that passage may have been a bit more nuanced—pointing us away from ourselves, our activity, and our organizations and back to God.

This is what we learn from Jesus, who withdrew in solitude, who gave himself to silence, and in the unrelenting demands of humanity practiced stillness in his own inner cell.

In the inner cell and through the subversive memory of Jesus we learn how solitude allowed him to give his life outside the gates of Jerusalem by rejecting the centrality of the temple and the commerce of the empire. In the inner cell we learn how in silence Jesus finds words so that those who are poor and forced to the margins are named. In this quiet place we learn how in his stillness Jesus voluntarily enters the inner cell of the tomb and emerges from it still bearing the wounds of his crucifixion.

And it's this simple and subversive Christ who calls Paul to "do good better."

By grounding our social and cultural engagement in a deep contemplative spirituality we can do good better, too.

Mary and Martha; Mom and Me

Stephen Henderson

As Jesus and his disciples were on their way, he came to a village where a woman named Martha opened her home to him. She had a sister called Mary, who sat at the Lord's feet listening to what he said. But Martha was distracted by all the preparations that had to be made. She came to him and asked, "Lord, don't you care that my sister has left me to do the work by myself? Tell her to help me!" "Martha, Martha," the Lord answered, "you are worried and upset about many things, but few things are needed—or indeed only one. Mary has chosen what is better, and it will not be taken away from her."

—Luke 10:38–42 NIV

Can't we just have eggs?"

This anguished cry from my mother came on a summer morning in a rented beach house on Cape Cod. At this point in the early 1980s, my three sisters, brother, and I were already adults, yet we weren't so distracted by our own family responsibilities that we couldn't gather for a week's vacation with our parents. These were happy reunions, if occasionally

147

fraught with moments when our diverging sensibilities were revealed.

My attempts at individuation were probably most evident in ambitious cooking experiments, which, to Mom's dismay, even occurred at breakfast. One day I'd gotten up early to mince garlic, dice tomatoes, pit black olives, and make a chiffonade of basil leaves. I was prepping my version of *oeufs à la méditerranéenne*, and my mother wasn't pleased. Any fuss over food was suspicious to her, if not downright sinful. She wanted her eggs *plain*, save for a pious pinch of salt and pepper.

A born-again Christian and wife of a conservative Baptist preacher, Mom lived a circumspect life, one carefully cordoned off from what she habitually referred to as "the world." She didn't go to movies, watch TV, read novels, or flip through fashion magazines.

This rigorous self-restraint extended into the kitchen. It's not that Mom was a bad cook; there was something ascetic about her disinterest in new flavors and recipes. It was as if she believed that blandness was next to godliness. By far the most exotic spice I knew her to deploy was paprika—and this only rarely.

What explains my mother's gastrophobia? I now suspect it was her study of Luke 10:38–42, which is the perplexing Bible story of two sisters, Mary and Martha, and their opposing opinions on how best to treat a VIP guest—none other than Jesus Christ. Before considering Martha and Mary's divergent styles of entertaining, though, it might be helpful to offer some historical context.

First, Jesus relied on the kindness of strangers. He didn't have the benefit of a trusted travel agent or the mechanism of a "worldwide evangelistic crusade" behind him to set up a seamless itinerary of e-tickets, Hertz reservations, and non-smoking hotel rooms with king-size beds. On the contrary, Jesus mostly walked from village to village, hoping (and, doubtless, praying) that he'd encounter someone who would want not only to hear his message but also to provide him with food and shelter.

As such, Martha's welcoming of Jesus, which Luke 10:38 makes a point of specifying takes place at her house and not Mary's, suggests Martha wants to support Jesus' ministry.

So does her sister.

Indeed, when Jesus arrives, Mary is starstruck and very excited for whatever this visit may portend. Grabbing a front-row seat, she immediately plops herself down at Jesus' feet. Presumably Martha is just as keen to hear what Jesus has to say, yet she's also conscious of her role as hostess. Concerned Jesus and his traveling companions might be hungry and thirsty, she begins to bustle about, getting food ready.

I like to imagine Martha whipping up a quick batch of hummus, or making sure the pita bread is warm. Truth to tell, Martha may also have taken a few extra seconds to fluff up the pillows or sponge off the kitchen counters. We all know how embarrassing it is when someone we admire shows up unexpectedly only to discover what slobs we really are. Would you want the son of God to see your underwear dangling from the doorknob if he needed to use the bathroom?

Whatever sort of hospitality she had in mind, Martha soon realizes she could use an extra set of hands. When she sees Mary cooling her heels out in the living room, Martha is irritated, and—admittedly, not to her credit—she brings this frustration to Jesus, not to her sister. After hearing her complaint, Jesus gently chides, "Martha, Martha. You are worried and upset about many things, but only one thing is needed.

Mary has chosen what is better, and it will not be taken away from her."

A standard interpretation of this story gives the impression that Mary is the good sister. She's *the spiritual one*, the one who understands that nothing in life matters except opening one's heart up to God. Martha, on the other hand, is made to seem slightly ridiculous, a Galilean forebear of her namesake, Martha Stewart, who's more concerned with place cards and color-coordinated napkin rings than with seizing this opportunity to feast on Jesus' wisdom.

Other biblical scholars put a feminist spin on the narrative. In Hebrew society of two thousand years ago, they remind us, women were openly despised by many rabbis and discouraged from learning of any sort. Men controlled the higher realms of thought through their study of the Torah, while women were to busy themselves with humbler concerns: caring for the home, the children, and, yes, making the hummus. By saying she must free herself from domestic drudgery, Jesus is doing the unthinkable: he's encouraging Martha to "man up."

The question remains, though: once Jesus is done preaching and it's time for lunch, what then? It's not like Martha could just pop a few frozen burritos into the microwave or pull out her cell phone and order a rush delivery of sesame noodles.

As I see it, Jesus' behavior would be more exemplary if he'd said, "Martha, Martha. How thoughtful of you to realize we might soon be feeling a little peckish! But why don't you relax and listen? Then, a few minutes from now, howzabout Mary, the disciples, and I come help you throw something together?"

Or, since Jesus was, by all reports, able to single-handedly pull off miraculous feats of mass cookery—the feeding of the five thousand, say, or the water-to-wine switcheroo he accomplished at the wedding at Cana—he might also have said,

"Martha, Martha. Please join your sister and sit down next to me! After a while, when we're all hungry, you'll discover lunch has taken care of itself out there."

Jesus didn't say either of those things, however, which makes this New Testament story problematic, especially in the United States, where certain Scripture verses, and certain preferred ways of interpreting them, have a sneaky way of seeping into the collective consciousness—not to mention into federal laws. It's often noted how so-called "Bible-based" attitudes have affected US policy on LGBT rights and marriage equality, women's reproductive health, and attitudes toward environmentalism and global warming. I believe Jesus' oddly dismissive rebuff to Martha has done much to engender America's oddly dismissive attitude toward food also.

Sure, among the affluent and well-educated, there's a growing enthusiasm for organic produce, free-range poultry, and line-caught fish, not to mention the slow food movement. However, a vastly larger group of Americans make time for all sorts of things—shopping, playing sports, watching television, updating their Facebook pages—but could care less about cooking.

In 1970, Americans spent 26 percent of their food budget on eating out. By 2010, this number had risen to 41 percent. Maybe not surprisingly, during the same period, rates of obesity in the United States more than doubled, and one out of three American adults is now estimated to be overweight.

Industrialized food manufacturers have quite profitably convinced us that knowing how to peel a shrimp or stir-fry kale requires specialized knowledge nearly as arcane as being able to play the harpsichord. In his recent book *Cooked: A Natural History of Transformation*, author Michael Pollan describes a condition called "learned helplessness," whereby most Americans have outsourced their own sustenance to such a degree that they're now incapable of feeding themselves.

When I have people over to dinner, I'm frequently amazed when my guests say things like, "You did this all yourself? I'd never have the patience!" Or "I wish I had time to cook!"

Hearing these comments, with their not-so-vague air of condescension, I sometimes feel dissed. "Um, wait a second here . . . I've gone to all this trouble, and your response is to hint that I should have done something more important with my time?"

I wonder if this isn't how Martha felt after Jesus scolded her.

Which somehow brings me back to my mother, whose time, it should be noted, was largely not her own. As with most ministers' wives, you see, Mom was my father's unpaid assistant. It went without saying that whenever there was a meeting at the church—morning and evening services on Sunday, Wednesday evening prayer meetings, women's missionary fellowship on Thursday—she had to be present. In whatever free moments she had, though, Mom very deliberately devoted herself to Mary's "better part" and chose to read the Bible, pray, and counsel other women in the church that they should do the same.

As a result, we seldom entertained people at our house, and many family meals involved "labor-saving" products such as powdered mashed potatoes, spaghetti sauce from a jar, and frozen fish sticks.

Do I really wish my mother had spent all her time learning how to perfect a crème brûlée? Certainly not. Instead, I question the either-or alternatives Jesus presents to the two sisters in Luke 10:38–42. If Mary represents the viewpoint that "man does not live by bread alone," then Martha's response is, "Yeah, right; but a person can't survive on a diet of words."

In my life, I've spent a lot of time thinking, studying, and listening to teachers. Along the way, I've also taught myself how to cook and to become what I hope is a gracious host. I've come to realize that the work of preparing a meal, be it for family or friends, will often nourish my mind, body, and soul more than the food itself.

Not always, of course.

Every meal isn't a sacred experience. I occasionally crave a slice of greasy pizza, and I can inhale a bag of potato chips or a pint of Häagen-Dazs just as fast as anyone else can. Yet that's kind of the point. When we snarf something up, it often lets us down.

Cooking requires planning and effort. It's not wasted time, however, because while making a meal, maybe especially if it's a dinner for an honored guest, I always learn so much. Read between the lines, and just about any recipe will reveal profound mysteries.

What are the marvelous cycles of seed and regeneration, birth and death, that create garlic, tomatoes, black olives, and basil? How has my life progressed to the point of standing here, on a summer morning on Cape Cod, with an eggbeater in my hand? Who are these hungry people, soon to arrive at breakfast? What do I hope to learn from them, and is there something I'd like to teach?

The next time you make a meal—or, if you're lucky enough, the next time you have someone cook for you—keep these questions in mind and savor the answers as they melt in your mouth.

Tastes good, doesn't it?

God Breathed

Gareth Higgins

All Scripture is God-breathed and is useful for teaching,
rebuking, correcting and training in righteousness...
    —2 Timothy 3:16 NIV

My earliest memories are colonized by celluloid dreams—
flying over spectacular, lit-up Manhattan with that guy who
wore red briefs over his blue tights, or magicking an acciden-
tal flood into an angry sorcerer's parlor with Mickey Mouse,
or bicycling over the moon.

We experience movies the way we remember things—
Norman Mailer once wrote that the resemblance of cinema to
death is one of the most ignored yet most obvious perspectives
through which to view the art. Our memories of the dead are
pictures we keep in the paradoxically ever-deepening tunnel yet ever-expanding kaleidoscope of our minds. When we
think about it this way, there's not much difference between
a photograph of Harrison Ford holding a sword on a rope
bridge in India and a memory of a person we love whose body
is now mingling with the dust of earth.

So when I'm remembering my childhood, I'm remembering

something that is, in one very real sense, dead. When I'm remembering movies, I'm remembering something that in a very real sense died when the final print emerged from the cutting room. When I'm remembering dead people, I feel like I'm at the movies.

What, you may ask (and I wouldn't blame you), has this to do with the collection of writings—the authorship or co-authorship of which remains uncertain (indeed, depending on the tradition, we don't even agree on what those writings *are*)—that we who may be a little lower than the angels usually call, simply, the Bible? Well, *it's* like that, too.

My youth was formed in the crucible of Northern Irish civil strife and angry, divisive religion, whose light side included more than a healthy dose of possibly randomly selected (certainly not all) and selectively interpreted biblical stories as the only foundation for living. I heard Daniel in the Lions' Den, David and Goliath, No Room at the Inn, Jesus on a Donkey, and Crucify Him! Crucify Him! so often that it was hard to distinguish between those tales and those of Elliott and E.T., the Goonies and their treasure map, or Marty McFly and the DeLorean.

So while there's considerable beef to be had with the way Scripture has been used to divide and conquer, and with the way religious institutions have corroded the difference between the spirit and the law to the point where both have been emptied of meaning, and with the way my—and your—very personhood has been subject to death-dealing social practices justified by an appeal to both Testaments and entrenched by the unarguable "all scripture is God-breathed," such analysis or angst or alternativizing is not my focus here. What I want—or sometimes think I want—is to be able to return to a time when I didn't "know" what the Bible said.

I'd like to experience it as if it weren't the undergirding text of the imperialistic culture into which I was born, whose privileges I inherit, and whose sins I cannot deny. I wish bad interpretations of the text had not been woven into a discordant symphony of autobiographical background music. I'd like some distance. In short, I'd like to remember the Bible as if it were not a movie.

Actually, there was this *one* time...

It was just before Easter in 2005. Pope John Paul II was mere weeks away from death, which means Belfast was a month or two away from the appearance of graffiti on a parking lot wall overlooking a main route into the city that inquired of local Catholic residents WHERE THE FUCK IS THE POPE NOW? and followed it up with a flourishing HA-HA so as to make sure they knew we were laughing. I say "we" because just as I am an heir to both the shadow and light side of scriptural interpretation, it's too easy to deny a share of responsibility for the actions of my co-religionists. I'm at least half Protestant, so I'm at least half part of the community that produced people who thought the best way to mark the quiet death of an old man was to mock his extended family. I'm at least one-quarter Catholic, so I guess I'm allowed to be pissed off, too.

A few weeks prior to John Paul II's death, I had been in Bethlehem and Jerusalem and Ramallah and Beit Sahour and Tel Aviv—the magical world of the Movie Bible. I visited the Mount of Olives and the Western Wall and the Al-Aqsa Mosque and the Temple Mount and the place they call the Church of the Nativity and the place they call the Church of the Holy Sepulcher and the place they call Golgotha.

No one can be certain, of course, whether all these are the *actual* locations where the events for which they are named took place, but there was a deeper reality at work during my visit. We were walking, as they say, where Jesus walked. That sentence is so redolent with interpretive complexity that it bears repeating.

We were walking where Jesus walked.

And where Solomon judged it wise to offer to cut a baby in two to settle a family dispute.

And where Ruth found her way into a man's heart by uncovering his feet.

And where Samson pulled the whole thing down around him for zeal and shame.

And the sower and the seed and the well and the mercy and the bread and the fish and what my national poet, Seamus Heaney, called "the man sick of the palsy / Was lowered through the roof, had his sins forgiven / Was healed, took up his bed and walked away."

And where the stories—and a large part of the Story—began.

It's close to indescribable, the feeling of being where the tales your grandmother told you were invented. It's like entering a Bavarian forest and catching a glimpse of a crimson-robed girl being chased by a wolf; or standing where a beaten-down boxer stood at the top of the Philadelphia Museum of Art steps; or dancing on the Yellow Brick Road. It's magical and unreal and *surreal* and more real than you ever imagined.

And so I stand and pray at the Western Wall and under it, where the noise of the intercessors feels like an indoor thunderstorm; and I kiss the floor in the Church of the Holy Sepulcher, where Jesus may or may not have been buried, and I am thinking not so much of Jesus but of the thousands of people and millions of journeys that have kissed the same floor; and I traverse the grounds of the Church of the Nativity and note the irony of its being empty of tourists because of heightened security and repressive border restrictions implemented partly at the behest of people who claim to inherit the mantle of a king born in a stable whose very identity cannot be divorced from the promotion of human freedom. And I sit with Palestinian families who serve sumptuous meals from the limited food they are able to get into their town, which looks up at a walled Israeli settlement that has no trouble accessing fresh fruit; and I sit with Israeli academics and discuss how they don't like the situation, either, but we're in a café that was once suicide-bombed, and *wouldn't you give up some liberty for the sake of safety?*

And so I sit. And I rest.

I'm confused, but I know I'm alive. I'm alive in the place where the Story started. And most of all I'm learning that I do not know what I do not know.

———

Where I grew up, "all Scripture is God-breathed" was used as a weapon—a bat to beat the truth into wayward questioners, a magic wand to ward off disagreement, a guillotine to decisively cut off any possibility of dialogue. It seems to have been rarely invoked by people who actually have been to the places where the stories were written. It wasn't usually spoken of with a sense of wonder, humility, or joy. It was simply a tactic for winning.

In Jerusalem, it may seem like no one is winning. Except maybe the taxi driver I meet at the place they call Golgotha. Yeah, maybe him.

Golgotha, or at least the place they call Golgotha, is a couple of holes in a wall—caves dug into or naturally occurring a few feet off the ground, a lump of clay where everything was finished and fixed and transformed, utterly. I wander there among cab drivers hawking their services in front of a fleet of dented yellow Mercedes limos and wonder and don't feel much beyond the vague notion that the axis of history deserves a better monument than a cab stand.

I'm thinking all Scripture is God-breathed, but knowing that doesn't make you God. And the Bible isn't the *only* word. And the journey toward figuring out what you don't know is the beginning of wisdom.

Immersed in such skeptical/arrogant/honest reverie, I don't notice when a quick-handed pickpocket dashes into a zippered compartment on my backpack and nabs my passport. I just keep wandering, questioning, doubting my faith in humanity because of our propensity toward turning the sacred into theme parks, enshrining my ego on the altar of white European male privilege, proving myself an heir to the colonialist spirit by a sin of omission: I don't exactly scorn these people, but I don't exactly respect them, either. I've begun to suspect that, because I grew up in a culture that thought it knew the Bible, I have the right to claim some ownership of the land where it was written.

I'm allowing myself to acknowledge that even a statement professing humility may itself conceal a subtle yet insidious sense of smug self-satisfaction when something pokes me in the back. I turn around and am confronted by one of the Palestinian taxi drivers trying to get my attention. I assume he's trying to milk me for a hiked-up fare to where I need to get to next, so my feet begin the time-honored process of gingerly stepping backward, out of his orbit, out of my way.

But he says, "No—I don't want your business. I am sorry for what he did."

What *who* did?

He indicates another man now shrinking away, embarrassed. What did he do?

"He stole your passport. It's not fair. You are a visitor. I am sorry. Welcome to Jerusalem! Please, have a good time. I am sorry."

And he gives me back the passport and I shake his hand and thank him, but the moment is so fleeting that I don't begin even to understand its layers of complexity before he's gone, back to his taxi.

All Scripture is God-breathed.

"I give you the land as an inheritance."

"Love your neighbor as yourself."

"Ask and you shall receive."

"For I know the plans I have for you."

All Scripture is God-breathed.

The Scripture is the word, and it is the land, and it is the people.

I wouldn't say that you can't claim to understand Scripture if you've never been to the land where it was born, but I wouldn't deny that I have never seen it the same way since I did.

And I wouldn't say that you can't claim to understand Scripture if you don't read it in the original languages—without a commentary—but I wouldn't deny that I know I'm missing something because I'm invested in an ancient text whose original languages I've never bothered to try to learn.

And I wouldn't say that most of Christendom's culture is dominated by a pop-movie version of Bible stories so unrooted that they might as well be the vignettes in a *Saturday Night Live* episode, or that they devote the same kind of attention to love as the source of all being that *American Idol* devotes to the songs of Bertolt Brecht, but I wouldn't deny that I sometimes wonder.

And I wouldn't say that just because your co-religionists paint WHERE THE FUCK IS THE POPE NOW? HA-HA! on a wall to insult others who are mourning or that your experience of the Bible comes alive in the face of a taxi driver a few thousand miles away should lead you to join with a group of friends and paint that graffiti over with the word SORRY, because while it's not the Alpha and Omega, and it's not the whole word of God or the witness of Scripture or even a minor epistle, it is, at least, a start.

I have a passport because a Palestinian taxi driver nonviolently intervened with a man made in the image of God who was trying to steal it beneath the gaping eyeholes of the cliff known as Golgotha, where humanity did what it does worst, and love does what it is, and everything returns and is reconciled and alive and all Scripture is God-breathed.

And knowing that doesn't make you God.

But maybe, just maybe, we're being breathed, too.

Willing and Doing

David B. Fletcher

> I do not understand what I do. For what I want to do I do not
> do, but what I hate I do.
> —Romans 7:15 NIV

The book of Romans shows Saint Paul in all his confident, didactic glory, laying out with relentless logic the grand narrative of human depravity and the role of the law, grace, and salvation. This is Paul at his most magisterial. With grim assurance he condemns the Gentiles for rejecting the God seen in nature and subsequently for embracing nameless sins, and then turns to the Jews and gives them even rougher treatment.

Yet anyone reading the book of Romans has certainly been brought up short by Paul's surprisingly personal admission of his own frustration at trying to lead the sort of life he expects of his readers. Paul frankly admits, "I do not understand my own actions" (Rom. 7:15 ESV). That sentence is arresting: the man who explains the mysteries of God's interaction with humanity from the beginning of creation to the end of time does not even understand the acts he himself is doing.

Worse than that, when he looks at his actions he finds them contrary to his own notion of what they should be. Perhaps this should not be at all surprising. "Know thyself," the ancient Greek maxim, is a remarkably difficult assignment. Paul as much as admits he hasn't fulfilled that command.

What is it about himself that Paul finds so puzzling? The problem seems to be in the connection between his willing and intending to act and the actual performance of the act. He tells us that "I do not do what I want, but I do the very thing I hate" (Rom. 7:15 ESV). He expands his self-diagnosis by admitting, "I can will what is right, but I cannot do it" (Rom. 7:18 RSV). "For I do not do the good I want, but the evil I do not want is what I do" (Rom. 7:19 RSV). Paul finds that he wills as he should, but something falls short in the execution of his good deeds. He finds that he is doing the very opposite of what he intends, or at least what he thinks he intends. The man who would exhort the Corinthian Christians, "Be imitators of me, as I am of Christ" (1 Cor. 11:1 RSV) now finds himself in an embarrassing and distressing situation in which he would not seem to be a good model for anyone to imitate.

Psychologists might speculate about the processes going on in Paul's life, and biblical scholars can speculate about the place of this remarkable interlude in Paul's theological essay. Yet in a way, it is not puzzling that Paul is experiencing this distress. It seems to be part of the human experience, and surely we all feel it in our own lives.

I don't think I'm alone in admitting that Paul's predicament is my own. I have the best intentions (some of the time), I clearly understand what I must do, and I intend to do the act most in tune with what I think I really do value the most. Yet like Paul, I am later surprised as I look back and discover that this is not at all what I've actually done. I intend to exercise and to watch my diet, particularly because I must manage my diabetes. I set goals and establish workout routines and diets. Without consciously deciding to disregard them, I find that I have not followed those excellent plans. In similar manner, I take on writing assignments and sketch out a schedule for completing them, fully intending to get them done not only on time but actually before the deadline. A while later I find myself nagged by editors who can't understand why they haven't received my work.

Paul is not the first person to puzzle at the disjunction between the desire and will to do good and the evil that one actually performs. The Bhagavad Gita, the great text of ancient Hinduism and part of the epic Mahabharata, was composed somewhere between the fifth and second centuries BCE. This text tells the story of Arjuna, a prince on the eve of a battle, distressed by the thought of the carnage about to take place. He is particularly concerned because he has relatives on both sides of the conflict. He seeks consolation and advice from his chariot driver, who turns out to be none other than Krishna, the eighth incarnation of the supreme god Vishnu. They have an intimate conversation about Arjuna's dilemma as well as the great themes of Hindu theology.

Arjuna shares with Krishna a question that has vexed him as it will vex Saint Paul: "Krishna, what makes a person commit evil against his own will, as if compelled by force?" (Bhagavad Gita 3:36). Arjuna describes having a sense that he is acting under compulsion when committing evil acts. These are acts that in some sense he does not really desire to do.

Paul seems to be struggling with this sense of compulsion as he gives further analysis of his predicament. He finds that there seems to be a law, something of a Murphy's Law of the moral life, that guarantees that things will go wrong. "So I find it to be a law that when I want to do what is good, evil lies close at hand" (Rom. 7:21 NRSV). This law, Paul finds, is that for all his good intentions, evil is always lurking to undo them. While he finds he "delight[s] in the law of God in [his] inmost self," he finds in his "members" this law wages war against those intentions, imprisoning him in the "law of sin" (Rom. 7:22–23 NRSV). As he reflects on this inner turmoil, he declares "Wretched man that I am! Who will rescue me from this body of death?" (Rom. 7:24).

This intimate look at a man racked with moral and spiritual anguish leaves us with questions: What is this internal force that seems to be derailing Paul's attempts to live up to his own values? If Paul is wretched, what hope is there for the rest of us? Surprisingly, at this juncture Paul bursts forth with praise, making the acclamation, "Thanks be to God through Jesus Christ our Lord!" (Rom. 7:25 NRSV).

This is a surprising non sequitur. How does that doxology answer these deep questions? Does this mean that *Jesus* is the answer to Paul's predicament, that *Jesus* rescues Paul from this "body of death"? Or is there no answer to his plea, but nonetheless Paul declares his commitment to follow Jesus, whether he receives his answers or not?

Unlike Paul, Arjuna gets an immediate answer: Krishna tells him, "It is desire and anger, arising from nature's quality of passion; know it here as the enemy, voracious and very evil" (Bhagavad Gita 3:37). That answer is not far from the analysis that Paul gives of his situation. Paul blames the "sin that dwells within" him for the actions that he disavows (Rom. 7:17, 20 NRSV), a "law of sin that dwells in [his] members (Rom. 7:23 NRSV). Krishna's account is that desire and anger are the causes of evil that derail our best intentions. He goes on to account for these phenomena in *prakriti*, a word that translates as "nature"—an active physical force in the material world that pulls it away from the world of spirit. Krishna advises Arjuna to exert spiritual effort to learn to see the world differently and react to it more appropriately. Paul offers no remedy but seems rather to leave the matter with this recognition: in his flesh he is "a slave to sin" (Rom. 7:25 NLT).

Paul raises an interesting question in the realm of moral motivation, as interesting to the ethicist as it is to the ordinary person trying to live a good life in accord with worthy ideals. Whether we are ethicists or ordinary people, we assume that we are capable of first *willing* to act, and then of *following up* that intention with action. We instinctively believe that "ought implies can," and that we have some control over our own motivation, without which we would not be free and true moral agents at all. For such reasons, Paul's admission that "I can will what is right, but I cannot do it" (Rom. 7:18 NRSV) is troubling. If I can will to act in accordance with the ethical norms I profess, why would I find myself unable to carry out that choice? Can I be held responsible for failing to eat right and exercise, for not getting the writing assignment in by the deadline, or for failing to "respect the dignity of every human being," as I promised in baptism?

Perhaps Paul had it right all along. We are in a puzzling and agonizing predicament as we look into our own hearts and the wellsprings of our actions. Perhaps we cannot do better to conclude this discussion than to rejoice, with Paul, in our ability to offer thanks to God through Jesus Christ.

The Bible:

Full of Sound, Fury, Sarcasm, and Poop Jokes

Susan E. Isaacs

> Eliyahu [Elijah] began ridiculing them: "Shout louder! After all, he's a god, isn't he? Maybe he's daydreaming, or he's on the potty..."
>
> —1 Kings 18:27 CJB

I am grateful that I grew up in a church that revered the Scriptures; but sometimes it created a wall between God and me. I'm a comedienne: I've always seen life through the skewed lens of humor, but there was no room for levity in my church. My mom suggested I write Bible skits. *Seriously?* There weren't any jokes in the Bible! Well, except for the stuff that was unintentionally funny, like when Joshua climbed the hill of foreskins. And sarcasm? Forget it. I once had a church elder tell me that sarcasm was "fallen humor."

I pulled myself together in college and got serious about my faith. And I mean *serious*. I had a quiet time every morning.

I implemented the college-group acronym for prayer: PRAY—
Praise, Repent, Ask, Yield. (No J for "jokes" in that acronym.)
I needed to approach God with humility, but some of my unc-
tuous prayers would have elicited Monty Python's God to
reply, "Stop groveling! I hate it when people grovel!"

Imagine my relief to discover how much spit and vin-
egar actually exists in the Bible. Most of us miss it, because
we haven't studied enough Greek and Hebrew to identify
the wordplay, puns, and sarcasm. We're conditioned to read
everything as though Charlton Heston were saying it. But
when I realized it, it was as if the clouds parted and Terry Gil-
liam's cutout Almighty appeared.

Regarding sarcasm: one Sunday my pastor preached on
Job, chapter 11. Job's been getting a mouthful from his accusers. The final insult comes when Zophar tells Job to repent
and "your world will be washed in sunshine" (v. 13–20 MSG).
Makes you want to hurl, right? But then Job fires back at his
accusers. In chapter 12, he says (sarcastically), "Surely, surely,
my discerning friends, you are the ones! And when you pass
away, the sum total of all wisdom will perish from the earth"
(v. 2 VOICE).

There's plenty of wit in the New Testament as well. When
the Pharisees continue to grill the man born blind, whom Jesus
healed, the man gets exasperated. "I've told you over and over
and you haven't listened. Why do you want to hear it again?
Are you so eager to become his disciples?" (John 9:27 MSG).

Nathaniel initially scoffs about Jesus. "Nazareth? You've
got to be kidding" (John 1:46 MSG). When Jesus tells Nathaniel he "saw" him under the fig tree, suddenly Nathaniel is a
believer. Jesus replies—and I'm paraphrasing here: "That's all
it took? You ain't seen nothin' yet." Of course my pew Bible
read, "Can anything good come out of Nazareth?" and "You

will see greater things than these" (John 1:46, 50 ESV). And we recited it with a humorless tremolo.

(Man, I wish *The Message* had been around when I was a kid.)

Even Jesus has a good comeback on Good Friday. He's been arrested, interrogated, flogged, mocked, and interrogated again—and now the Pharisees want Pilate to execute Jesus. Pilate goes to Jesus, "So you're a king?" Jesus' reply is translated as, "Are you saying this on your own, or did others tell you this about me?" (John 18:34 MSG). My pastor recently told me the tone is actually sarcastic: "So you just figured it out, or did someone tip you off?" If Jesus can fire off a bon mot on the worst day of his life, don't we have the freedom to lob one off occasionally?

My favorite sarcastic moment is in 1 Kings 18. When the prophets of Baal can't get their god to light the fire on their altar, Elijah taunts them. "Cry aloud, for he is a god. Either he is musing, or he is relieving himself, or he is on a journey, or perhaps he is asleep and must be awakened" (v. 27 ESV). According to William Lee Holladay's *A Concise Hebrew and Aramaic Lexicon of the Old Testament*, the verb used for "relieving oneself" can be translated as "having a bowel movement."

What's Elijah really saying? "Maybe he's taking a dump."

Right there in the Bible.

But wait, there's more! On the day of Jesus' resurrection, the women ran back to the cowering disciples to tell them about the empty tomb. But "their words seemed to them like nonsense" (Luke 24:11 NIV). The original Greek for "nonsense" is *laros* (λῃρος). My pastor said she couldn't repeat the translation from the pulpit, but it was "an exclamation . . . of the barnyard variety."

In Philippians 3, Saint Paul recites all his credentials prior to his conversion. "I consider them [*skubalon* (σκύβαλον)], that I may gain Christ and be found in him" (Phil. 3:8–9 NIV). Most Bibles translate *skubalon* as "garbage" or "refuse." But *skubalon* is a vulgar word for "poop." Why does Saint Paul resort to scatology? Because isn't everything we use to prop up our egos just shit in comparison to knowing Jesus? (Of course, we can't print Saint Paul's real words in the Bible; polite society might throw a *skubalon* fit.)

We should have the same freedom to complain to God, especially in the midst of some tragedy from which we've not been spared. And the Bible is littered with examples.

"Leave me alone so I can smile again before I am gone and exist no more" (Ps. 39:13 NLT).

"You have taken from me friend and neighbor—darkness is my closest friend" (Ps. 88:18 NIV). This Psalm doesn't even bother to end on a hint of optimism.

Jeremiah might be the king of kvetch. He hears God's call to be his prophet and accepts. In return, he's mocked, beaten up, thrown into ditches, and left for dead. Jeremiah feels like God tricked him into this prophet job, so he lets God have it in chapter 20, verse 7. My polite pew Bible reads, "O LORD, you have deceived me, and I was deceived; you are stronger than I, and you have prevailed" (ESV). But in his book *The Prophets*, Rabbi Abraham Joshua Heschel renders the verse as: "O Lord, Thou hast seduced me, and I am seduced. Thou hast raped me, and I am overcome." It doesn't get much more graphic than that.

I don't want to encourage anyone to debase holy writ or use these examples as an excuse to be rude—of course we should hold the Bible in the highest regard. But isn't it encouraging to know that canon Scripture contains a full range of emotion and language? That the characters in the Bible didn't sound like Charlton Heston all the time? And that even God himself can get sarcastic? I mean, look at God's response when he finally answers Job: "Where were you when I laid the foundations of the earth? Tell me, since you know so much" (Job 38:4 NLT).

Do we fully comprehend the fact that God knows us completely—there's nothing we can do or say that will shock him? That God knows what it's like to live on this planet, to be subject to disappointment, heartache, tragedy, and violence? Or do we think God expects us to flop around like a depressed, boneless chicken and talk like Charlton Heston?

Skubalon no!

James and John, the sons of Zebedee, were known for being hotheads. When they got pissed off that other people were healing in Jesus' name, Jesus told them to take it down a notch. "What does it matter who preaches the gospel?" But Jesus didn't punish or demote them. In fact, he gave them a nickname: Sons of Thunder.

I've been going through another Dark Night of the Soul recently. I told my spiritual director that I hadn't lost my faith, but I had lost hope. God seems silent and disinterested. She asked me to meditate on Rembrandt's painting *The Return of the Prodigal Son*. I bought a large lithograph of the painting, hung it on my wall, and looked at it a long time. I returned to my director with this. "Yeah, I see the son, all right: shoeless and destitute. I see the older brother, the onlookers. But there's no dad in my story! The space where Rembrandt's tender, welcoming father is? It's a black hole! If God *is* in my picture, he's the curious rubbernecker way off in the back!"

Off I went, ranting and weeping and snotting my way through a box of Kleenex. When I had cried out my last wet booger, a curious response came to my heart: "That's my girl."

171

Part of me wanted to fire back. "Okay ... Anything else?"
But I left with a smile. And that's more than I came with.

Can we allow ourselves to let it rip once in a while? So what if we go overboard with the kvetching? God might take us down a notch, but we will never lose his love or *delight* in us.

What's the worst that could happen?

He might give us a nickname.

And isn't that a sign of endearment?

The Starlit Way:

Confronting Doubt with Jesus

Anna Broadway

"You do not want to leave too, do you?" Jesus asked the Twelve. Simon Peter answered him, "Lord, to whom shall we go? You have the words of eternal life. We have come to believe and to know that you are the Holy One of God."
—John 6:67–69 NIV

Lord, to whom shall we go?"

On the brink of what seemed an inevitable divorce from the only God and religious tradition I'd ever known, those words arrested me.

In the passage from which they come, Jesus has just asked some of his closest followers if they, too, plan to leave him, as many others have. But one of his twelve closest disciples responds, "Lord, to whom shall we go?"

For all my years of Bible reading, I'd never heard that exchange for what it was. Then again, I'd also never seriously considered quitting God and my faith before.

The first time I really heard that verse from John 6, I was on my final retreat with a student religious group that I would soon leave for good, at the start of the crisis of faith that coincided with my senior year of college. Around me, the northern Arizona pines yielded to the early October breeze with a sigh that echoed my internal restlessness. Though the air was sweet and cool, it would be months yet before the temperatures back home on the valley floor in Phoenix dipped anywhere near this comfortable.

Sitting on the weathered bench of the small outdoor amphitheater, I felt like an outsider among so many friends who'd spent their summers on short-term evangelistic projects around the country. As we sang emotional praise songs and then listened to the weekend's guest speaker, I shifted restlessly and avoided eye contact.

Singing always feels like a kind of assent to me, like you have to mean what you sing. Unlike the hymns I grew up with, which my local church still favored—standards like "Holy, Holy, Holy" and "Fairest Lord Jesus"—the worship music at the retreat keyed off our *feelings* for God, positive emotions I no longer had. But silence would draw attention; I knew most songs well enough to improvise a harmony.

Ultimately, the only way I got through one of the songs that weekend was by quietly changing some lines (such as "I'm so grateful") to something that felt more honest (such as "I'm so confused"). When I sang the more truthful refrain, I almost wept.

No one would have expected such reticence of a student leader, least of all me. Only a few months before, I'd decided to risk *more* on God by giving up my summer to practice and research evangelism methods in Berkeley, California, with several other students from around the country. Instead of using the hottest months to earn extra money and develop skills for the "real" job I'd need in just a year, I decided to spend those two months on more "spiritual" work.

Yet several weeks after crafting and mailing support letters telling friends and family why I was "serving God" instead of taking a regular job for the summer, there I sat, doubting God's very existence.

"Lord, to whom shall we go?"

Under the circumstances, the last thing I expected to hear was a text that spoke so pointedly to my crisis. Whatever the speaker said after reading that verse was lost on me as I sat there with Simon Peter's question reverberating inside me.

Where would I go if I left the church? Until then, I hadn't even considered the alternatives.

All summer long, our conversations in Berkeley kept coming back to "authenticity," which for us had meant candor about our doubts and questions and the messiness of our attempts to follow Jesus. One of the rare happy parts of that strange summer was the communion we'd found in questioning all our old certainties.

Still, at twenty-one, I was too young to have seen once-fervent followers of Jesus turn away from him. Though I was majoring in religious studies (which some would blame for my spiritual crisis) and knew a bit about the other major religious traditions, I didn't know where people went when they left God.

Had God been a fellow human and our relationship a marriage, I might have been better prepared for cooling ardor. Though my parents were still happily married, and though I'd never even had a boyfriend, I knew romances had their ups and downs. I knew—if only in the abstract—that people changed, and that this could change their relationships in unexpected ways.

But I didn't realize it could happen with God as well. I grew up in the church, so I first asked God's forgiveness for my sins when I was six. Though mine would be a loveless faith until college, I spent most of my formative years trying to be a good Christian, to have a relationship with God. Somehow, though, the models I observed during those years showed me more about spiritual "success" and perseverance in suffering than how to survive seasons of uncertainty and doubt. I had little concept of the steep ups and downs, the tight, lonely canyons through which the Christian journey could wind. In my mind, a sputtering of the faith that had blazed so hotly during my freshman and sophomore years of college could only mean imminent spiritual disaster.

And yet for several months I'd felt a growing distance from God. My almost daily times of prayer and Bible reading had gradually ceased giving life and become a more and more leaden ritual. No matter how hard I tried to find meaning or connection with the text, nothing could revive the old sense of encountering a spiritual being in that devotional practice.

Not even my eight weeks in Berkeley had helped. It would take me years to understand why what we attempted in those tumultuous two months, our grand attempt to overhaul evangelistic practice, was doomed to failure even before we started our research. I went home in August profoundly troubled and confused, feeling like I was waking up after an unknown explosion had knocked me out.

Worst of all was the mystery of why *God* had allowed that. How could the one I'd gone to Berkeley to seek and share with others so gravely let me down? Why had he evaded me? Ironically, I remember trying to read the Psalms that summer. Yet despite how many of them lamented God's confusing behavior and seeming absence, I couldn't get past David's combat metaphors and over-the-top words of love and adoration for God's provision and faithfulness.

> You have made known to me the path of life; you will fill me with joy in your presence, with eternal pleasures at your right hand (Psalms 16:11 NIV).

> You give me your shield of victory, and your right hand sustains me; you stoop down to make me great (Psalms 18:35 NIV).

That was not the God I'd been struggling to find each time I opened my Bible. Indeed his silence had grown so loud that by summer's end I started to wonder if there was even a God up there beyond the stars to encounter.

Mind you, I had read all the Psalms and other Old Testament lamentations of God's inaction and seeming absence. But perhaps because my only cover-to-cover Bible readings took place before I had entered high school, I had not fully grasped the authors' spiritual crises.

As a pre-adolescent reader, I had not pondered the inner life of an Israelite in exile or the profound doubts one might feel about the God who supposedly freed your enslaved ancestors centuries before yet failed to intervene for *you*. In any case, I was too focused on trying to churn through the lengthy readings involved in my read-the-Bible-in-a-year program to deeply meditate on each passage, anguished or otherwise.

But what could the exiles have thought as they slowly settled into their new, assigned homes in Babylon, far from the hills and rivers God had given their families long ago?

Surrounded by people who worshipped and ate and drank very differently from the way they did, did they wonder if the name of one's god even mattered?

After a time, God sent that beleaguered group a message through his prophet Jeremiah: " 'For I know the plans I have for you,' declares the LORD. 'Plans to prosper to you and not to harm you, plans to give you hope and a future. Then you will call on me and come and pray to me, and I will listen to you. You will seek me and find me when you seek me with all your heart. I will be found by you' " (Jer. 29:11–14 NIV).

During a low point my freshman year of college, I'd come upon that partly familiar passage while desperately giving the Bible a second chance after several years of not reading it. Seizing on what seemed like a promise in the text, I decided to seek God as earnestly as I knew how, in case he was real enough to help me with the weight gain and deep loneliness that the first few months of college and life on my own had brought.

Despite my childhood Bible reading and early prayers for salvation, I'd always known I did not love God, so I was surprised by the change in my heart that followed that encounter with Jeremiah 29. As I began to seek *God* through my Bible reading, rather than the knowledge or accomplishment I had pursued in earlier years, something changed. For the first time in my life, I really began to have a sense of relationship— and with that, love quickly followed.

In retrospect, the two years between my freshman and senior years of college entailed a honeymoon stage with God, but at the time, I thought I'd finally found that normal "Christian life" people talked about. I thought it would go on like that forever.

"Lord, to whom shall we go?"

None of my early spiritual teachers denied that our faith

would face threats, but it seemed that the most dangerous threats were questions you couldn't answer. *Why would a good God allow suffering? How did we get here? Was Jesus really God's son?* I and my siblings and fellow Sunday school students were taught that faith in God rested on things like fact and reason, not fickle *feeling*. We were taught the logical answers, the only ammunition midcentury Christians needed to defend and explain their faith to skeptics.

By 1999, the summer I went to Berkeley for the summer of missions, those answers were showing their age. Some people within the church even called logical answers irrelevant to the so-called postmodern questions Christians increasingly had to combat from nonbelievers. During my eight weeks in Berkeley, I was supposed to learn how to explain my faith to the new, postmodern skeptic, who doubted truth as much as God's existence.

Instead I came home realizing how much these serious questions were my own.

My spiritual life started unraveling. The Bible left me unmoved when I read it, and prayer felt like a monologue without an audience. Not even the "facts" that ought to sustain me went unscathed. At bottom, each proof went back to a human source, a human claim, a human observer, and what had I been learning everywhere but that human sources were biased? We were never *completely* objective, so how could I trust even one of them? How could I trust *myself*?

"Lord, to whom shall we go?"

Could other traditions claim greater objectivity? No. Indeed, by definition, any and all religious experiences and traditions could be apprehended only on human and therefore limited terms. No event or truth was protected from the distortion its observers' limitations might introduce.

Not that I was particularly drawn to any other tradition.

Insofar as I was pondering a spiritual divorce, this owed not to some sudden crush on another faith tradition (such as Buddhism, which I learned about in my religious studies program) but to frustration with the God to whom I'd committed myself. I wanted an escape from the present confusion and misery of my Christianity, yes, but the only better experience I'd known was the past state of that relationship.

And what would I even renounce or discard if I left? Would I embrace lying or envy or murder? What a wicked thought! Although I would perhaps have liked to consider sex outside marriage, men showed no interest in being my boyfriend—much less husband—and on the whole I thought the Bible's ethical framework was quite sound.

Where I disliked parts of Christianity, the problem usually seemed to stem from a faulty human interpreter rather than the Bible itself. And where I felt unhappy . . . well, that almost always came back to God. I was angry and distrustful of his plans for my romantic future: the marriage I'd thought would conclude my college years proved elusive. I was angry and confused about God's distance.

To whom would I go if I left this God? The disciples told Jesus they stayed because he had the words of life. And I didn't really want to leave, either; I just couldn't square my experiences and questions with the picture of God I'd been given.

Could I become an atheist?

Had my belief in God died?

Our retreat speaker said something else that stayed with me. In a private conversation with me and a couple of similarly questioning friends, he told us we shouldn't confuse our paradigm of God for our faith itself.

On the desert floor, where we spent the school year, the

sky seemed fairly starless on most nights except for the odd bright light. Shooting stars might as well have been a thing of myth for all we could see in the shallow brick and stucco canyons of Phoenix and Tempe. But up in the higher desert near Sedona, where our retreat took place, no city lights washed out the glittering multitudes above. Out there, a night well spent might include dragging blankets and sleeping bags outside to spend a long while staring up at the stars and trying to pick out constellations.

In both locations, we observed the same phenomena, yet our paradigm of sky from the Tempe valley floor was quite different from the paradigm we constructed among the red rocks a few hours north.

It's been almost fifteen years since that perplexing yet quietly pivotal weekend.

For months afterward, I continued to founder in what felt like impenetrable darkness (though perhaps it only seems so when you've left a place of frequent supplemental lights). As I continued the journey, however, in hopes that my feet were on a real, if unseen, path, I gradually started to see things I never saw before.

I don't necessarily like walking this way, and I'm not wild about being *still* single at the age of thirty-six, but sometimes when I look up and catch more of the limitless majesty above, I catch my breath at the beauty.

That awe has only grown with each step, no matter how steep the hike.

Though I may often dislike the journey, Lord, *with whom else would I go?*

You have the words of eternal life.

Stillness

Alice Currah

O LORD, hear my prayer, listen to my cry for mercy; in
your faithfulness and righteousness come to my relief.
    —Psalms 143:1 NIV

Baring my soul naked before God should feel safe, comforting, and natural—like a baby girl who feels secure in her
daddy's arms, knowing she is the apple of his eye.

Yet even though I know that God—the creator of the universe—fashioned me together as a complicated, multifaceted
quilt, my struggle with unbelief is my constant companion,
affecting me every day.

My hunger to search for God beyond the walls of the
church has led me down a path I did not choose for myself; I
believe God chose it for me. To know God, my Abba Father,
for myself—and not from the pulpit, from dogmatic theology,
or from the well-intentioned church people who maintain
these things—has taught me that if I want to really know God
in a deep, personal way, I must seek his heart and not his hand.

Wrestling with unbelief has less to do with my faith in
God and more to do with trusting him to the point of constant

surrender. Seeking God's heart challenges me to allow him into my deepest fears, hurts, and unfulfilled dreams. To stand soul-naked before him without a facade to clothe me— covering my insecurities or projecting a false confidence in the hope of winning him over—also gives me permission to doubt.

With my faith truly on the line, my spiritual journey has always been a cinematic adventure. Life-and-death battles, heroes, villains, angels, and devils have all played critical roles, but my relentlessness in pursuing God has made my story always about redemption and unwavering grace. It has caused me to look at the world with eyes of compassion.

Believing in God is easier for me than trusting in his love for me.

When I lay my head down each night, too often I allow the weight of my burdens to anchor me in a sea of my own self-pity. It is at that moment I hear God calling to me to relax and be still. With my eyes closed, I try to avoid his invitation. Ashamed by the way I've failed in the day that's gone before, I intentionally avoid having a conversation with my heavenly Father. Then guilt sets in.

This plays out nightly, and I'm aware of how silly it is to avoid God when he knows everything I am feeling and thinking. Yet he allows me to ignore him. Others would judge me for this, but God doesn't. God knows my heart, and he sees a very wounded girl when he looks at me. He knows the reason I avoid him during my nightly meditation time is not because I don't want to converse with him but because I often cannot let myself come before him with flaws, bruises, and brokenness.

Yet it is through the brokenness that I know he desires to reach me and free me from my own bondage of pride. Still... it is too difficult for me. What eats me up inside is knowing just how patient God is. He *will* wait for me. That much grace is too much to comprehend: I often cannot even allow much of it to penetrate the many walls I have built up over the years. Yet brick by brick, God dismantles my fortress of self-inflicted protection.

In my humanness I struggle with God's perfect grace and love. This is another reason why unbelief taunts me. I know I can be a horrible person, yet God challenges me and dares me to let him in. He wants to show me that his grace is actually sufficient. His quiet whispers in the night invite me to let him carry much of the burden that I refuse to release. I don't let it go because my identity is so intricately wound up in it.

Who would I be if I let him take my wounds from me? I can't even imagine, and that scares me. Yet I'm tempted— tempted enough to have taken God up on his offer many times. Each time, he has showed me clarity, peace beyond understanding, and infectious joy. He has shown himself faithful even when I wasn't. Still, I require him to prove himself each and every time I trust him. I know it sounds ridiculous, but still, he proves himself, shows himself trustworthy to me, and does not condemn me.

The only thing I think God asks of me is that I surrender my lies and the pain I've held on to like a security blanket. Slowly I've been letting go, opening up my clenched fists, asking God to heal me and make me whole.

My heart is fully confident in God's goodness, but I'm still broken, bound by my pain. I am a work in progress. I am a vivid mosaic of pieces God is still re-creating, placing each broken piece of glass side by side for what will be a beautiful "work of heart" to accompany an adventurous story about a little girl who loved God because she was told to, to a woman after God's own heart—full of flaws, but fully in love with him because he never gave up on her and was faithful to his word.

Broken and Bent

Ellen Painter Dollar

Since it was the day of Preparation, the Jews did not want the bodies left on the cross during the Sabbath, especially because that Sabbath was a day of great solemnity. So they asked Pilate to have the legs of the crucified men broken and the bodies removed. Then the soldiers came and broke the legs of the first and of the other who had been crucified with him. But when they came to Jesus and saw that he was already dead, they did not break his legs. Instead, one of the soldiers pierced his side with a spear, and at once blood and water came out. (He who saw this has testified so that you also may believe. His testimony is true, and he knows that he tells the truth.) These things occurred so that the scripture might be fulfilled, "None of his bones shall be broken."
—John 19:31–36 NRSV

Well, shoot.

Is it blasphemy to wish the soldiers hadn't been so attentive that morning—that they had gone ahead and broken Jesus' legs, even if it meant the Scripture wasn't exactly fulfilled? What if I admit that I would be even more interested in a story in which Jesus broke his leg while he was still alive, when one of the tables he turned over in the temple landed on his shin or something? It would give me some comfort to know that Jesus knew the agony of a broken leg—the searing, awful pain, followed by weeks of frustrating immobility as it heals.

Because of a chronic bone disorder (called osteogenesis imperfecta, or OI), I've had about three dozen broken bones in my lifetime; my daughter, who inherited the disorder from me, has had about a dozen. I would like knowing that Jesus understood a teensy bit about the pain and limitations we live with.

But not only does Jesus not ever have a broken leg, pre- or postmortem, Jesus also never engages at length with someone who has a chronic illness or disability. Jesus healed people with chronic illness—the paralytic whose friends lowered him through the roof and the woman with the twelve-year hemorrhage, for example. But we don't have any stories in which Jesus spends the afternoon conversing with an old lady hobbled by severe arthritis or a young man with lungs compromised by cystic fibrosis. Perhaps Jesus had such conversations, but we don't get to read about them. When it comes to chronic illness, the gospel narrative offers two possibilities: Jesus notices and heals you (not always in that order—e.g., the bleeding woman) or you don't make it into the story at all.

So essentially Jesus will either notice me and heal me (I'm forty-five years old; it hasn't happened yet) or I'm on my own.

Thanks a bunch, Jesus.

Jesus' heal-or-nothing approach to illness and disability has left a confusing mess behind for those of us exploring the intersections between health, illness, medicine, and faith. (Maybe Jesus isn't solely to blame. Maybe Jesus had lots of conversations about physical pain and chronic illness and about why he healed some people and not others, but no one recorded them. Whatever the reason, the Gospels don't give us much to work with.)

Christians have inserted all sorts of horrid theology into the vacuum of scriptural wisdom around living with chronic illness and disability, inventing inane platitudes that don't help and often hurt. Faced with scary diagnoses, life-altering accidents, and the cries of those weary of the burdens of chronic pain, treatments that can seem worse than the diagnosis, or social exclusion, we pull these platitudes out of... out of where? Not Scripture, that's for sure. Out of nowhere. Out of the cramped, musty corners of our souls, where fear lives, the fear that makes us desperate to explain other peoples' pain away so we can feel assured such pain won't move into our family. Out of our asses.

"Everything happens for a reason."

"God helps those who help themselves."

"God won't give you more than you can handle."

Let me repeat: none of these platitudes comes from the Bible. They are terrible theology and even worse pastoral care. That last one, about God not giving you more than you can handle, is a bad (blasphemous, actually) paraphrase of an actual verse, 1 Corinthians 10:13: "No testing has overtaken you that is not common to everyone. God is faithful, and he will not let you be tested beyond your strength, but with the testing he will also provide the way out so that you may be able to endure it" (NRSV).

In some translations, "he will not let you be tested beyond your strength" is translated "he will not let you be tempted beyond what you can bear." This verse is about temptation, not adversity. It reassures us that God always provides another way, a better way, when we are drawn to the temptations "common to everyone." When we are tempted to be self-serving, to drown our worries in alcohol or drugs or food or reality TV, when we are tempted to cheat on our spouses or neglect our children, God is there, calling us back from the brink, reminding us that there is a better way, steering us toward love, honesty, and truth.

This is a wonderful verse, an important verse. But it is not telling us that God won't "give" us more than we can handle. What poppycock. First of all, I know a bunch of people who have had to deal with more than they can handle. I bet you do, too. Second, God doesn't "give" pain, misfortune, and agony. What kind of God would shower pain on people and then say, "It's okay. I know you can handle it!" What kind of God would sit up in heaven, making these sorts of calculations? "Okay, you there—you get a few months of unemployment, maybe a house foreclosure. You over there—you get a dead child. Because I know you can handle it."

Another idea that creeps its way into our theology is that we should be grateful for misfortunes because of all that we learn from them. This idea at least has a little more scriptural merit. Jesus' crucifixion and resurrection, after all, provide the consummate example of redemptive suffering—suffering bringing about transformation, the best possible thing (eternal life) arising from the worst possible thing (a tortured, painful death).

So can our suffering be redemptive? Should I be grateful for all my and my daughter's broken bones and surgeries, for the chronic pain, for all the times we are unable to do things we'd like to do because of our physical limitations?

Yes, our suffering can be redemptive. Our suffering can transform us and those around us. Wonderful things can arise from bad things.

Living with OI has certainly made me wiser in some ways. For example, I can see right through our culture's idolatry of the body—the idea that we can be happy and fulfilled if only we attain an ideal weight or sculpted muscles or a certain definition of beauty. I know from hard experience that there is no diet or superfood or exercise routine that can bring about perfect health and well-being. My bone disorder has also brought about particular blessings in my life. For example, my experience living with OI and having a child with OI has been the subject of my most successful writing; in a way, I am a writer, and have developed my unique voice, because I have this disorder.

But I am not grateful for my bone disorder. First, I know that OI is not necessary for wisdom; there are many wise people (good writers, too!) who haven't had three dozen broken bones, a dozen surgeries, and chronic pain.

But more important, I can be grateful for the good things that have arisen from life with OI without being grateful for OI itself. Put in theological language, there is a huge difference between saying that my bone disorder was intended (presumably by God) to teach me important things and saying that my bone disorder has ended up teaching me important things.

I can believe that God is capable of using hard circumstances for ultimate good. I cannot believe that God creates hard circumstances for ultimate good or that we should be grateful for such circumstances themselves rather than for the good that arises from them. Gratitude for suffering is (or should be) offensive to most reasonable people: should a couple who met in a displaced persons camp after World War II and lived a long, happy life together be grateful for World War II, with all its deprivation, violence, and horrors?

Gratitude for suffering is also inconsistent with biblical narrative.

The biblical promise is that there will be a new heaven and a new earth, in which "God himself will be with [his people]. He will wipe away every tear from their eyes, and death shall be no more, neither shall there be mourning, nor crying, nor pain anymore, for the former things have passed away" (Rev. 21:3–4 ESV). The ultimate gospel message is that God will save us from sin, and brokenness, and evil, and sickness, and death—not make us cry and then teach us a lesson as he dries our tears. And there are many Scriptures (such as the Psalms of lament— all that weeping on beds, all those fainting spirits) in which peo- ple utterly devoted to God bewail their suffering without a hint of gratitude for what they might learn from their pain.

So Jesus healed some people but not others, and he didn't fill us in on why that was. The platitudes that Christians trot out in an effort to be helpful are not very helpful, nor are they biblical. Is there anything helpful to be said from a Christian perspective about the pain of chronic illness and disability?

There's this:

When my daughter (the one who inherited OI) was two years old, she broke her femur in our living room when she slipped on a book on the floor. Without thinking, I responded to her initial scream by picking her up and putting her on my lap. That movement, of course, added to her agony. She shrieked and shrieked. Her blond curls became soaked with sweat, her face wet with tears.

A femur fracture is a terrible thing, excruciating and debil- itating. The weeks that followed that moment in our living room were terrible in their own way, as she was immobilized in a fiberglass cast that went from her chest all the way down to her toes. But those first moments after she fractured, as the

two of us sat on our living room floor, as I began to understand what had just happened and how much pain she was in,
were beyond terrible. They were some of the bleakest, saddest
moments of my life.

A few days later, I e-mailed a friend to let him and his wife
know what had happened. I tried to articulate just how awful
things were, though I knew my words were pale representa-
tives of the blazing agony in my heart and in my daughter's
leg. Our friend wrote back, saying, "I don't know what to say
except that I believe Jesus was there on the living room floor
with you as your daughter screamed."

I don't know why those words helped so much.

It's not as if Jesus did anything while he was supposedly
there on the floor with us. Those moments on our living
room floor were still terrible. But the image of Jesus there on
the floor with us did help.

Jesus is with us, in our bleakest moments of physical pain
or emotional agony or both. God is with us. That is the message that has helped most as I have wrestled with this bone
disorder, with all the ways OI has seared and scarred us as
well as taught and challenged and enriched us. This is the
fundamental message of the cross, that Jesus is with us in our
bleakest moments, in our deepest sufferings, because Jesus
knows from hanging on the cross how it feels to be captive to
all the forces in the world that want to break us.

Jesus knows what it feels like to feel forsaken, even when
the hard thing you are doing is the very thing God has called
you to. Jesus' life pointed toward the cross; my whole life has
pointed toward having my children, including my fragile
child, whose suffering I understand all too well.

That day in our living room, Jesus was with us as my
daughter sweated and shrieked.

Another day some years later, when my daughter broke her femur again, Jesus was with us again, but in an even more tangible way. When she was nine years old, my daughter was riding a scooter with some friends at a local playground, hit a crack in the pavement, and went down. She broke several bones, including her femur. We called an ambulance. As my daughter lay in agony on the hot asphalt, an EMT lay down next to her and, from that awkward position, quickly and almost painlessly started an IV, through which my daughter received morphine to ease her pain for the ambulance ride. That EMT's willingness to get down on the ground with my daughter, along with his skill, were the embodiment of God's grace in one of my family's most difficult moments. Jesus was, literally, there on the ground with us.

Do I still wish Jesus had some firsthand experience with broken bones? Sure. But even without his sharing that particular pain, I am comforted by the knowledge that Jesus is with me whenever I am mired in hurt, physical or otherwise, whether I feel his presence in that moment or not (most of the time, not). The cross testifies that Jesus is with us in our suffering because Jesus knows how it feels to despair, and that God is capable of redeeming even the worst pain, bringing light out of dark, life out of death.

That witness is far more powerful than any platitude.

SLUT!

Cathleen Falsani

For Herod himself had sent men who arrested John, bound him, and put him in prison on account of Herodias, his brother Philip's wife, because Herod had married her. For John had been telling Herod, "It is not lawful for you to have your brother's wife." And Herodias had a grudge against him, and wanted to kill him. But she could not, for Herod feared John, knowing that he was a righteous and holy man, and he protected him. When he heard him, he was greatly perplexed; and yet he liked to listen to him. But an opportunity came when Herod on his birthday gave a banquet for his courtiers and officers and for the leaders of Galilee. When his daughter Herodias came in and danced, she pleased Herod and his guests; and the king said to the girl, "Ask me for whatever you wish, and I will give it." And he solemnly swore to her, "Whatever you ask me, I will give you, even half of my kingdom." She went out and said to her mother, "What should I ask for?" She replied, "The head of John the baptizer." Immediately she rushed back to the king and requested, "I want you to give me at once the head of John the Baptist on a platter." The king was deeply grieved; yet out of regard for his oaths and for the guests, he did not want to refuse her. Immediately the king sent a soldier of the guard with orders to bring John's head. He went and beheaded him in the prison, brought his head on a platter, and gave it to the girl. Then the girl gave it to her mother. When his disciples heard about it, they came and took his body, and laid it in a tomb.

—Mark 6:17–29 NRSV

Baby, please, baby, please slow down
Baby, I feel sick
Don't make me stick to my promise
—from "Salomé" by U2

I must have been a teenager the first time I heard the story about the girl whose dancing so pleased the Roman leader Herod that he rewarded her by ordering the execution of John the Baptist and giving her the prophet's head on a platter.

The dancing girl's name was Salomé, the teacher or preacher told me, even though there is nothing in the Bible to indicate that this is true. In fact, the writers of the two gospel accounts of the alleged events that led to John the Baptist's beheading (found in Mark 6 and Matthew 14) don't bother to give the dancer a name. She is referred to, simply, as the daughter of Herodias, the wife of the Roman ruler Herod.

The application of Salomé as the dancer's name comes from a first-century manuscript known as *Antiquities of the Jews* (ca. 94 CE), by the Jewish-Roman historian Joseph ben Matityahu (a.k.a. Titus Flavius Josephus), who wrote:[1]

---

1. Joseph ben Matityahu, *Antiquities of the Jews* 18: 4.

Herodias...was married to Herod, the son of Herod the
Great, who was born of Mariamne, the daughter of Simon
the high priest, who had a daughter, Salomé; after whose
birth Herodias took upon her to confound the laws of our
country, and divorced herself from her husband while he
was alive, and was married to Herod, her husband's brother
by the father's side, he was tetrarch of Galilee; but her daughter Salomé was married to Philip, the son of Herod, and tetrarch of Trachonitis; and as he died childless, Aristobulus,
the son of Herod, the brother of Agrippa, married her; they
had three sons, Herod, Agrippa, and Aristobulus...

Whether her name was Salomé or not, the dancing girl and
her mother, Herod's sister-in-law and illicit wife, are painted as
two of the great villainesses of the Bible. Salomé, I was taught,
was a slut, and so was her conniving mother. But is that actually true? Or is Salomé, like Mary of Magdalene, a victim of
misogynist interpretations of Scripture and cultural bias?

Throughout a long stretch of Christian history, Mary Magdalene was called a prostitute—one who had been redeemed
through her faith in Jesus Christ, yes, but nevertheless a
woman of ill repute. That is, she was characterized as such
until contemporary biblical scholarship provided a corrective
to her traditional story.

What does the Bible *actually* say about Mary Magdalene?

Well, although she is mentioned in all four gospels, little is
said about her before the crucifixion. But in Luke 8:1–3 (NIV)
we read:

After this, Jesus traveled about from one town and village
to another, proclaiming the good news of the kingdom of

God. The Twelve were with him, and also some women who had been cured of evil spirits and diseases: Mary (called Magdalene) from whom seven demons had come out... and many others. These women were helping to support them out of their own means.

Whether Mary Magdalene truly was possessed by demons or had been suffering from physical or mental ailments that were popularly attributed to demonic possession, it is clear from Saint Luke's account that she was part of Jesus' cadre of followers and helped support his ministry and that of his twelve male disciples.

It is also clear from further gospel accounts that Mary Magdalene was present for the crucifixion and stayed to the bitter end, even after all the other male disciples (with the exception of Saint John the Beloved) had fled. She was present for his burial in the tomb provided by Joseph of Arimathea. She was the first person Jesus chose to reveal himself to after his resurrection, and she was the first evangelist. That is, she was the first person to tell others—the male disciples—the good news that Jesus had come back from the dead, just as he had promised.

Mary Magdalene was one of Jesus' intimates, a friend, faithful follower, and part of his "chosen family," along with the twelve disciples. Some scholars argue that next to the Blessed Virgin Mary (Jesus' mother), Mary Magdalene is the second-most important woman in the Bible.

So why was she labeled as a hooker for so many centuries?

The simplest explanation, perhaps, is that the idea of a woman being among Jesus' closest followers and friends was untenable in a social milieu that viewed women as considerably less important or valuable than men. Calling her a prostitute was a way to impugn and demean her significance in the gospel story. A woman of ill repute on whom Jesus took pity, healed from demonic possession and allowed to tag along with his motley band of disciples and other followers, holds far less import in the arc of history than a woman who chose to follow and support Jesus' ministry, sticking by him to the bitter end and beyond.

If Jesus treated Mary Magdalene—she of the fairer, weaker sex—as equal to his male compatriots, what would that mean for the way women were supposed to be treated by society in general?

What would Jesus do?

It's much easier to dismiss her as a slut (albeit a redeemed and reformed one) and sweep her off to the side as a footnote in the gospel story than it is to confront the scourge of gender bias, patriarchy, and misogyny that has plagued too much of human history.

Taking a closer look at the gospel accounts of Herodias and her daughter—the would-be Salomé—revealed a layer of the bleak story of John the Baptist's demise that had eluded me in the past and changed the traditional ways I had understood it for much of my life.

In the account in the Gospel of Mark, the dancing girl is referred to in the Greek as Herodias's "daughter" (*thugater*), and then, a few sentences later, when she goes to her mother to ask what she should tell Herod, she is referred to as "the child"—*korasion* in Greek, which has a more specific meaning than simply "child." *Korasion* is a diminutive form of the Greek word for "child" and means "little girl."

If so-called Salomé was a *little girl* and not some hyper-sexualized ancient Lolita, the story takes on an even more nefarious import. Some scholars argue that the Greek word interpreted generically as "dance" also had a more specific meaning as a circle dance or playful dance. Picture Shirley Temple tap-dancing rather than a nubile young woman working the stripper pole or a teenage seductress doing the Dance of Seven Veils, as she is portrayed in Oscar Wilde's play *Salomé*, which has more to do with how the dancing girl has been popularly understood through the ages than with the biblical accounts themselves.

If Salomé was a little girl, she was an innocent exploited by her mother and stepfather first as entertainment and then as an unwitting accomplice to murder. That she felt the need to ask her mother's advice about the reward she should seek from Herod makes it all the more plausible that she was a young child who didn't know quite what to make of Herod's offer to give her "up to half" of his kingdom.

That offer, by the way, likely wasn't meant to be taken literally. It was a colloquial expression at the time, not unlike someone today saying something like, "If you do this favor for me, I'll buy you a pony."

In the gospel accounts of John the Baptist's beheading— in the Gospels of Mark and Matthew—the dancing girl is not named, which indicates that she was insignificant, which is how children at the time were perceived, lending further credence to the idea that so-called Salomé was an innocent little girl who danced to show off for her stepfather and the tipsy dinner guests at his birthday party.

That her mother used her to demand the beheading of John the Baptist, the hairy, eccentric prophet who had publicly criticized Herodias and Herod for their illicit marriage, casts another pall on one of the darkest stories from the gospels. There is no redemption or grace in the Salomé tale. A child is exploited by her wickedly immoral parents, and an innocent man loses his head. There is no Jesus, no forgiveness, no resurrection, no good news.

So what are we to learn from this tale of woe?

I'm not sure. But I do know (now) that it's neither a cautionary tale about the evils of dance (as it has been characterized by more than one preacher in the history of Christendom) nor a moral one about the destruction wrought by lascivious young women and dirty old men.

Salomé was a victim and a pawn, much like the man whose head she presented on a serving plate to a drunken audience of adults who understood the depravity of the situation, even if it eluded her.

But she wasn't a slut.

Apocalypse Later

Jay Emerson Johnson

Here is wisdom. Let him who has understanding calculate
the number of the beast, for it is the number of a man: His
number is 666.

  —Revelation 13:18 NKJV

I freely confess how much I relished anticipating the battle of
Armageddon. That memory takes me back to my teenage self,
to a world long since past yet still remarkably vivid. Living
then in an evangelical, quasifundamentalist subculture—let's
just call it *fundagelical*—I believed that the Apocalypse defined
what it meant to be Christian. Apart from that galvanizing
moment of the world's end and the glorious second coming of
Christ, very little else about Christianity made much sense.
Some might imagine the End Times as Christianity's caboose.
For me, it fueled the engine of my faith.

  Consider this slice of memory from the 1970s, as an adolescent boy goes to bed in a cozy suburb of Chicago. I'm propped
up, leaning against a stack of pillows, and reading the Bible.
The house is quiet and dark, except for the small pool of light
created by the lamp on my bedside table. While my parents

sleep, I underline key biblical passages with a fine-point pencil and a transparent six-inch ruler. Next to me on the bed sits a book by Hal Lindsey, *There's a New World Coming*, his commentary on the biblical book of Revelation. His bestseller, *The Late Great Planet Earth*, holds far less interest for me, as I assume he wrote that book for the uninitiated masses. I want the insider's scoop, the blow-by-blow, verse-by-verse analysis of how the world will (soon) end. I'm sixteen years old, and as I ponder all the signs of the times pointing toward Armageddon, I'm deathly afraid Christ will come again before I have a chance to have sex. Never mind the prerequisite of marriage, which seemed impossibly out of reach even then. A gay identity lurked around the edges of my life in those years, not fully formed but certainly gestating its own apocalyptic anxiety. Revealing that kind of sexual desire would exclude me from the new world coming.

This memory explains a lot, not least the ambient sense of fear I associate with my childhood faith. I grew up believing that Christianity provided but one essential thing: the assurance that born-again believers would not be "left behind" in the "Rapture," that moment of Christ's coming at the end of time (1 Thessalonians 4:16–17). I could, of course, cite dozens of biblical passages on this; the New Testament would lie in tatters on the cutting-room floor if we tried to excise from it all traces of the Apocalypse. Martin Luther noticed the same thing some five hundred years ago.

As Luther uncovered the abuses of medieval church power, boldly nailed his theses to the cathedral door in Wittenberg, and generally scoffed publicly at the pretensions of prelates, he generated a good deal of apocalyptic alarm. He had avoided the book of Revelation early on in his career, refusing to write a commentary on it and insisting that it never should have been included in the canon of Christian Scripture. "I can find no trace of good news in it," he would say.

Later, when the rhetorical war of words with the pope took unsettling turns, Luther suddenly found some edification in that final biblical book. The pope, he reasoned, clearly fit the bill for the Antichrist, that fabled "beast" whose appearance would signal the end of time (Revelation 13:3–5). In due course, Luther wrote a commentary on the book of Revelation, leading his contemporaries to dub him the Angel of the Apocalypse. They had no doubt about the world's imminent demise, and they were quite correct. Given how Luther's reform movement dismantled the tightly woven structures of European society and medieval Christendom, the world as those sixteenth-century Germans had known it rather quickly unraveled, as worlds of many types so often do.

It's a simple word, really. Like so many of our words that carry more burdens than they ought to bear, *apocalypse* comes from the Greeks. This word derives from the verb *apoka-lupto*, often translated as "to reveal" but literally meaning "to uncover." That's it. Nothing about this word, by definition, carries the promise of disaster or the potential for a Hollywood blockbuster. It could, with no trouble at all, describe a moment of rather mundane insight, like clearing off the clutter on your desk and finding—actually *uncovering*—the wallet you thought had been stolen. Yet for all that unpretentious practicality, the word *apocalypse* still manages to create quite a fuss: doomsday prophecies, religious cults and mass suicides, marshaled armies.

Remarkably enough, to wreak all this havoc *apocalypse* need not refer to a revealed secret with any specificity, like where or when a terrorist will strike or who sold a small parcel of enriched uranium or how a particular virus initiated an epidemic. When that word, like a barely audible whisper in the dead of night, hovers around troubling circumstances, the vast imprint of Western religious culture does the rest. When *apocalypse* sneaks into consciousness, it drags a long and bloated history behind it. Beginning quite modestly as an ordinary verb in the marketplaces and academies of Athens, it then wandered through the scriptoria and monasteries and outlying provinces of the Roman Empire, accruing ever larger chunks of a fantastical religious imagination. From there it trekked across the Atlantic to a brand-new world, incubated in the spiritual fervor of New England Puritans, and eventually made its way to my twentieth-century bedside table.

As I reflect on this biblically inflected past I need to admit something else. I still relish the idea of a final confrontation between good and evil, longing of course to see good triumph. J. R. R. Tolkien's *The Lord of the Rings* certainly shaped that desire when I read it in high school, but no less when I saw Peter Jackson's film adaptation of it on the big screen. Like so many others, I nearly rose from my theater seat cheering as Gandalf led a liberating army of good guys (on a white horse, no less) to defeat Saruman's evil minions.

That deep desire for victory—barely distinguishable from revenge, the honest among us must confess—marks far too many Christian sensibilities and postures generated at least ostensibly by the Prince of Peace. Despite the church's own history of violence, the gospel still challenges me to ponder what grace means, not for me alone but also, and especially, for those I despise. Oddly enough, Christianity compels a redeeming logic that can appear opposed to its own canonical texts. That's a rather queer posture toward religion, indeed—and it has saved me more than once.

Coming out as gay while also nestled in the bosom of

fundagelical Christianity reveals more than sexual secrets. That moment uncovers a brand, no less indelible than a tattoo, marking a life of exile. The world of comfortably familiar spiritual practice and all its attendant social entanglements— that world ends. Far too many end their own lives in the wake of that apocalypse; just one such ending is, of course, too many. Yet by some amazing grace, I refused to end. I clung stubbornly instead to the hope of that very same tradition, the hope that inspired equally the writer of that last book of the Bible.

I remain a Christian today—deeply, occasionally even joyfully, and, still more, apocalyptically. But neither fear nor revenge fuels that embrace. I rely instead on the rhythms and patterns of Christian faith for their intimations of hope, especially in world-ending moments. All sorts of "worlds" end quite regularly. The question is not whether they will end but how we will live through the endings.

If the biblical book of Revelation still proves useful for a twenty-first-century world, it will encourage us to sift through the many complex layers of our sociopolitical distress and uncover reasons for hope. I mean quite deliberately to avoid optimism here, and even more to avoid any talk of certainty. Life comes with no guarantees, as human beings learn at nearly every turn. But hope is different. Along with faith and love, Paul included hope among the three indispensable features of a Christian life (1 Corinthians 13:13), even with all its uncanny, ephemeral, and invisible character (Romans 8:24–25). The fleeting though resilient energies of hope matter when they breed a posture of trust toward others rather than fear or suspicion or senseless hostility.

Another slice of memory, this one more recent, is the wake of the September 11, 2001, terrorist attack in New York

City. I watched that apocalypse unfold on television, thankfully accompanied by good friends, as the Twin Towers fell. They knew I had focused my graduate studies on Christian eschatology, and they kept looking at me during commercial breaks, pointedly and expectantly. So...is this it? they wanted to know. I knew exactly what they meant and stumbled my way through inadequate academic answers. I realized later what the only answer that matters is. In moments like that, when terror strikes, what matters most is the love we share for each other, the kind of love that binds us together and inspires both hope and something like trust. Ironically, I suppose, I had learned that as a fundagelical youth, many years before anyone had ever heard of Osama bin Laden.

That very evening I decided to clean out my garage. Odd, I know, but when the world around you descends into chaos it sometimes helps to create a little order on your own. Built for two cars, my garage would barely hold one, crowded with all those boxes I had been carting around with me every time I moved but had never bothered to unpack. If the world as we knew it sat on the brink of disaster, it made sense (at least to me) to catalog what, exactly, would go down with the ship.

I remember this: moving randomly from one box to the next, shuffling through old notebooks and school papers, uncovering a collection of Bibles in various translations and paraphrased editions. I smile. How many Bibles does one person to need to own? I reach to the bottom of the pile and pull out a small Bible with a red leather cover, a Revised Standard Version. I suddenly recognize this Bible as an old friend, the one that had accompanied me throughout high school. I'm amazed I still have it. I open it and flip through the pages, noticing all the neatly underlined passages; it feels like reading a long-forgotten journal.

Apparently I made very few marginal notes back then, maybe half a dozen in all. A small "H.L." adorns the space next to a verse in the book of Daniel, and I realize that it stands for Hal Lindsey, who frequently turned to that text for apocalyptic inspiration. I find the word *Dad* in Paul's second letter to the Corinthians, near the verse about having "treasure in earthen vessels" (4:7 RSV). It was one of my father's favorites. Then I stumble across "Bob and Roger," followed by an exclamation point, next to these words in the letter to the Philippians: "For God is my witness, how I yearn for all of you with the affection of Christ Jesus" (1:8 RSV).

I look up from the page, temporarily bewildered. I have no recollection of who those men were and why they deserved notation in my Bible. After a few moments of head-scratching, the revelation occurs, and my smile widens. Bob and Roger were high school classmates. I can see them sitting next to each other in the back row of my geometry class, but I remember them best in their baseball uniforms. Bob may have played outfield, tall, lithe, and blond, with radiant blue eyes. Roger stood a bit shorter, more compact, with darker skin and brooding eyes; he was a better hitter than Bob. I failed miserably in sports, including baseball, but Bob and Roger never made fun of me in gym class and even came to my defense among those who did. That explained, at least partially, my infatuation with both of them.

It never occurred to me in high school to call my feelings for Bob and Roger a "crush." I had not yet uncovered any language for a sexual attraction to other men. I worried instead about their souls. Religious concern felt safe and familiar, and it made sense to worry about the Rapture—of the Pauline kind—and whether these two boys would be left behind. I can see myself, leaning against propped-up pillows under the glow of the bedside lamp, and underlining those words from Philippians. The physical stirrings of affection for Bob and Roger threatened to inspire more in that moment than underlining, so I made a marginal note and offered a prayer.

Those stirrings of desire eventually took root in my life and blossomed, no biblical substitution required. Yet I still wonder, after all these years, what became of those boys of baseball who had shown me such kindness. Retrieving those memories just then, surrounded by fundagelical artifacts, kept me from thinking too much about terrorist attacks and what they may have triggered. More than a few Christians started to read the Revelation to John a bit more assiduously in the aftermath of 9/11 and as the first bombs fell over Afghanistan. I kept such speculations neatly contained, even though it gave me pause to watch a war unfold near cities with such biblical names as Nineveh and Babylon.

I learned something from cracking the covers of my adolescent Bible just then, in that peculiar time. Moments of apocalypse unfold at their own pace, and as some worlds fall, others rise up to take their place. Sometimes this process transpires on a grand scale, among nations and governments and religious sects. Other worlds encompass much smaller spaces. A personal cosmos might fade away and reveal something new, perhaps for only a handful of witnesses. That's why I smiled, standing in the midst of all those boxes and Bibles in my garage, remembering Bob and Roger. The apocalypse I both desired and feared as a teenager came later, in its own time.

Daydreaming of Bed Linens

Bill Motz

About noon the following day...Peter went up on the roof
to pray. He became hungry and wanted something to eat,
and while the meal was being prepared, he fell into a trance.
He saw heaven opened and something like a large sheet
being let down to earth by its four corners. It contained all
kinds of four-footed animals, as well as reptiles and birds.
Then a voice told him, "Get up, Peter. Kill and eat." "Surely
not, Lord!" Peter replied. "I have never eaten anything
impure or unclean." The voice spoke to him a second time,
"Do not call anything impure that God has made clean."
This happened three times, and immediately the sheet was
taken back to heaven.

—Acts 10:9–16 NIV

I have a confession to make: I'm "Bible Bill." Occasionally
I put on a superhero costume and perform at my church
as a Bible-toting caped crusader against sin. It's all good
tongue-in-cheek fun, and the congregation gets a laugh out
of watching a middle-aged man strut around the sanctuary
in tights.

Upon my victory over evil, I shout out my catchphrase, *Sola Scriptura!* You theology geeks already know that the phrase is Latin for "by Scripture alone" and that it is a central doctrine of the Protestant Reformation. The idea is that the Bible is the final authority when it comes to determining correct theology and practice.

I got the nickname Bible Bill back in high school, when I'd walk the hallways wearing a cross around my neck and toting a small New Testament in my back pocket. I loved that little book, and any time I had the opportunity, I'd open it up and share the amazing, life-giving word of God with what I hoped would be a receptive listener.

But I have another confession to make: adult Bible Bill struggles with Scripture. What used to seem so clear-cut and focused now feels murky and muddled. It's like being in a love-hate relationship with a dear old friend: some parts of the text fill me with joy and an overwhelming sense of truth, others anger me and make me feel that there's no way God could ever have intended them to be included. Though I try to keep the discipline of daily study alive, I'll admit to more than a little trepidation when I reach for my Bible.

Maybe that's why I've been thinking a lot lately about this strange little story in Acts and its impact on my understanding of the authority of Scripture—the idea that God has revealed himself and his will in these sacred texts, the Old and New Testaments, and that we can rely on them as a foundation for faith and life. If that's true, then this story in Acts is a troubling passage.

Most of the time, we Christians conclude that Peter's vision has to do with God receiving the Gentiles into the community of the chosen. (That and the idea that we can now eat bacon-wrapped shrimp.)

But the problem is, Peter's vision clearly spits in the face of the Mosaic law. God goes to great lengths in Leviticus laying out what is clean, what is unclean, and even how long something remains unclean. God commands: "Do not defile yourselves by any of these creatures. Do not make yourselves unclean by means of them or be made unclean by them. I am the LORD your God; consecrate yourselves and be holy, because I am holy" (Lev. 11:43–44 NIV). God equates observance of this law with holiness. This is a big, big deal, and members of the Hebraic community could get tossed out for neglecting it.

So suddenly Peter has a dream, and God's revelation to Moses and thousands of years of tradition get chucked out the window? Can you imagine the same thing happening today? How would the Christian community respond if someone like, I don't know, megachurch pastor Rick Warren woke up from a nap and said, "Wow. Had the strangest dream. Turns out that thing I thought was forbidden isn't. God wants us to use Ouija boards in worship." We know what would happen. He'd be run out of the pulpit as a heretic, lambasted for leaving the precious parameters of orthodoxy.

The early Christian community struggled with the implications of Peter's dream, too. Most of the believers at the time were Jews who believed that Jesus came as the fulfillment of Mosaic law. They still kept kosher; they went to the temple; and they continued to observe the Jewish festivals and sacrificial system. But more and more Gentiles were coming to believe in Jesus, too. So should they become like Jews and observe the law?

This became a heated debate within the young church. Some of the Jewish believers were telling Gentile converts, "Unless you are circumcised, according to the custom taught by Moses, you cannot be saved" (Acts 15:1 NIV). Paul and Barn-abas sharply disagreed with them, so a church council was called in Jerusalem to make a decision. What was the role of the law, if any, in this New Covenant?

Think about the ramifications of this question: Was God's direction to Abraham and Moses still valid? As good Jews, they would know that circumcision was *the* sign God estab-lished with Abraham of their covenant. "For the generations to come every male among you who is eight days old must be circumcised...Whether born in your household or bought with your money, they must be circumcised. My covenant in your flesh is to be an everlasting covenant. Any uncircum-cised male, who has not been circumcised in the flesh, will be cut off from his people; he has broken my covenant" (Gen. 17:12–14 NIV).

Not a lot of ambiguity there.

But taking the sheet vision and the subsequent outpouring of the Holy Spirit onto the Gentiles as evidence, Peter argued, "He did not discriminate between us and them, for he puri-fied their hearts by faith.... We believe it is through the grace of our Lord Jesus that we are saved, just as they are" (Acts 15: 9–11 NIV).

James then concludes the discussion by saying, "It is my judgment, therefore, that we should not make it difficult for the Gentiles who are turning to God. Instead we should write to them, telling them to abstain from food polluted by idols, from sexual immorality, from the meat of strangled animals and from blood" (Acts 15:19–20 NIV).

Wait. What? That's the distillation of the law for the Gen-tiles? Avoid food offered to idols, sexual immorality, strangled meat, and blood? What happened to the "everlasting cove-nant" part of circumcision? Honestly, we should be shocked by their decision. Where's the exegesis we expect from our theological leaders? Where's the parsing of the text to find something as close to the original intent as possible? Where's the discussion of dispensational theology, which would preserve the idea of God's revelation to our faith ancestors as being authentic *for its time*—and would replace it with a better, more complete covenant that reflects the next step of God's salvific work?

But the apostles don't do any of that (at least as it's recorded in Acts). Instead they turn to that theologically dreaded duo: experience and feelings. Their *experience* shows them that God has accepted the Gentiles "as is," without the law or circumcision. Their experience has shown them that they, as Jews, have been unable to live up to the expectations of the law. Because they believe that they are saved by faith and not by works, they *feel* like they shouldn't put the burden of the law onto the Gentiles.

Bible Bill finds this disconcerting. So much for the "God said it, I believe it, that settles it" mind-set. Apparently the early church's response was: "Except when it doesn't."

To be fair to the apostles, this somewhat cavalier attitude toward Scripture didn't start with them. Jesus begins his discussion of the law in the Sermon on the Mount by saying, "Do not think that I have come to abolish the Law or the Prophets; I have not come to abolish them but to fulfill them. For truly I tell you, until heaven and earth disappear, not the smallest letter, not the least stroke of a pen, will by any means disappear from the Law until everything is accomplished. Therefore anyone who sets aside one of the least of these commands and teaches others accordingly will be called least in the kingdom of heaven, but whoever practices and teaches these

commands will be called great in the kingdom of heaven"
(Matt. 5:17–19 NIV).

That is good, solid *Sola Scriptura* thinking.

But then Jesus proceeds to make all sorts of modifications
to the law with his "you have heard that it was said…but I tell
you" statements. He assigns the penalty of murder to anger.
He widens the definition of adultery to include lust. He nar-
rows the allowable reason for divorce. He vetoes the use of
oaths. He throws out the proportional justice system of an eye
for an eye in favor of turning the other cheek. And that whole
"healing on the Sabbath" business gets him in trouble again
and again.

So it's understandable, therefore, why the Jewish community had issues with the young church and started seeing it
not as a *fulfillment* of Moses' law but a rejection of it. Orthodox Jews were known throughout the world (and still are)
for a few key tenets: they observe the Sabbath, they don't eat
unclean foods, and the males are circumcised. It's central to
being a Jew. It's part of what sets them apart from everyone
else.

On the other hand, it's obvious that the church doesn't follow the law anymore. There's no clean/unclean distinction.
We don't make sacrifices. Most males in the United States are
circumcised, but that has to do with hygiene, not covenant.
And if we observe the Sabbath at all, it's on the first day of the
week, not the seventh. We do all this for good theological reasons, but for all intents and purposes, the Mosaic law is dead
in the church. What the Christian community has said is,
"Ignore parts of the Old Testament as no longer being valid.
Some of it still is, but not all of it. It's all God's word, but it
doesn't all apply." (We do the same with the New Testament,

by the way. Or am I the only one who attends a church where women wear jewelry and pray without covering their heads?)

So how are we supposed to know what still applies and what doesn't?

I've heard some theologians say that you have to read Scripture and look for the "eternal truths"—those principles that go beyond cultural and historic boundaries and remain valid no matter what. The command against murder is one of those. Stealing, too. The "Numbers 5" test to see if a wife has been unfaithful by making her drink holy water mixed with tabernacle dust? Well, not so much.

The "looking for eternal truths" method, then, becomes highly subjective and quickly breaks down. We know from 1 Corinthians 8 that Paul thinks it's really no big deal if you eat meat that was sacrificed to an idol; just don't do it in front of a weaker brother who would stumble if he saw you do it. And obviously the strangled meat and blood taboos long ago left church orthodoxy.

That leaves one last rule: sexual immorality. Maybe that's why sex is such a hot-button issue for the church; it's the one connection to the law we have left. Is that why we still look to Leviticus for questions of sexuality while ignoring the chapters on clean versus unclean, diet, and blended cloth? But even that one remaining taboo—sex—gets a little loosey-goosey if we consider the multiple wives and concubines of the patriarchs, relationships later prohibited for church leaders in the New Testament. And though Jesus states that divorce is permissible only in the case of unfaithfulness, Paul expands it again to allow a believer to divorce if his or her unbelieving spouse wants out (1 Corinthians 7:15).

Where does that leave us, then, with this idea of the authority of Scripture? What do we do when we want to know God's point of view on certain issues? Usually, we argue. We find the verses that support one view over another. We break into camps, vilify our opponents, and sometimes we actually take up weapons.

Take the issue of slavery in the United States. Entire denominations broke apart and re-formed over the debate. Sermons packed with Scripture were preached on both sides; each convinced that they had correctly interpreted the word of God. Eventually, the conflict led to a civil war, and the theological debate was ultimately decided by the cultural outcome. The Scriptures didn't change, but you don't hear many pro-slavery sermons anymore.

A similar thing happened around racial segregation and women's ordination, and my hunch is that it's happening again now with LGBT issues. We like to pretend that we're "Bible-based," getting our direction from Scripture alone. But in reality, just like the early church, we're using our feelings and experience to help us make sense of theological conundrums.

For instance, I know several gay Christians who are filled with the Holy Spirit. If I use the same math that the apostles did in Acts . . .

I think we have to be honest with what the Bible is and is not. Though it would be much simpler if it were, the Bible's not a systematic theology. It contains rules, but it's not a rule book. It is a library with a wide collection of literary styles, including poetry, parable, wisdom sayings, apocalyptic allegory, and lots and lots of narrative that tells the story of people wrestling with God.

That's the problem with the Bible: it's messy. God does things we think God should not do and doesn't do things we think God should do. There are things about Scripture that we love and things that embarrass us, like a drunk uncle at a wedding. It's silent where we want it to be loud and loud where we wish it were quiet.

And I have a strange feeling God likes it that way. He likes to have us wrestle with the mess of it all.

Returning to the vision of the sheet, Peter knew the Scripture. He followed the law. He was a good Jew. God could have used some other analogy than the sheet to show that the Gentiles were now welcome into the community of faith. He could've used Jesus' illustration of vine grafting or given Peter a vision of another fold of sheep joining with the shepherd's flock. But he didn't.

Instead of those nice, neat images, Peter was given a vision that challenges and even violates his very core. It is a central taboo, one that would make him physically ill to contemplate. It rocks his understanding of holiness at its very foundation. And it sets in motion a series of events that forever changed the church's connection to its Jewish roots.

Sola Scriptura! If the authority of Scripture is to inform how we live the life of faith, then I'm encouraged that the early church also struggled, wrestled, and argued. It makes me feel like Bible Bill is still in good company.

I wonder...does God still lower the sheet today? If he does, what's inside of it that makes me uncomfortable? And what will be the implications for my theology?

Early-Morning Matters

Jack Palmer

If anyone loudly blesses their neighbor early in the morning,
it will be taken as a curse.
> —Proverbs 27:14 NIV

I love the Proverbs.

They are tidbits of insight into the world around us, words of encouragement and warning in equal measure; wise sayings that we can carry with us for a few moments, a day, or a lifetime.

I come at the Proverbs from no theological height. To be honest, I come to almost nothing from any height. However, my hang-ups about my height are for others to deal with, not you, dear reader.

But what I do believe about these biblical Proverbs is that they reflect the desire of someone—whoever the author or authors of these nine hundred or so verses actually is or are—to live in a way that is pleasing to God and generally to make living alongside others a little bit better.

They are not theological fortune cookies—a biblical afterthought to accompany a sizable bill. And yet we rarely treat them with the same reverence or authority as we do other parts of the Good Book.

But the more I read these acorns of wisdom, the more they take root; and the more time I give them to sink in, the more they produce fruit.

Even the ones that on the surface just seem a bit odd.

Consider Proverbs 27:14 as an example.

"If anyone loudly blesses their neighbor early in the morning, it will be taken as a curse."

Now, for me, reading this initially elicits an image of King Solomon locked in some kind of Homer Simpson–Ned Flanders feud with his neighbor—yes, King Solomon is Homer Simpson in this example (try not to think about it too much; it's not supposed to be an airtight illustration). Each morning, an overly chirpy, overly friendly neighbor who just has to bless him a little bit too eagerly and too loudly greets King Solomon on his porch. The neighbor (a.k.a. Flanders) tells him how wise he is looking—nay, how regal. The neighbor loudly proclaims how overwhelmingly awesome Solomon is at 6:30 a.m., when all Solomon wants to do is drink his coffee and read his paper in peace (or whatever the equivalent tenth-century BCE ritual was).

Let's be honest: people don't need other people all up in their grille like that first thing in the morning, however nice the compliments may be.

And so how did Solomon respond? Well, he happened to be writing this book called Proverbs at the time this feud was going on, which was super convenient. All he had to do was drop a cheeky little line into it that called out his neighbor, put on record that such loud blessings were never kosher that early in the morning, and the world would be safe from such early morning overexuberance. Job done. (Drops the mike.)

Or so he thought...

Solomon, in all his wisdom, recognized a plague that would continue throughout the ages, one that would cause distress, weeping, gnashing of teeth, and sometimes just good old-fashioned rage.

I am, of course, referring to... the morning person.

Yes, in this sentence, squashed between hundreds like it, King Solomon—the king who, when offered anything he wanted, chose wisdom—calls out the morning person.

I hope this isn't too much of a slap in the face for all of you who like to be up with the lark (or up with the Partridge, if, like me, you enjoy a good Alan Partridge reference). It must be tough to hear. Solomon, of whom God says "there will never have been anyone like you... nor will there ever be" (1 Kings 3:12 NIV), isn't a fan of how you do things in the ay-em.

For me, however, as a decidedly non–morning person, the verse plants a giant grin right across my face. (King Solomon even received his wisdom in the middle of the night rather than while he was doing his early morning devotions. He was a night owl, like me—getting stuff done in the peace and quiet of the wee small hours.)

As I spent time thinking about this verse and why on earth it is included in the Proverbs (somehow I don't think the neighborly feud story I suggested is the reason—for one thing, Solomon lived in a palace, not a row house, where his annoying neighbor could pounce on him on the porch), I thought I would do a little background research. Surely there must be some examples of Solomon doing stuff in the morning.

One of the great things about the Bible is how descriptive it is—how the writers take such care to set the scene. And one of the ways they do this is by telling us when things happen.

We know when Jesus picked out his dream team: "When

morning came, he called his disciples to him and chose twelve of them, whom he also designated apostles" (Luke 6:13 NIV).

And we know when he liked to pray: "Very early in the morning, while it was still dark, Jesus got up, left the house and went off to a solitary place, where he prayed" (Mark 1:35 NIV).

But Solomon? Nothing. In the Bible, there is no mention of him doing anything "in the morning." Well, that's not quite true. There is one reference, in 2 Chronicles 2:4, when he is explaining the purpose of the temple he will build and the burnt offerings that will be made there every morning and evening. Other than that? Nothing. Nada. דבר שום (yes, I translated *nothing* into Hebrew). If you want something done in the morning, apparently Solomon was not your man.

If you want to find the morning person in the Old Testament, there is one standout contender—Joshua. He loved his morning activities. Mustering armies, crossing the Jordan, taking up the ark of the Lord—he couldn't get enough of his early morning activities. But apparently that just wasn't how King Solomon did things three-hundred-odd years later.

So was Solomon hiding under his duvet at noon on a Monday like some lazy college student? Of course not. Dude had a kingdom to run. He would have been up at a reasonable time. Had a good breakfast. Read the morning scrolls. Maybe even worked out a little. But he had the God-given wisdom (quite literally) to know not to rub people the wrong way before the day had even started!

Of course it is okay to be up at a reasonable time. But it's the accompanying "loud blessings" that cause problems. In shame I remember the looks of utter disdain I used to get from my housemates when I would bound into the kitchen at breakfast time, the grin of an untrained and slightly dim-witted puppy slapped across my face, gleefully proclaiming that morning was here and that we should all be very happy about it.

Those looks.

Those looks could kill. And in the end they actually did. They quickly killed off my phase of being the morning person.

Since then, when I wake up, there is most definitely no loud blessing of anyone. Only cursing. Horrible, disgraceful, only-appropriate-for-HBO cursing that the day is once again upon us and I am to be forcibly removed from my bed.

Now, I moved past the morning-person phase before I knew this Proverb existed. But as bizarre as it may sound, this Proverb has become a real encouragement to me. A friend and former pastor of mine wrote that it is "a humorous proverb on untimely behavior." But for me, it has become even more. It reminds me that every character in the Bible is human (well, Jesus had the whole fully God–fully man thing going for him, but most everyone else is human) and liable to get annoyed at the actions of others. And it reminds me that we all have our own patterns of time and rhythms of life. And that that is okay.

So it's okay (I think) that I'm not great at getting up in the morning to read my Bible and that I am better at opening it up at midnight instead.

It's okay (I hope) that I'm not exactly a bundle of joy before about 10:00 a.m. and would prefer to be left to do my own thing until the caffeine has kicked in.

This isn't to say that there aren't any aspects of my life, mornings or otherwise, that I should be working on. Of course not. That would be a fairly depressing and defeatist attitude to take on life. But the humanity of this Proverb is what really gets me. It is honest and challenging, affirming and thoughtful. And of course, most important, it's a clear divine revelation that the morning person needs to take a long, hard look at himself or herself in the mirror and decide if his or her morning blessings are just a little bit too loud.

So here's to you, non–morning person! May the wisdom of Solomon be with you as you curse the sun's rising and don't feel fully human until nearly noontime.

Embrace your suspicion of the crack of dawn and know that you can rebuke the morning person, secure in the knowledge that the wisest person to walk this earth would have done the same!

The Miracle

Timothy King

By faith Abraham obeyed when he was called to go out to a
place that he was to receive as an inheritance. And he went
out, not knowing where he was going. By faith he went to
live in the land of promise, as in a foreign land, living in
tents with Isaac and Jacob, heirs with him of the same promise. For he was looking forward to the city that has foundations, whose designer and builder is God. By faith Sarah
herself received power to conceive, even when she was past
the age, since she considered him faithful who had promised. Therefore from one man, and him as good as dead,
were born descendants as many as the stars of heaven and
as many as the innumerable grains of sand by the seashore.
—Hebrews 11:8–12 ESV

Now faith is the substance of things hoped for, the evidence
of things not seen.
—Hebrews 11:1 KJV

I kept the steering wheel together with duct tape. The gas
tank could only be accessed if someone with small hands

popped the trunk, reached past the lining, and pulled on a small spring. But in my opinion there was only one thing wrong with the car: the radio didn't work. If you turned it up all the way, you could make out some muffled music, but nothing had been the same since I had slid off the road during a snowstorm the previous winter.

And yet it was a car.

I was eighteen, and I loved it.

Perhaps it was my tendency to overlook the imperfections of this car that led me to forget one of its flaws the day my friend Mike and I went hiking. During that accident the winter before, the car had sustained some significant damage, most of which had been fixed. But when it came back from the repair shop, the car's thermostat had stopped working. In order to make it possible to turn on the radiator, a friend's father had installed a manual switch that connected directly to the battery. If the car began to overheat, I'd throw the switch, crank the heat, and the car would cool quickly. But if the switch remained engaged after the rest of the car turned off, the battery would slowly drain.

We drove two hours that morning to pay homage to the Old Man of the Mountain, who had collapsed a few months earlier. In life, he had been made up of a series of five ledges at the top of a cliff face that, when viewed from the right angle, formed the image of a man's face looking eastward. It was thought that retreating glaciers some two thousand to ten thousand years earlier had created this natural wonder. The Old Man was on our New Hampshire driver's licenses, our license plates, and our highway signage. In fourth grade, I'd learned the Daniel Webster quote "Men hang out their signs indicative of their respective trades; shoe makers hang out a gigantic shoe; jewelers a monster watch, and the dentist hangs out a gold tooth; but up in the Mountains of New Hampshire, God Almighty has hung out a sign to show that there He makes men."

The Old Man was especially dear to my family because my mother's father had been part of a team of engineers that had worked to preserve its face. The same slow and steady movements of rock that had created the face were slowly destroying it. With wire supports and steel rods, engineers attempted to retard the progress in the hope that they might preserve the face for generations to come.

But early one morning in 2003, tectonic plates deep beneath the earth's surface that had been in motion since the earliest days of history caused a slight tremor—no more than a shiver—and shook the mountain.

The inevitable occurred; the old man fell.

Mike and I had picked the range of mountains just east of where he had stood as a fitting place to say good-bye. We started late and hiked fast. Once we had climbed the first peak we jogged from ridge to ridge and passed hiker after hiker. We stopped at one peak to drink some water and talked to a couple who had started our same route early that morning. They were going to stay at a shelter that night. But we were determined to finish the same route all in one day.

Our boots landed hard on the ground beneath us as we ran down the trail. We hit a rocky stretch and began a series of seamless movements bouncing from rock to rock. Our bodies engaged in complex calculations as we landed perfectly on one rock and used our momentum to leap to the next. Without conscious thought, our muscles contracted, our feet relaxed, and our knees held just enough tension to absorb each shock. Gravity, momentum, and trajectory all were calculated without mistake over and over again.

In the brief moment when my foot would make contact with the ground, I would plan my forward trajectory. My path was dictated by that contact, no matter how brief it was. My only job while in the air was to stick with the plan. I was to keep moving forward and trust that the ground would be there the next time I put my foot down, that the rate of gravitational acceleration would remain roughly constant, and that friction from the atmosphere surrounding me would continue to be negligible. Each step was taken in agreement with unseen forces and predicated on a trust that what had been true in the past would prove to be true in the future.

Abraham, Hebrews 11 tells us, "went out not knowing where he was going." God told him to leave his home. He did. God didn't tell him his final destination. But he left anyway. Normally when Abraham's story is told it makes it sound like he never questioned his decision to go. Never doubting that it was the right plan, he just put his head down and did it, moving forward no matter how hard the task became. No matter how brief the contact with the ground was, he trusted that his job was just to keep going in that same direction. Abraham knew those unseen forces were at work in the same way that day as they had been the day before and would be forevermore.

If that was Abraham, I can't relate. If Abraham was a man whose resolve was always strong, always focused, and always sure, then I am not sure there is anything I can learn from him. That kind of unwavering confidence is not simply beyond my capabilities, it is beyond my comprehension.

But the story of Abraham is not so one-dimensional. He might have gone out not knowing where he was going, but it seems he spent a lot of time regretting that decision. According to the story told in the book of Genesis, while Abraham was living in the ancient land of Gerar he told everybody that his wife, Sarah, was just his sister. It was *technically* true. She was his half-sister. Abimelech, who was king of Gerar, sent for Sarah and "took her." And then Abimelech finds out in a dream that he just took Abraham's wife, and God isn't happy about it.

It's around this time that I'm sure Sarah lost any confidence that her husband knew what he was doing. She would certainly object to his inclusion in any list of folks who had the whole "faith is the substance of things hoped for, the evidence of things not seen" thing all figured out. But their marriage recovered from that setback, and they went on to have their first child, Isaac, when they were both in their nineties. But marrying your stepsister and then handing her over to the king in order to garner favor with the local authorities is certainly a misstep worth noting—especially considering it was the second time it had happened. (Abraham had pulled the sister-wife trick with the pharaoh of Egypt eight chapters earlier.)

While ultimately celebrated as a paragon of faith, Abraham is not a person whose beliefs were always solid and sure. I don't think anyone in his position would be. If God had asked him to do easy things he probably would have been much more confident—bounding down the path, leaping from rock to rock in a display of complete trust. But God asked Abraham to do great things, and so he doubted.

Faith wouldn't have been necessary if his tasks were easy. While there may have been moments when he leaped from rock to rock in a seamless display of trust, Abraham also seemed to spend a good deal of time with his face in the dirt.

Mike and I stumbled into the trailhead's parking lot exhausted, dirty, and sweaty. This late in the evening it was almost deserted. There were a few cars left scattered around the lot. We hadn't passed another soul for several miles and didn't think there were many more hikers who would be coming down that trail after us. We took a deep breath. We hadn't talked about this part. The parking lot where we'd left my car was seven miles away. (Oops.) We had gone out not entirely knowing where we were going. There had been a turn we passed a few miles back. That turn wouldn't just have cut the length of our hike by four miles, it also would have taken us on a loop that would have brought us right back to my car.

That's when we spotted him. He was walking out of a restroom and toward a car. We tried to look harmless, but we were two guys with big hair and hemp necklaces who were pretty filthy and smelled even worse. We explained our situation and that our car was just down the highway. If he were headed that direction anyway, might he help us out?

He hesitated. He said he would like to help us but would have to check with his wife. His car was full. It was a four-door sedan with two adults and two kids, both in car seats. We stood nearby as he had a brief and heated discussion with his wife. We could tell he was on our side. They went back and forth. She pointed to the backseat, he pointed to the trunk. She held out five fingers and then held out six. We looked at the car. She was right; five seats and six people. The math was not on our side. He pointed to the trunk again. She threw up her hands and went to the backseat, removed a car seat, and moved it to the trunk. He came over to tell us that it would be tight but we could have a ride. We breathed a sigh of relief.

The conversation was strained but polite. While the husband drove, I sat in the front passenger seat and Mike sat in the back next to the children, one of whom was now sitting on her mother's lap. The husband, having just gotten his way, was silent. His wife made a point of being extra friendly, asking about us and our how our hike had been. I imagine the husband had told his wife that she should be nicer to strangers. The wife probably informed her husband that she was in fact a very nice person but that didn't mean she thought giving strangers a ride with their kids in the car—especially when they didn't have enough seats—was such a great idea.

We arrived at the exit where our car was parked pretty quickly. Our car was another mile down the road, but I politely suggested that they had already been a great help and didn't need to drive the extra mile; they could drop us anywhere. They wished us good luck, the husband unlocked the doors, and we stepped out onto the grass by the off-ramp. The wife got in the front seat holding her child, and without getting the car seat they took off straight for the highway on-ramp.

Our muscles were cold now, and our feet felt raw. That last mile was a slow one, but we got to my car. There were a few other vehicles in the parking lot, but it looked like they all belonged to overnight campers. The sun had dipped behind the mountains, but we still had another hour of dusky light left. We collapsed in the car and took off our boots. I put the key in the ignition and turned. Nothing. Not a sound. Not even a whine. The dashboard lights were dark. And that little red switch to the left of the steering wheel that turned on the fans to cool the engine was still in the on position.

I'd forgotten to turn it off. And now the battery was dead.

We pushed the car to the edge of the road and put up the hood. It wasn't a heavily trafficked road, but we felt sure someone would be by soon to give us a jump. After a half hour, though, only four cars had passed. One stopped but didn't have any cables. Two slowed down without stopping, and the driver of the fourth never even looked as he sped by. Dusk was over, and most of the scant light we had now came from a waning moon. Our chances of getting a ride in the dark were pretty slim.

That's when we remembered the Flume. It was a big gorge, a tourist attraction half a mile down the road. We had passed it on the way to the parking lot. It was downhill all the way to the visitors' center. I put the car in neutral and got behind the steering wheel. We couldn't see any cars coming in either direction, so Mike pushed the car into the road. The car began to pick up speed, and he jumped on the trunk. The car rolled faster, and he got nervous and yelled that he was going to jump off. He lunged, rolled on the ground beside the road, got up, and started chasing the car down the hill.

I kept my eyes peeled for the entrance to the visitor's center. *Shouldn't be too much farther.* I looked back and saw headlights coming. I kept rolling, and they got closer. It was a logging truck. Not a full semi but much larger than my sedan. And it kept getting closer. Maybe the driver wasn't paying attention and didn't notice a car slowly coasting down the hill without any lights. The entrance to the visitors' center was near. I looked back, and the headlights almost blinded me in the rearview mirror. It felt as if time had slowed and the lights of the truck were bearing down on me inch by painful inch.

There was no traffic coming the other way, so I pulled to the other side of the road. The turn was closer now, but the lights felt like they were almost at my back bumper. I yanked the steering wheel to the left, toward the entrance to the visitors' center. The headlights followed again. I gripped the steering wheel and sucked in a breath. The sound of a thousand accidents played over and over on the television in my mind.

The folly of the entire trip was wrapped up into that moment before impact.

Mike and I are a lot alike. That's how we met.

We both were lifeguards and swim teachers at the YMCA. I worked at the one in Goffstown, and he worked at the one in Manchester. Every once in a while I would take a shift in Manchester, and he would take one in Goffstown. I kept having coworkers tell me that I needed to meet their friend Mike. He had big curly hair like mine and wore hemp necklaces, too.

I started dating a girl and though it didn't last long, she kept telling me that I reminded her of another guy she used to date named Mike. He had big curly hair and wore hemp necklaces, too.

A couple of kids from my church youth group had met this guy named Mike (who had big curly hair and wore hemp necklaces) during a play they were in together. And then, on our way to a Ben Harper concert, a friend from school told me that we had to find her friend Mike, who was meeting us at the show. In fact, she told me, I would probably like him. You guessed it: he had big curly hair and wore hemp necklaces.

It felt as if there were no way we could *not* have met. All those circumstances had conspired years before to bring us to that moment in the dark, with the dead battery and the logging truck bearing down on us fast.

I closed my eyes and braced for impact. The headlights swerved to my left. The truck's brakes locked, and the entire rig came screeching to a stop. I hit my brakes as well. Mike jumped out of the cab and onto the ground. The driver came around from his side and looked at me with surprise.

"There was someone in her?" the truck driver asked.

The truck driver had seen Mike jump off the back of the car and then get up and run after it. He couldn't see inside the car and assumed it was a runaway vehicle. He picked Mike up off the side of the road and told him they would catch up to the car. They didn't communicate about exactly what they were doing as they attempted to catch up to the car that was coasting down the hill. The driver had pulled up directly behind my car and had closed in slowly. He wasn't sure what he could do to stop a runaway car, but he was sure he could do something.

Time hadn't slowed, but the headlights really had been bearing down on me inch by inch.

The truck driver pulled out some jumper cables. He told us it might not be the best idea for him to use a big truck to try and jump a small car, but because the visitors' center was empty we figured our best hope was to give it a try. I sat in the car ready to turn the key. Mike attached the cables and gave me the go sign. I turned the key, heard a snap and pop from the battery, then the engine turned over and the radio began to blare some classic rock. I turned the volume knob down. The surge of electricity through my vehicle had healed the radio. We thanked the trucker and got back on the road.

When I told the story later I would always finish with what I thought was the most exciting part: the healed radio. It was as if everything had gone wrong just so I would get the radio working again. Sure, if the first guy had given us a ride all the way to the car he might have been able to give us a jump. Or if one of those other cars had stopped and had jumper cables we might have gotten going again without Mike having to jump off the back of a car and me having a panic attack from what I thought would be a fatal wreck. If none of that had happened we would never have gotten a jump from a truck that would somehow fix my radio.

Yes, the truck could have also blown a fuse in my car or created some other sort of expensive damage, but it didn't. It healed my car. If I hadn't left the switch on at all, if we had left earlier in the day, if we hadn't run along the ridges or run the last mile, if the husband and wife hadn't argued and delayed our departure. The entire day seemed to be specially designed and beautifully orchestrated for the purpose of fixing my car radio.

But if the God that I believe in is one who makes his presence and power known through an ability to orchestrate the repair of my car radio, I'm not sure I've discovered a God worth believing in at all.

I believe in a God whose presence can be felt in both the mundane and the extraordinary, in the majesty of the mountains and the intimacy of a still, small voice. But that belief does not rise and fall upon the evidence of a divine presence interfering in the world around me to get me what I want or to fix all that I deem wrong.

When I think of faith, I don't recall bounding down a mountain path with my body in harmony with the unseen laws of the universe or the series of perfectly executed motions that allowed God to fill in each and every gap. When I think about faith, I remember what it felt like to push a dead car onto a highway at night with an eight-ton logging truck bearing down on me, and how just when I think it's the end, that I'm about to meet my maker, I get the jump-start I need to limp back home again.

In the midst of a world that is so clearly broken, in the midst of lives laced with tragedy, goodness and beauty are still constantly evident. That is the miracle.

When the Old Man of the Mountain fell, it was not a sign

for me that the world is irredeemable and in inevitable decay. Instead, the fact that it ever stood at all was a testament to creation's underlying goodness.

I believe in miracles not because I think God orchestrated a day of vehicular malfunctions in order to heal my busted radio but because I had a friend who helped me push my car onto the highway, held on as long as he could, and then flagged down a passing trucker to catch up again as soon as he fell off.

Abraham's faith inspires me not because of the high praise it affords the man but because holy writ tells us about the myriad ways he screwed up, over and over again, and yet found redemption anyway.

Running from "Healing" to Healing

Calenthia S. Dowdy

[Jesus said,] "Is it not written, 'My house shall be called a house of prayer for all the nations'? But you have made it a den of robbers."

    —Mark 11:17 RSV

One humid summer morning near the center of Philadelphia, a middle-aged black man ran down the street alongside a public bus, huffing and puffing as the hospital robe he was wearing—tied at the neck but open in the rear—flew in the wind.

When the bus operator noticed the man running alongside his bus, his first reaction was annoyance: "Another derelict nuisance." Not wanting to risk running over and killing the man, the bus operator stopped the bus in the middle of the street and opened the door. The running man hopped inside.

The driver looked him over curiously, noticing the plastic hospital band around his wrist and nonskid socks he wore with his robe. The bus had passed a hospital a few blocks back, and the driver must have wondered: Has this man just escaped from the hospital?

The running man mumbled to the driver, "I don't have any money, but I only need to go a few blocks." The bus operator responded, "Okay." And there he stood in silence, the running man at the front of the bus, until he reached his stop. Then the door opened, and he jumped off.

I don't know what the situation of this running man was, but from all appearances he looked like he woke up that morning, perhaps grumbled to himself, "Fuck this," got out of his hospital bed, and left the hospital.

It reminded me of the time when I was a kid and my own dad was in the hospital after a heart scare of some sort. After a few days he decided to unhook himself from the needles and monitors. Then he said he had had enough and felt fine and that he was going home.

So he went home and appeared to be fine from then on.

Hospitals are healing institutions, and we need them, but I know people who have reported feeling more ill inside the place that's supposed to make them better than they did before they were admitted. They claim they experience a more rapid healing once they leave the hospital. Plausible? The reality is that people choose to leave hospitals early all the time, before their doctors recommend it and prior to a formal medical discharge. *They want out.* Far from healing them, hospitals sicken them.

While I don't necessarily share that view of hospitals, I understand it because it resonates with my feelings and experiences of church.

Yes, church: that spiritual institution that purports to offer healing for the human soul. Similar to that running man, I have been the running woman in the city streets, trying to get home after escaping many bad church experiences.

The earliest was when I was about sixteen years old, and one of the other girls in church turned up pregnant. The pastor and church leaders had her and the boy who got her pregnant (also a church member) come to the front of the church to confess to the congregation that they had sinned against God and against us. It was a public shaming, and their humiliation was palpable. I remember feeling so sad for them that I wanted to get up and run out the church doors, but my parents wouldn't let me.

As an adult, I ran from church several times. I escaped and planned never to go back…until I found a "better" church. Certain congregations felt toxic to me, and my soul was in turmoil in certain congregations, including the one I was raised in. Some churches sought to suppress my ministerial longings and squelched my calling and giftedness because of my gender.

"God said women should not lead in the church."

"Women are to follow their husbands."

"Women are the weaker sex and need protecting by men."

No healing there.

I found more affirmation for my talents outside of church than inside it. So I ran.

For the past fifteen years or so, my commitment has been to cross-cultural, transracial ministry. The majority of churches I joined or partnered with were led by white Americans. The racial discomfort and subtle pressures to conform to majority-culture ways of thinking, doing, and worshipping were apparent to me in many of these settings.

I recall a fellow parishioner once saying to me, "Well, *you* people do it this way, but I think you'll see that our way of doing it is much better." These churches often loved having me in their congregation, but their objective was to change me and colonize me—to *heal* me?—instead of recognizing that we could transform each other in community with one another. These experiences were painful. Unhealthy. Sickening. So I ran. I don't advocate running, and I don't hate church. I'm far from being a "hater": the truth is that I love the church and the body of Christ, so my critique is from a heart of deep hope.

Here's the awful thing about church: the people there are just like me—flawed, ill, and contagious. In my search for spiritual healing, I have often had to leave the institution and go outside because what was happening inside wasn't healthy.

Jesus himself had a few run-ins with church people. In Mark 11:15–19, Jesus and his friends arrive in Jerusalem only for Jesus to immediately begin throwing people out of the temple. He kicks out everyone who's set up shop there, buying and selling. Jesus knocks over the tables belonging to moneylenders and kicks over stalls of pigeon merchants. All this activity was going on inside church! Jesus didn't let anyone even carry a basket through the temple. He told everyone there, essentially, "My house is supposed to be a house of prayer for all people, but you have turned it into a hangout for thieves." The religious leaders were angry about what Jesus had done. They also panicked, because he was persuasive with the crowds. Jesus was a troublemaker, and the clergy had to figure out how they might get rid of him—even if it meant killing him.

Jesus responded with righteous anger when he saw that his house of spiritual healing had become a sick place. The temple was supposed to be the center of holiness, an open place where everyone could come for healing and to worship God. But it had become a house of lies and exploitation. Even religious leaders took part in temple abuse. They welcomed bribes and profited from dishonest gain, prostitution, and debauchery. Those deemed "acceptable" were permitted entry to the temple, and those marked "unacceptable" were barred from it.

That night, Jesus left the temple and exited through its gate. It was outside this religious institution where his most poignant healing ministry occurred. *Outside* the temple and *outside* the cultural gates to the city, Jesus met real, hurting people. After turning over the tables inside the temple, Jesus went "off the grid" and tore down walls outside it.

So let's go outside, where Jesus is. Let's go where the action is. Let's not spend our time with privileged insiders, trying to be like them. They abuse Jesus. This "insider world" is not our home. We must keep our eyes peeled for the city that is yet to come. Let's take our place *outside*, with Jesus, no longer pouring out the sacrificial blood of animals but pouring out sacrificial praises from our lips to God in Jesus' name.

In *Christ Outside the Gate: Mission Beyond Christendom*, Orlando Costas wrote, "Salvation lies outside the gates of the cultural, ideological, political, and socio-economical walls that surround our religious compound and shape the structures of Christendom. It is not a ticket to a privileged spot in God's universe, but rather freedom for service."

Jesus shows us that our healing and mission are not inside the safe dysfunction of the institution but rather outside, in the streets and on the sidewalks, with other broken people just like us, in search of healing.

I understand that running man because I ran, too, from "healing" to real healing.

Maybe God wants us to know that our spiritual salvation is tied to our physical salvation: location and place *matter*. We are whole when we are outside the church gate, face-to-face and shoulder to shoulder with the grit and grime of a diverse humanity that, like us, is in need of Christ's healing.

That's our home.

The Good Shepherd

Victor Conrado

Then Jesus told them this parable: "Suppose one of you has
a hundred sheep and loses one of them. Doesn't he leave the
ninety-nine in the open country and go after the lost sheep
until he finds it?"
     —Luke 15:3–4 NIV

After eleven years living among the Samburu tribe of Kenya,
I grew to appreciate the parable of the lost sheep—if for no
other reason than it makes for a great children's sermon.

In Samburu culture, children younger than twelve take
care of the cows, goats, sheep, and camels. These animals
comprise the family's wealth, and children better watch
them well. These children clearly get the point of leaving the
ninety-nine sheep in search of the one that gets lost. It belongs
to the family, and they'd better do their best to take care of it.

At night, after their free playtime, some of the children I
knew chose to go to school to learn how to write and read.
About once a year, I'd get the children together and tell them
the parable of the lost sheep, and then I'd let them play hide-
and-seek either in the classroom or the sanctuary. To begin

the game, I'd count to ten and then come looking for the children like a shepherd looking for his lost sheep. Only I'd intentionally overlook one of the children each time we played, then I'd pretend that we were running out of time and needed to end the game. Regularly, the children would grab my hand.

"Oh, no!" they'd say. "You can't go on until you find the last sheep."

Of course, that's the point I was hoping to get across.

It worked like a charm every time.

If we pay close attention to this parable, we can see that its point is clear: God is like a good shepherd who, having lost one of his sheep, will leave the others and go after the one that is lost until he finds it and brings it back to the fold.

Raymond E. Brown, a biblical scholar and one of the editors of the *Jerome Biblical Commentary*, says, "God's mercy, indeed, is as foolish as a shepherd who abandons ninety-nine sheep to save one..."

If we examine it more closely, this parable challenges us in a number of unexpected ways. I'd like to take a look at what this parable says about who God is and what God does. I'd also like to think about what it says about human beings and what it teaches us about community.

The parable of the lost sheep brings us before a God who does not close the door to anyone.

Once more:

Which one of you, if he has a hundred sheep and loses one of them, would not leave the ninety-nine in the open pasture and go look for the one that is lost until he finds it? (Luke 15:4 NET)

The usual answer is "No one!" That's not the way we

think. If you have a hundred sheep and you lose one, well... too bad! One sheep out of a hundred is an acceptable loss. Hey, it's only 1 percent.

When you think about it, our whole lives are based on the idea that there is an acceptable percentage of failure. We are at peace with this concept when we deal with other people, nature, and the environment. We send our young people to war knowing that not all of them will come back home. Well, it is a small sacrifice compared to the good that they do. (Besides, we are being kept safe here at home.) We start every school year knowing there will be a certain drop-out rate. Not everyone will graduate. We're happy when the employment rate is below 5 percent. We don't expect every-one to be able to keep a job. Marriages begin, but we know some will end. There is a percentage of failure. We accept it. So as far as we're concerned, losing only one sheep out of a hundred is not so bad. You might even say it's impressive.

But with God, every sheep counts. And that's the first les-son of the parable: with God, nothing is lost. Often we give up too easily. We are used to considering numbers and percent-ages—not individual, cherished human lives. Not so in the kingdom of God.

We live in community with each other—all of us are inter-related—so when we talk about being "lost" we really refer to being separated from each other. In other words, the sheep was lost because, at the start, it was *part of the flock*. Being lost has to do with a broken connection. To say someone is lost is also to point to the effect that the lost one has on the others in the community.

This is a correlation I've come to appreciate more and more over the years. The more intimately we're connected to another person, the more we agonize when we're separated.

The less we're connected, the less we're affected. When we talk of military personnel overseas, patriotism and sacrifice come to mind. But something completely different happens when one of them is *my* son or my daughter, *my* brother or my sister. My friend.

This is the essence of the kingdom of God: we're family! We are brothers and sisters in Christ, joined by our common allegiance to him. And because we belong to the body of Christ, when only one is missing, something of *us* is missing as well.

How many times have we heard that parable during a church service and thought that we are among the ninety-nine because we happen to be in church that day? And what happens when we go back home and look in the mirror and encounter the one who is lost? Every single time I did the children's sermon in Kenya, the kids got it right—they wouldn't allow me to go on until the last sheep was found and brought back to the fold. Likewise, the kingdom of God isn't complete until *everyone* is safe, secure, and accounted for. We live in community with each other, or we don't live at all.

As a missionary priest living among the Samburu, I realized that the easy way to look at those who attended church on Sunday was to pretend that they were "perfect." They were the ninety-nine good sheep who heard the call of the Lord and came to listen to him. I know this was just how I wanted to see those people on Sunday. But this is how I was trained to think and act. We created a way of life inside the church that did not allow for lost sheep. But one Samburu elder once told me that the nature of the sheep is to get lost at a certain moment of its life.

The good news is that the good shepherd comes looking for them, and he searches until he finds them, and when he does, he brings them back to the fold. That's a model we'd do well to follow in our lives and witness within the church—not to be content with those who show up on Sunday morning but to be persistent about reaching out to those who don't.

May we remember that no one is lost to God. We must not think in the world's terms, of "acceptable percentages of loss," but instead—like our good shepherd—we must seek out those who are lost and alone, missing from among us, and welcome them back to the flock with God's love.

Move Down! Clean Cup!:

Pulling Back the Covers on Revelation

Christian Piatt

Then I heard a loud voice from the temple telling the seven angels, "Go and pour out on the earth the seven bowls of the wrath of God." So the first angel went and poured his bowl on the earth, and foul and evil sores came upon the men who bore the mark of the beast and worshiped its image. The second angel poured his bowl into the sea, and it became like the blood of a dead man, and every living thing died that was in the sea. The third angel poured his bowl into the rivers and the fountains of water, and they became blood. And I heard the angel of water say, "Just art thou in these thy judgments, thou who art and wast, O Holy One. For men have shed the blood of saints and prophets, and thou hast given them blood to drink. It is their due!"

—Revelation 16:1–6 RSV

The book of Revelation and I have a complicated relationship. We flirted a little bit back in high school, at least until it got me kicked out of church. I suppose I had a little something to do with that, given that I was an uppity teenager, full of questions and doubt, in—of all places—a Baptist church in Texas. But mostly it was Revelation's fault. That's how I remember it, anyway.

Ironically, my youth leaders at the time had invited us to pick our next Bible study topic, and I was the one who requested Revelation. At the time, I was into heavy metal and horror movies, and it seemed like Revelation was the closest thing to a visual complement to the sound track of my life. I mean, what's not to like? Fire, destruction, dragons...all the good stuff without any of those rules about being kind or giving all your stuff away. So I was in.

The problem was, it didn't take long before we got into the lengthy and growing list of all the folks in my life who were headed south for a permanent vacation, if you know what I mean. The list included all my Jewish friends from school, who were among the most faithful and kind people I'd ever met. They invited me in to take part in their Passover Seders, their bar mitzvahs, and their Hanukkah celebrations. They seemed to live the way their faith directed them to live, and many of them believed that Jesus was a great prophet. Heck, maybe even with a little divinity sprinkled on top.

The thing is, they hadn't been baptized and hadn't made a (translated: the one and only) public confession of faith, so they were screwed. The whole lot of them. And then we moved on to my dad, who wasn't a churchgoing kind of guy. But to me, he was my dad, my hero. So to have someone so easily write off his immortal soul was more than a little bit of a shock. When I asked what they suggested I do about it, they told me to go home and tell him to invite Jesus into his heart.

Um, yeah.

Then there was the matter of biblical interpretation. I had always taken the fantastical stories in Revelation—among many others in the Bible—to be just that: stories. I figured they had some truth or greater wisdom to offer, but I didn't ever really think they were meant to be taken literally. Of course I hadn't shared this little secret with my youth leaders, but on one particular day, my sense of discretion was fairly clouded by my distress about the fate of most of the earth's population, including most of my friends and loved ones. So I figured, what did I have to lose?

"Seriously, guys," I finally said. "You're telling me that actual dragons are going to fly down from the sky?"

"Yes."

"And rivers will literally be turned to blood, complete with plasma and corpuscles and stuff?"

"Yep."

"How does it keep from clotting?"

"Excuse me?"

"These rivers of blood. I mean, they're exposed to air, right? So how do they keep from scabbing over?"

This went on for a good fifteen or twenty minutes, by which time we had laid out on the table a number of revelations of my own, including:

- I didn't believe the earth was five thousand years old;
- I didn't buy the theory that scientists secretly manufactured the fossil record to accommodate their nefarious anti-God agenda;
- I thought God was a real jerk, and I wasn't particularly interested in spending eternity with a brazen sadist;
- nonetheless I thought God's love was likely big enough to offer grace to Jews (gasp!) and maybe even to atheists (what?!?); and

• any God who would set his son up to be slaughtered to satisfy some contract with the same people who killed him was a pretty crappy dad, by all accounts.

You could have heard a gnat fart by the time I was done. But damn, it sure felt good to get it all out, all the stuff I'd been sitting on for years. Five days a week I'd go to a school where they challenged me to think critically and ask questions, and then I'd come to church, where I was expected to absorb and assimilate without question. For the first time I recognized the ideological line in the proverbial sand, and, not unlike Adam and Eve in the metaphorical garden, I realized I was over here, and the rest of my church folks were somewhere waaaaay over there.

"If you can't believe every word in this book, exactly the way it's written," said my youth leader, his face turning six shades of crimson as he wielded his floppy King James Bible over his head, "then it doesn't mean shit!"

And then he threw it at me. Yes: he threw the Bible and nearly hit me in the head with it. Soon thereafter, we both agreed it was probably best if I found another place to frequent on Sundays, as it was clear the whole "Christian" thing just wasn't taking.

Thanks a lot, Revelation.

———

I'd wager that the book of Revelation is the most talked about and yet most misunderstood book in the Bible. For one, it's Re-ve-la-tion, with no *s*. Every time I've heard a preacher announce that he's speaking on this Lord's day on the book of Revelation*ssss*, I tune out.

Get the name right, pal.

Second, although a good number of people know that Revelation was believed to have been written by John, there's plenty of confusion about who this John guy actually was. By most Bible nerds' estimations, this is not the same John to whom the Gospel of John or the Johannine letters (1, 2, and 3 John) are attributed. This John supposedly was writing Revelation from prison, as he had been jailed for being a vocal leader of this sassy new Christian movement. He was sent to live in exile on an island called Patmos, just off the mainland of Greece, in the Aegean Sea. So most of the time, he's called John of Patmos.

The debates about what's being said in Revelation and why are actually as interesting as the Scripture itself. Of course, there's always the "take it literally word-for-word" angle, though suffice it to say that I'm not in that camp. I'll explain a little bit more about why later, but I'd argue this isn't what God—or John—was going for.

Some people believe the whole book is written in code, as a way for John to get his secret messages out past the island prison guards and to his fellow subversive Christians. But if that's the case, reading it feels a little bit like reading the cryptograms on the back of the Ovaltine can without your trusty Little Orphan Annie decoder ring. What's the point, right? And it makes the name of the book particularly ironic if, rather than revealing something, the text is actually an ancient and mysterious secret code that we've yet to entirely decipher. Makes for a good story, but there are major points off for obfuscating biblical wisdom.

Another theory is that John was going crazy and that the whole book is little more than the ramblings of a nutcase suffering from an extreme case of claustrophobia. But again, how does reading the delusions of a wacko help me better understand the kingdom of God? Maybe this is why the Council of Nicaea—the group of church leaders back in the day who got to decide which books would be included in the official Bible and which didn't make the cut—almost voted against including Revelation as inspired, sacred text.

My personal preference is to approach the whole thing as elaborate metaphor and fantastic poetry, all of which doesn't have to be literally, factually accurate in order to point toward a greater truth. So then we, as readers, have two opportunities: first to enjoy the imagery and beauty of the words, and then to try to discern the wisdom beneath the over-the-top imagery.

I know for some this is more or less heresy to even suggest, but if parables and metaphor were good enough for Jesus, why can't they work for other authors of Scripture? That's one of the things I've always wrestled with most when I'm trying to engage with Scripture—when someone tells me, "Yeah, Jesus told stories about prodigal sons and mustard seeds as illustrations to make a bigger point, but this bit here about burning bushes and that one about flying dragons, that's all totally real."

In the immortal words of Ace Ventura: "All rightee, then." You have fun with that. I'll be over here using the power of critical thought endowed to me by my creator.

Revelation falls within the time-honored genre described by most Bible nerds as apocalyptic literature. And we have this book in particular to thank for the frequent misunderstanding of the word *apocalyptic*. Although in contemporary culture we talk about the Apocalypse as some cataclysmic, earth-shattering event that will be the end of life as we know it, that's really overselling the word. It actually comes from the Greek word *apokálypsis*, which just means "unveil" or "uncover." In this sense, apocalyptic literature is meant to reveal something that has been hidden, which really helps to explain why the book would be called Revelation, if you think about it.

So if we're not going to take all this literally, and if it's not some fancy code or the ravings of a lunatic, what exactly is supposed to be revealed in all this? My wife, Amy, went to seminary a number of years ago, and she had a professor who basically distilled the sum total of Revelation down into two words: "God wins." In the end, the forces of evil will not prevail, and God will triumph over all the bad stuff. And while I tend to agree with her professor, I think we still have to do a little more unpacking to understand what we mean when we say that God wins.

In order to figure this out, it helps to understand what we think of when we talk about "justice." For the most part, human beings think of justice in pretty cut-and-dried terms. There's a winner and a loser; someone bad gets what he has coming to him. This kind of justice is obsessed with fairness, with getting even, making things *right*. I call this type of justice retributive justice. And there are plenty of texts throughout the Bible that justify our reliance on this kind of justice. For example, how else can someone interpret "an eye for an eye, a tooth for a tooth" in Exodus 21? But if we consider that before this law came along, the law of the land, as we read in Genesis 4, was that a person who does wrong should be "avenged sevenfold," then the act of taking only one eye actually constituted a dialing-back of the law, a reversal of the system of ever-escalating retribution and violence. And then Jesus comes along and does them all one better with "turn the other cheek." Helps us understand what he means when he says he was coming to fulfill the law, not abolish it. Things were headed in the right direction; they just weren't all the way there yet. And Jesus was pointing the way.

So Jesus was trying to guide us away from our addiction to retributive justice and toward a more *restorative* kind of justice. This justice is more concerned with making things whole, with reconciling divisions and brokenness, with holding out hope that oppressor and oppressed, lion and lamb, actually have an opportunity to live together in peace. Sucks for the winners, right? If we're on the winning team, we want to see our opponents suffer for being on the wrong side of history. We want to take the images from Revelation and place our enemies in the shoes of the remorseful people who are "left behind." We want to sit at the right hand of God and munch on a giant state fair turkey leg to the sound track of much weeping and gnashing of teeth.

Sorry, says Jesus. If one is lost, we're all lost. It's about restoring this entire mess to wholeness, not about picking winners and losers. And given this frame of reference, I've actually come to love the book of Revelation again. It's no longer the blueprint for my loved ones' demise but rather a fantastic vision of the great shake-up that's to come, when God makes sense of the sum total of all our screw-ups. Will it be tough, maybe even a little bit messy? Could be. After all, every new birth tends to come from some sort of violent rupture that tears at the seams of time and space, making room for something new that wasn't there before. But in my mind, I like to think of it as being a little bit more like the Mad Hatter's tea party in *Alice in Wonderland* than like some half-baked Kirk Cameron movie.

Move down, move down! Clean cup, clean cup!

I don't know about you, but my cup is a mess. It's got chips all over it, and try as I might to care for it, I drop it a hell of a lot more than I should. I kind of like the idea of a fresh start. Not just for me, but for those people I can't stand. If I'm right, chances are I'll have a seat at the table, right next to my good old youth minister, come kingdom time.

God help us both.

Womb Work and the Uncomfortable Idea of Redemptive Suffering

Rachel Marie Stone

We know that the whole creation has been groaning as in the pains of childbirth right up to the present time. Not only so, but we ourselves, who have the firstfruits of the Spirit, groan inwardly as we wait eagerly for our adoption to sonship, the redemption of our bodies.

—Romans 8:22–23 NIV

It was the middle of the night, and the contractions were coming unnaturally hard and fast as the result of a hasty inducement of labor. That I was laboring without pain medication had nothing to do with being heroic or dedicated to a particular philosophy of childbirth. Thanks to surgery I had when I was seventeen, my spine was filled with scar tissue, and I was simply not allowed to have an epidural. In between contractions that contorted my mind and body, in the midst of pain that overwhelmed every breathing technique and visualization exercise I'd practiced for months, I had ten or twenty seconds to catch my breath and prepare for more agony. After six hours of muscle spasms, gritted teeth, and inarticulate groans and cries, I used one of those ten- or twenty-second breaks to look into my husband's eyes and whisper, "Why does God want me to suffer like this?" His eyes filled with tears, and, being truly wise, he said nothing at all, but he did not leave my side until the ordeal was over six hours later.

Why does God want me to suffer like this?

To pay for Eve's sin, of course—at least that's what I'd been taught to believe. Even after I held my baby in my arms, triumphant and exceedingly proud not only of my beautiful child but also of my own body's power, I felt shaken and disturbed by the pain I had experienced. I certainly hadn't forgotten it all as soon as I saw the baby, in the clichéd way that I was "supposed" to. I didn't forget it, and I didn't cherish it. For months I could not listen to the songs I had listened to early in labor (for the record, Yo-Yo Ma *and* U2) without experiencing intense anxiety, but I sensed the pain's value.

So many kinds of pain, such as a stubbed toe, a broken arm, and a toothache, seem (and sometimes are) pointlessly absurd and useless in a way that the pain of birth tangibly, visibly, audibly isn't. *Look at my baby. Look what my labor, my pain, has brought forth.*

The idea that pain and suffering might have some sort of redemptive value makes me roll my eyes as I conjure images of patiently suffering saints, eyes cast heavenward, waiting for the illumination that is sure to follow their affliction. I imagine cheesy Victorian heroines who are "too good for this world" happily embracing the news of their impending death, because now they'll *really* get close to God. Why does God want *them* to suffer? Surely to enlighten them, to make them realize some deep truth, to make them new and better people. It's an idea I find irritating, and yet when I think of the pain of childbirth, I think there may be something to the idea that suffering can be redemptive.

Early in the pages of Genesis, the meaning of death is bound up with birth and with redemption. On the day that the woman ate of the fruit, God "greatly increased" her pains in childbearing. The suffering of a woman in bringing forth life was a reminder of death. This paradox is intensified when you consider that the biblical narrative also tells us that God has conquered death by being born of a woman, as a baby. A sword will pierce Mary's soul and, even still, Saint Paul writes, the whole creation groans in labor pains, awaiting its transformation. These are only a fraction of the birth images employed by biblical writers—who, we may safely assume, were males writing largely for other men. Still, birth must have assumed enough of a role in the lives of men *and* women to have been a meaningful image, capable of evoking deep truths about life, suffering, God, and hope. Throughout the Bible, God makes cameo appearances as a midwife and as a laboring mother; sometimes God's people are in labor, some-times God's people are as a baby being "delivered." A very good case can be made for birth as a primary and shaping Christian metaphor: you must be *born again.*

Still, I've heard only one sermon that discussed a literal childbirth in relation to the spiritual truths it illustrates, and— no big surprise here—it wasn't delivered by a male pastor.

Emerging from a woman's womb is, like death, a great human equalizer. In Ecclesiastes, the Preacher reflects that not even great wealth prevents us from leaving this life in the condition in which we arrive. As we came, so shall we go, naked and without possessions.

Job likewise considers the womb as a place that establishes human equality:

> If I have rejected the cause of my manservant or my maidservant, when they brought a complaint against me, what then shall I do when God rises up? When he makes inquiry, what shall I answer him? Did not he who made me in the womb make them? And did not one fashion us in the womb?[2] (Job 31:13–15 ESV)

In the nineteenth century, the writer Harriet Beecher Stowe transformed her agony over the loss of her "most beautiful and loved" son Charley to cholera at just eighteen months of age into the beginnings of the book that helped elicit compassion for those living under slavery. Frequently in *Uncle Tom's Cabin*, her most famous work, she calls upon mothers to recognize the common humanity that they share with slaves and to realize that the system of American slavery, in which families were ripped apart at the auction block, was an unimaginable violence. Perhaps it is wrong to use the words *recognize* and *realize* to describe what Stowe did. Above all, she invited people to *empathize*, to be moved to compassion. "Most mothers are instinctive philosophers," she wrote.

If philosophy is about discovering the truth that leads to the best sort of life, then the Hebrew Bible certainly confirms Stowe in this. In the story of the two harlots who stand before Solomon—with but one live baby between them—it is a love that is "willing to forfeit even justice for the sake of life" that defines the mother. In the Hebrew, says scholar Phyllis Trible,

---

2. For the observation that the womb is a "place of human equality," see Phyllis Trible, *God and the Rhetoric of Sexuality*, vol. 2 of Overtures to Biblical Theology (Philadelphia, Pa.: Fortress Press, 1978), 36.

the meaning of the word *womb* (*rehem*) is "compassion." She writes, "In biblical traditions, an organ unique to the female becomes a vehicle pointing to the compassion of God."[3] While the majority of biblical metaphors for God are masculine, only God—never God's creatures—is said to be *rehum*. Merciful. *Womblike*.

The Bible has been used to justify all kinds of nasty ideas about women. They are more easily deceived, because Eve ate the forbidden fruit first. Sin is passed to the next generation from women,[4] especially through their wombs. Women must be silent and submissive. But the Bible also celebrates women as brave and strong and capable of love that transcends all law, even justice (e.g., the "harlot" who would relinquish any claim to her child rather than see it killed). If the Bible locates the womb as the place where humans begin to fail, or if it assumes that all women must be mothers to be complete, it also understands that the womb is the seat of tremendous creative power, justice, and compassion. It is but an imperfect picture of the kind of self-giving love that God has for God's creatures—a nourishing, protective, merciful, compassionate love; a love that, like the mother in the Solomon story, brings truth to light.

"To give to the light" is the literal meaning of the Spanish phrase for "to give birth." Giving to the light, to my mind, is a metaphor expressing a movement toward generosity and truth. A woman gives when she has a child; she gives life, and she gives of herself, of her very body and blood. Only a woman's womb can do that, with God's help.

---

3. Trible, 38.

4. In *The Great Christian Doctrine of Original Sin Defended*, Jonathan Edwards says: "It is most plain, that man's being born of a woman is given as a reason of his not being clean."

But what made biblical writers identify the womb as the seat of compassionate, self-giving, truth-seeking love? One possible explanation might be that, for them, the womb defined women, much as it seemed to in ancient Egypt, where it was thought that the uterus was free-floating and wandered through the body, causing all sorts of mental disturbances and physical maladies. Ancient Greeks agreed. Their explanation for seizures and depression involved blaming the uterus, and it's their word for uterus—*hystera*—that gives us the word *hysteria*. Irrational behavior was largely associated with women, and in particular with their wombs. Hysterectomy (the surgical removal of the uterus) and oophorectomy (the removal of an ovary) were used to "treat" mental illness in women. In 1847, Frederick Hollick, MD, wrote in his book *The Diseases of Woman*:

> The Uterus, it must be remembered, is the *controlling* organ in the female body, being the most excitable of all, and so intimately connected, by the ramifications of its numerous nerves, with every other part.[5]

Not long afterward, Dr. Edward H. Clarke of Harvard Medical School argued in his book *Sex in Education* that educating women was potentially dangerous because the uterus and the brain were at odds with each other. This went right along with the Victorian notion that to be sexually "continent" was the most rational choice, and having too many orgasms would diminish men's and women's intellectual and rational capabilities. These thoughts on sexual continence

---

5. Frederick Hollick, MD, *The Diseases of Woman: Their Causes and Cure Familiarly Explained* (New York: Burgess, Stringer, 1847), 205.

weren't exactly sexist, then, but nevertheless it was wombs and menstruation that kept women firmly lashed to the earth and the things of the earth.

Despite the fact that people have long defined women by their wombs—and not in a positive way, at that—the Hebrew Bible, surprisingly, doesn't disparage the womb but honors it. Neither does it ascribe the womb's most salient quality (which Trible identifies as a love that "protects and nourishes but does not possess and control") to women alone.[6] I think it's more likely that the biblical writers identify the womb with compassion and love out of great respect for what many women's wombs can do. They offer hospitality and suffer god-awful pain for the sake of another. Even those who are "barren," to use that biblical word so redolent of sorrow—either because of life circumstances or because they are male—can do the compassionate, "wombing" work the Bible metaphorically envisions.

God, who has no body at all, certainly does.

The English language uses birth metaphors with respect to other kinds of creative or transformative work. We *conceive* ideas and allow them to *gestate*. We may characterize the difficulties of a new endeavor as *birth pangs* or the letdown after a big and exciting effort as *postpartum depression*. The writer David Rakoff described the essence of being an artist as having the ability to "tolerate oneself long enough to *push something out*." Still, many of us tend to recoil from the fleshy reality of a literal birth, an attitude that is perhaps more Gnostic than authentically Christian but that nonetheless has a long history in Christendom. The second-century apocryphal gospel known as the Protoevangelium of Saint James imagines the birth of Jesus happening this way:

---

6. Trible, 33.

A great light appeared in the cave so that our eyes could not endure it. And by little and little that light withdrew itself until the young child appeared: and it went and took the breast of its mother Mary.

There is neither anguish nor blood—much less urine or feces or, heaven forbid, a vagina—in this birth story. The baby Jesus simply appears after an overwhelming light recedes, giving rise to the traditional Catholic version of the story, in which Jesus materializes, miraculously, outside Mary's womb "without [ahem] opening the passage."[7] Addressing Mary herself, Saint Augustine wrote, "In conceiving thou wast all pure, in giving birth thou wast *without pain*" (italics added).[8] (And how, exactly, did the saint presume to know this?) This painless and apparently vagina-free birth was confirmed at the Council of Trent and made part of the Roman Catechism, where it is written:

> To Eve it was said: In sorrow shalt thou bring forth children. *Mary was exempt from this law*, for preserving her virginal integrity inviolate she brought forth Jesus the Son of God without experiencing, as we have already said, any sense of pain [italics added].[9]

Perhaps in a similar vein, the second-century Gnostic theologian Valentinus insisted that although Jesus ate and drank, he did not defecate.[10]

---

7. Thomas Aquinas, *Summa Theologica* Q35, A2.

8. Augustine, *Sermone de Nativitate Domini* supposititious.

9. Catechism of the Council of Trent, part 1 ("The Creed"), article 3.

10. Fragment 3 of Valentinus, quoted in Ismo Dunderberg, *Beyond Gnosticism: Myth, Lifestyle, and Society in the School of Valentinus* (New York: Columbia University Press, 2008), 22.

Call it the problem of poop.[11]

Perhaps the irony in this scrupulous avoidance of vaginas and shit and pain is that the Christian hope of *re*birth centers on the cross: a place of blood, sweat, pain, and death; a place of bodily shame and anguish that becomes, finally, a place where death is conquered and the gift of new life is given. One does not need to take much imaginative license to see how the anguish of childbirth—even Mary's childbirth—anticipates the cross, where great suffering is transformed into glory.

A woman in childbirth is astounding to behold. It's at once as earthy and ordinary an experience as human life offers and as extraordinary and transcendent an experience as human beings can undergo. There are hours of struggle, and then, suddenly, there is no holding back. There is no escaping the radical transformation that takes places as a woman cries out, her swollen belly collapsing as a new human being emerges to breathe the air and look upon this world for the first time. All the ultrasounds in the world can't fully prepare one for that cataclysmic and irreversible moment of separation. I've watched even the most seasoned midwives and doctors—people who've been present at literally hundreds, even thousands, of births—break into a grin as they take in the kicking and wailing of a freshly born baby.

And so to say, with Saint Paul, that creation is "groaning in labor pains until now; and not only the creation, but we

---

11. See, for example, Milan Kundera in *The Unbearable Lightness of Being*: "Spontaneously, without any theological training, I, a child, grasped the incompatibility of God and shit and thus came to question the basic thesis of Christian anthropology, namely that man was created in God's image. Either/or: either man was created in God's image—and has intestines!—or God lacks intestines and man is not like him."

ourselves" (NRSV) is to express a hope for a world that is not merely touched up and prettified from the pain- and injustice-riddled place we now inhabit. It is, rather, to hope for a world that surpasses this one in almost every way; a world that is to this world what ultrasound images, heartburn, and labor pains are to cradling a newborn baby and understanding the certainty of the pain and pleasure she will bring.

I don't really believe the old line—almost surely penned by a man—that women "forget" the pain of childbirth. I haven't forgotten the pain, nor has any woman I've ever known well enough to interrogate on the issue.

Rather, the opposite is true: the memory of that pain forces me to remember the hopeful promise that even the profoundest suffering can somehow bring forth something new, something unexpected, something glorious.

This Is Buddha

Carolyn Reyes

As Jesus was on his way, the crowds almost crushed him. And a woman was there who had been subject to bleeding for twelve years, but no one could heal her. She came up behind him and touched the edge of his cloak, and immediately her bleeding stopped. "Who touched me?" Jesus asked. When they all denied it, Peter said, "Master, the people are crowding and pressing against you." But Jesus said, "Someone touched me; I know that power has gone out from me."
—Luke 8:42–46 NIV

I hate crowds.

I know everybody says that, but I really mean it. The loudness, the smells, and all those bodies—pushing past me, pressing against me, touching me. Yikes.

I'm one of those people who go to the farmers' market near closing time. Yes, the produce is often cheaper, but mainly I do it because there aren't as many people around. I can grab some discounted kale and butternut squash ravioli *and* avoid the sweaty armpits and equally assaultive wafts of patchouli stink.

We don't have a TV in our home. There are many reasons for this, mostly hippie-granola ones. Television sucks the life out of you. It inhibits creative thinking. I'm also trying to keep the ads at bay. I don't want my four-year-old learning how to be a good consumer. And I sure as hell don't want her to ask me to take her to Disneyland, because—well, among other reasons, there are crowds there.

I make exceptions, of course. I take my kid to gay pride festivities every year. Sometimes it's to the Dyke March or the parade in San Francisco, other times to the bounce house at Oakland Pride. And there's usually a smattering of protests throughout the year (we couldn't miss *all* the Occupy marches). I consider these to be sacrifices for the greater good as well as teaching moments for my impressionable young child.

My point in all of this is I couldn't imagine being Jesus in his time. Oh, the crowds!

And they're always trying to get to him.

I know I can't completely avoid the crowds. I also know the more I resist something I deem unpleasant, the more pain it causes me. I am acutely aware of many of the ways in which my desire to have things be different from the way they are causes me great suffering. It's my obsessive thinking about how much I want the gaggle of gum-smacking, screeching tweens to get off the crowded BART train that vexes me so.

No doubt they are objectively annoying, as confirmed by the eye rolling and head shaking of the twenty-two other middle-aged riders in the immediate vicinity who share my pain. That the minor irritation rises to the level of near desperation, however, is all my fault.

I can choose to heed the great wisdom of the old adage "Go with the flow," stay focused on my *Tricycle* magazine, and eventually get off the train virtually unscathed. But no! Instead I decide to pursue my negative thoughts about the preadolescent shenanigans and let my commute home after a busy day at work be as pleasant as a ride through Dante's fifth ring.

I have a spiritual practice I like to think I made up, but it is probably some 2,500 years old. It helps me deal with crowds (and gaggles of gum-smacking, screeching tweens and other nuisances), though that wasn't why I started doing it. Sometimes while walking to and from my office in the city's infamously seedy Tenderloin neighborhood, I silently greet each person I pass with the thought: "This is Buddha."

It is a sort of blessing for the passersby, but perhaps more important, it is a way for me to connect with what I know at my core—that there is no separation between me and any other living being. All those other bodies, smells, sounds, and personalities are disguises—mere distractions from what is truly "real," which is that you and I are one.

What would it mean to live as if I really believed this? I'm frankly afraid to let myself completely know the answer, because I am convinced it would require me to make monumental changes in the way I live. And, well, I don't really want to make monumental changes in the way I live, thank you very much.

But my practice does give me an opportunity, albeit a teeny, tiny one, to live as if I am each individual that makes up the crowds from which I try to keep my distance. For a brief moment, I let myself love this "other" person as I do myself.

I wish for her to make it safely on her crutches to Walgreens to pick up dish soap and an emery board.

I pray for him to be calm as he walks the last block to his art class to take an exam.

I hope she finds a safe, clean, warm, and quiet place to sleep tonight.

With each breath, my heart stretches a little wider, and my awareness of the present moment and my interconnectedness with all beings grows.

And who knows? After much practice, maybe someday, while in the midst of a maddening crowd, I will be able to tell that someone has touched the cuff of my jeans...

A Tale of Two Mottoes

Jack Heaslip

Unless the LORD builds the house,
the builders labor in vain.
—Psalm 127:1 NIV

RELIGIONE ET LABORE: familiar words in my late teens and early twenties. These three little bits of Latin looked down at me from a plaque in the assembly hall of the school where I was a pupil and where I began my teaching career. Religion and work. Sound principles and a safe pair of hands to deal with the second half of the twentieth century.

But is there a better way?

"Religione et labore" was the motto of a Protestant school in Catholic Ireland. It was a defensive statement made by an organization established to promote Protestant schools. In that sense it was sectarian. It was a school for "us" and not for "them." It was designed to keep "us" together and strong. Curiously, it was as accepted by the majority as it was by the minority. There was a generosity on the part of the majority that allowed this separate education pattern to exist and to flourish.

"Religion and work" epitomized the Protestant culture of a faithful religion and a determination to work hard and independently. Farmers, middle-class businesspeople, bankers, manufacturers. These were solid citizens seeking to perpetuate the supply of solid citizens.

But was there a better way?

"Religion and work" believed in itself, believed that what it was doing was right, that it deserved the commitment. It was reliable, and, in turn, it relied on its people.

It was man-made. Man religiously doing things for God. Dutifully. Obediently. Man decided what was good, good for man, good for God. Why should this ever change? Surely it was a winning formula!

But was there another way?

The school changed. Some said it progressed. Some resented the changes. A private all-boys day and boarding school became transformed into a state-run, coeducational, multidenominational, comprehensive school under Protestant patronage. It was a feat that would have impressed the most exacting natural history documentarian.

There was *another way!*

And it got another motto!

In the tradition of school crests and mottoes, Latin was maintained. This would keep it in the academic mold even in a school that no longer taught Latin as a subject. A new guideline, a fresh standard looked down from the school wall: NISI DOMINUS FRUSTRA.

Three words that most people couldn't translate as easily as they could the old motto. People looked and wondered, and a few even asked what it meant.

The context was the remarkable change. This motto had a significant source, coming as it does from Psalm 127—the first three words, themselves a summary of the Psalm: "Unless the LORD builds the house, the builders labor in vain."

Here was a passage from Scripture replacing a human description of what the aspiration of the previous school was. Now God was proclaimed the initiator. He was seen as personal, involved, interested, caring. He was the builder, the designer, the proposer—the necessary force behind successful activity.

The Psalm the motto comes from is a song of ascents in which God firmly, lovingly, excitingly, inspiringly takes the lead. The first two verses of Psalm 127 warrant quoting:

Unless the LORD builds the house,
    the builders labor in vain.
Unless the LORD watches over the city,
    the guards stand watch in vain.
In vain you rise early
    and stay up late,
toiling for food to eat—
    for he grants sleep to those he loves. (NIV)

How religion and labor are understood here is starkly different from what had been expressed in the previous motto!

Religion is no longer a "duty" to a distant God. Rather, the reader is invited to enter into an interactive relationship.

Vain, self-sufficient man is no longer applauded for his labor; he is chided for not understanding God's desire to provide for, and grant sleep to, those he loves.

"Nisi dominus frustra" blew me away.

This was a motto I could believe in. I still do! It still excites. In my experience it invigorates old and young. In a wider setting than school, it became *mine!*

The new motto inspired me in my work in the comprehensive school as much as it seemed to endorse the development and growth of my faith. The concept of the Lord building the house allowed me to view the community, pupils, and staff through the lens of God's eye. The demands of love and grace tempered and liberated our attitudes and practice. These reached young people with an ease and a natural understanding of graceful tolerance and respect. Youngsters "got it" in a way that their parents' generation did not.

For example, a small group of youngsters in a parish I ministered in were trying to choose a name for their youth group meeting. The name was important to them—it was like creating a motto. They nearly chose "Do it for God!" That sounded a bit clumsy but sincere and well intentioned. It was overtaken by "Do it with God!" Better! But it was superseded by "Do it, God!!" The DIG group was formed and named, and the youngsters instinctively picked up what is really pleasing to God. "Nisi dominus frustra!"

Their elders seemed to fit the pattern of religion and work, in which the burdens of responsibility were taken upon them as harnesses. The "workhorses" strained, heads down, ascribing worldly values to grace. "Terms and conditions will apply" could be heard, stated with the confidence of insurance salespeople. So much of this work appeared to be in vain. Religion was expressed in a joyless, worthy manner that failed to inspire, delight, or captivate me.

Really elder citizens, however, seemed more clued in to seeking God's building and design. The wonderful explanation given by a bishop as to why clergy often do their best work just as they reach retirement applied to them as well. The bishop claimed that as clergy undertake their final years of work, "they don't give a damn what people think of them anymore!" Somehow they are able to look for what the Lord is building, no longer telling him what he must build. Now God is not restricted to building only what his people approve of. Grace allows one to welcome and interact with, rather than confront, difference, variety, surprise.

And then...

The workhorses are put out to grass and allowed to kick up their heels in the meadow!

Seekers and Sparrows and Sunday School

Jenny Sheffer Stevens

Not one sparrow (What do they cost? Two for a penny?) can fall to the ground without your Father knowing it. And the very hairs of your head are all numbered. So don't worry! You are more valuable to him than many sparrows.

    —Matthew 10:29–31 TLB

I am the way, and the truth, and the life; no one comes to the Father but through Me.

    —John 14:6 NASB

Ask, and it will be given to you; seek, and you will find; knock, and it will be opened to you.

    —Matthew 7:7 NASB

I was a terribly nervous kid. Nowadays, my level of childhood anxiety would probably warrant therapy and/or medication, but then I was just "a worrier." Practically from the cradle, I had an extravagant imagination for irrational fears.

The normal: spiders, ghosts. And the not-quite-as-normal: revolving doors, spontaneous combustion.

I was raised in a conservative, independent Baptist church. We were evangelical, but I never heard that term; we were just "Christians"—a thing you either were or were not. You were saved or unsaved, a believer or a nonbeliever. Being a Christian, as I understood it, essentially meant that you went to our church or one exactly like it. Catholics, for example, were suspect at best. You had to have "a personal relationship with Jesus Christ." The central feature of Christianity was that you were going to heaven when you died, while everyone else was destined for hell.

Every Sunday I put on a dress and good shoes and went to Sunday school. I loved it! The singing, the Nilla wafers and Hawaiian Punch, the flannel graph—sandpaper-backed images of the baby in the manger or the triumphal entry into Jerusalem that stuck to a fuzzy board. I loved the Bible verse memorization contests, and I was class champion many years running (the only kid who could beat me is now a pastor, so fair enough); a little later I loved a boy at Sunday school; but most of all I loved the Bible stories.

Throughout my childhood, a revolving cast of devout and well-intentioned older ladies—ranging from the tall, thin, smartly dressed, and austere to the dowdy, soft bosomed, and extremely kind—were our Sunday school teachers. One in particular, a little hunched woman with a winky smile and a great flair for the dramatic, sort of followed us from grade to grade. She was a spellbinding storyteller who made the Bible come alive right there in the Primary Room in the church basement. I remember how she transfixed us with Moses, Lazarus, Noah, the miracle of loaves and fishes. She excelled at depicting the passion of Christ, using a knotty finger to show where the nails had gone through his palms and raising aloft her gnarled hands to bring down an invisible crown of thorns on her head.

The following is a sampling of the principal concepts I remember from Sunday school:

- Jesus wants me for a sunbeam.
- There's a fountain flowing deep and wide.
- Zaccheus was a wee little man. (Mama, don't let your babies grow up to be tax collectors.)
- I am to be made a fisher of men.
- Somewhere, there is a field with missionaries in it. This field is also populated with witch doctors, lepers, and people who have strange piercings and don't use toilet paper. Its exact location is unclear, but it would seem to be somewhere in Africa, or possibly Bangladesh. I am expected to go there someday, to "enter," bearing a suitcase full of Bibles. It is possible, even probable, that while there I will contract blood poisoning.
- What appears to be a fancy birthday cake is actually a hollow plastic form with a coin slot in the top, a dressed-up offering plate into which you should drop your birthday pennies so that you can give them to Jesus.
- Some very bad people captured Jesus—the gentle, pale man in the pictures, always carrying a lamb and in the company of a posse of small children whom he has suffered to come unto him, who knocks on your heart's door, saying "Behold!"—and they killed him in a horrifyingly violent manner. I cannot precisely remember the first time I heard this, but I can say with certitude that I was not yet in kindergarten when I grasped that all this had happened because of my sins; the chronology was perplexing, but I accepted it, and I was sorry I had done those things.

• The big sins included drinking, smoking, swearing, and dating a boy who was not a Christian (I entered middle school proudly proclaiming that I had *never* said a bad word, and I didn't really date any boys who weren't Christians, primarily because none of the ones I liked asked me out. You can imagine what a powerful witness this was); there was also something that was a Very Bad Sin unless you were married; it seemed to be somehow related to dancing, which was likewise verboten (an exception was made for ballet, and if it was part of your curriculum in gym class, square dancing; and I once heard my grandmother claim, in hushed tones, that "there is waltzing in heaven," but that is almost certainly apocryphal).

• If you died before you were six years old you had a free pass with respect to eternal life; after that, you're on your own, so it's a matter of urgent importance that you pray a special prayer that gets you Born Again: you need to say that you know Jesus died for you, and he must take up residence, at your express invitation, in your heart. Then you are Saved, Eternally Secure. I thought this was tricky—did you have to do it by the time you turned six, or did you have that whole year, until your seventh birthday, to get it right? I spent much of first grade parsing this detail, agonizing over whether I had ever actually done it (I had, about five times for good measure) and if I'd completed the task satisfactorily.

I was slightly obsessive-compulsive; I can't blame Sunday school for that.

Nonetheless, at church, things were presented with a simple, stark affirmation that they were True. There was no wiggle room; it was a credence that ran deep. When I was thirteen, a friend of mine died in a shocking accident. He was a bit older than I, nearly a decade past the crucial cutoff. He was, as far as I knew—by the only rubric I understood—"unsaved." I was tormented over the fate of his soul. I spoke to my pastor; he had no words of comfort. The benedictory hymn from that boy's funeral still gives me a sickening shudder: *Mine is the sunlight! Mine is the morning!* Even now I viscerally recall the recoiling, the clash of dread, shame, and senselessness in my gut as I stood in the pews of an unfamiliar church and sang that song, constrained as I was to regard its joyful promise as hollow, not applicable. Sorrow edged toward indignation, rage.

Either I was insane or God was.

So my early religious experience was not really a balm for my fretful nature. In fairness, my teachers were operating out of firm belief, a heartfelt burden for souls, and the fear that comes from feeling responsible for the everlasting life of their young charges. That I was to become—was already, innately—a seeker and a sort of mystic did not enter the equation; it would have scared and grieved them. As the parent of ecumenically inquisitive young children, I understand that better now.

But more on that in a moment.

In retrospect, the one really valuable and appropriate piece of information was this:

"Jesus loves me. This I know."

My mom and dad are conscientious, loving Christian parents. I know they didn't want to distress me. They taught me as they were taught. I'm not sure how it could have been different, even if they'd understood the way Sunday school stoked my natural anxiety and spiritual restlessness. I don't think even *I* really recognized its impact until much later, when I began to see it as sort of... appalling.

My gentle young mother gave me pieces of Scripture such as, "I am with you, and will keep you in all places" (Genesis 28:15 AKJV) to reassure and bolster me. And when I was about eight, she gave me a Children's Living Bible. It was my very own, and I cherished it and its soft cover, adorned with a Jesus-and-children pastel sketch. I loved to make notes in its delicate pages, as I had seen adults do—underline, circle, star!—indicating verses I liked or had memorized.

My most heavily marked verses were Matthew 10:29–31.

Not one sparrow (What do they cost? Two for a penny?) can fall to the ground without your heavenly Father knowing it. And even the hairs of your head are all numbered. So do not worry! You are more important to him than many sparrows.

I clung to that image because it seemed to offer some kind of comfort; but really, Matthew 10 is enigmatic and troubling. It doesn't say God will *catch* the sparrow, only that God knows it has fallen.

It also says:

I am sending you out as sheep among wolves (v. 16).

Everyone will hate you . . . (v. 18).

Don't be afraid of those who want to kill you. They can only kill your body; they cannot touch your soul. Fear only God, who can destroy both soul and body in hell (v. 28).

If you love your father or mother more than you love me, you are not worthy of being mine . . . (v. 37).

Wait…What? I'm eight years old! *Uh-oh*. I think I *do* love my dear mother and father more than you, Jesus, who lived two thousand years ago and whom I have never met. You seem really kind, and I didn't mean to hurt you, but this is all very confusing.

Here's the thing: there's no "children's" Bible. Sweet illustrations don't make it G-rated. The time I spent in it as a kid, immersed in church dogma and guided by the admonition that every word was literally, inherently True, drove me away from it later.

I had to learn to process it differently.

The Bible is a magnificent, mysterious, essential, sacred text, full, I think, of God's truths. It's also a nuanced, often opaque, confounding, manipulated, manhandled, and necessarily flawed document. To me it's obvious that much of its truth is metaphorical, many of its accounts allegorical. That doesn't make it less true! In fact, in a sense, it makes it *more* true but harder to untangle.

To only read it literally feels simplistic to me; I think it's fine for the church to approach it that way but regrettable that they view anyone who doesn't as lost. Sorting it out is intricate work. Genuine contemplation of the *meaning* of death and resurrection, of eternity, of Word Made Flesh should boggle the mind of any thoughtful adult. The Bible is often (mis)quoted as saying "you must have the faith of a *little child*," but I don't want my childhood back.

I went on to a conservative Christian college, and ironically, it was there that I really began to question, even rebel.

First I became an Episcopalian (so tantalizingly like Catholicism, with its liturgy, incense, and ritual!).

Later I became a yogi and learned for the first time that to live in my body—to move ecstatically, to *dance*—was calming and contemplative, holy; I could pray with my whole self and feel the presence of God on my yoga mat as much as I felt it in church or daily devotions.

Ishvara pranidhana: "I surrender, and lay all my actions at the feet of God."

I read the Bhagavad Gita, the Yoga Sutras of Patanjali; I chanted and *om*'d, placed a Buddha on my mantel right next to the cross, became enthralled with the Hindu concept of God's female expressions. I found myself awestruck by Joseph Campbell, the Sufi poets, the pure, devotional voice of Krishna Das.

And then I felt the old clutch of fear…

Dear God,

Do you know there's a sparrow missing from that neat little nest?

Is it falling, about to crash to the ground?

Or has it fledged, found its wings, and started flying up to the heavens?

Am I eternally secure?

Some people said, "You cannot be a Christian and a yogi." Excuse me? I had fearless joy and deep peace. If this was wandering, so be it; my spirit soared on this new path.

One mature Christian woman close to me said, "God is able to hold you."

That was grace.

I traveled along pretty intrepidly on my passionate, if patchwork, spiritual path. Along the way, I had kids. And like me, at a distressingly young age my firstborn began to worry, to wrestle with tough, murky questions. One night, he had a terrifyingly vivid dream of a baby dying; this dream even featured an original sound track—a haunting lullaby, sung by me. Oh, dear. All this from his four-year-old imagination. He was inconsolable. He began asking about God, death, and what comes after.

Whoa. Teachable moment. Now what?

I was desperate to comfort him, so I did my best. "No one knows exactly what happens after we die, because you have to die to find out. But I think our job on earth is to love God and talk to God and ask a lot of questions, to be thankful, and to treat people and the planet with kindness and respect. And I think that when you die you'll go to be with God. Sometimes we call it heaven. Some people imagine heaven as a place just for your spirit, but some people think heaven is an actual, wonderful city with shining streets and castles and parks and animals."

He pondered this and then said, eyes welling, "I don't really know if I want to go there, because it can never be as good as New York City."

Touché.

I want my kids to be curious spiritual creatures, dedicated truth seekers who feel safe and secure in God's love. But what surprised me is all that I realized I could *not* teach them: the onus of having to confidently convey "the Truth" to my children, to express what I really think truth is, posed a challenge.

It's what actually made me confront the fact that . . . I don't know.

But I know I can't take them to Sunday school.

There are two pitfalls in standard early childhood Christian education—allowing a relative stranger to coerce your young child, directly or subtly, into making a spiritual commitment he or she is ill equipped to make—and they are vexing counterpoints. One is the fact that, as I've said, most of the Bible is not kid stuff; it's too complex, violent, graphic, symbolic. *I* want to be the arbiter of what they're ready to process and when, using their questions as my guide. I don't want church to freak them out.

On the flip side, overexposure to the Bible can ultimately *de*sensitize them to the mystery and power of Scripture by introducing imagery and ideas they're not yet prepared to unravel. The distress and perplexity I experienced from some of my Sunday school lessons were real; but in truth I was more traumatized by the threat of leprosy or blood poisoning than the concepts of hell and crucifixion. The cross was— *is*—beyond comprehension. I couldn't begin to contemplate it then. But I thought I had it all down pat and wasted no time in educating all my friends, too.

Ooh... a little knowledge is a dangerous thing.

I see no way around it. If you think, in order to save her soul, you must prevail upon a child to *believe* a thing she is nowhere near mature enough to process with authenticity, then you must think that "becoming a Christian" functions as a magic spell. I think that's an abuse of the gospel... and possibly of the child.

My religious life as an adult has largely been about unlearning. It took me decades just to acknowledge that I don't believe the point of faith is inoculation against hellfire. The point of a life of faith is a *life* of faith. I want to spend less energy worrying about what's going to happen when I die and more energy concentrating on what's going on here and now. Faith is not something I possess as insurance against what happens after death; it's something I aspire to because I hope it will inform how I live. I want that for my children.

I cringe when Christians refer to being "saved," because it implicitly distinguishes between the are's and are nots, and because I think *saved* is a misunderstood and misused term.

I don't believe in hell.

If bearing children has taught me a spiritual lesson, it's that the creator's love must be unconditional and inexhaustible and that the very notion of hell is utterly inconsistent with everything I understand about God and Jesus. Creation and eternal damnation are mutually exclusive.

So *saved* from what? From a life of fearful despair, perhaps? From "myself am Hell" (Milton, *Paradise Lost*)?

Sin is not a checklist of naughty behaviors; sin is whatever draws you away from the heart of God, which is radical love that brings wholeness and peace. Salvation, if that's even the appropriate word, is not a golden ticket to heaven purchased by a rote prayer. It's a sustaining embrace, a deep blue pool of healing water you slip into slowly as you strive to quench an ontological thirst.

Conversely, I think the "eternal security" clause is rather silly—the belief that if you've said the special prayer you're saved for life (well, from death). I don't think you can fall away from God's mercy, but I think if you're falling back on a few words of belief you said once to keep you spiritually set for life, you probably aren't set for a spiritual life . . . know what I mean?

Having called myself a Christian since I was five years old doesn't make me a Christian any more than calling myself a sparrow makes me able to fly. On the other hand, my refusal to offer some secret born-again handshake just so I can fit a standard Christian mold doesn't make me a lost soul.

I've met God in diverse places. My faith is Christ-centric,

but the word *Christian* sticks in my throat. I think only God is in possession of absolute truth; in too many contexts and congregations, a key condition of calling oneself Christian is a chokehold on the truth, on belief, and, as a natural outcropping of that, a compulsion to draw lines between those who are in the fold and those who are not. I think that's none of my business and that drawing those lines is probably a sin.

I can't say that I actually have belief. I have gut knowledge and soul experiences that, to me, act as confirmation of the real presence of God in my life; but there's not much I can point to and say "I believe this" to the exclusion of other possibilities.

I don't really believe in belief. I'm not persuaded that the act or state of believing holds salvific power, because belief is slippery and unreliable. I can't be the kind of Christian for whom the whole deal is predicated on belief. How do I know if I really believe or if I just think and say I believe because I'm scared not to, as I did as a child? If something is not true, believing cannot make it so. "I am the way, and the truth, and the life; no one comes to the Father but through Me" (John 14:6 NASB). Either it is so or it is not so; my belief comes and goes, but if Christ's victory over the tomb is real, it must be complete. The Bhagavad Gita says, "The Unreal never is, the Real never is not." I love that. That resonates. I know what rings true in my soul; Lord, I believe, help thou my unbelief (see Mark 9:24).

To me, the greatest paradox of evangelical doctrine is that it does not permit God to intervene with people in any other way. If God is, as Christians contend, omniscient, then we must allow that God can connect with people in ways Christians do not concretely, academically comprehend. Or else we do not really believe in God's omniscience—we contend that God has parameters, which people can identify and circumscribe.

The Bible says, "Ask, and it will be given to you; seek, and you will find; knock, and it will be opened to you" (Matt. 7:7 NASB). I've heard Christians say they believe that anyone who is "truly seeking" will find the Truth; they mean, of course, find Jesus, and faith that fits a certain format. The problem is that when they meet a seeker who has *not* found Jesus as they understand him, the only way to reconcile this incongruity with their interpretation of Scripture is to disparage the nature or quality of the search.

Kick around a yoga studio for a while—you'll find some serious askers, seekers, and—ahem—knockers. To me, it's self-evident that God reaches people in individual, inscrutable ways; if not, Matthew 7:7 is patently untrue. The essence of a "personal relationship" with God is that it is uncharted territory; the worthiness of another's spiritual quest is distinctly out of our purview.

I'm not saying all religions and paths are simply the same or that none of this matters.

Human beings, from atheist to devout, never run out of ways to inflict all manner of evil on one another—card-carrying Christians included. Some very nonreligious people are Christlike, and some very religious people are not. And vice versa. There's no salvation litmus test; there's just the fruit of the spirit, the Golden Rule. Classifications such as pluralism and universalism and so on perturb me with their gross oversimplifications.

What I think is that God honors our sundry and clumsy attempts to move toward our creator, and that, assuming any of it is true, the ultimate intent and final state must be the restoration of all creation. Jesus can be the way, the truth, and the life, but God can reveal, infuse, apply, and manifest that truth for anyone in any way God chooses. We don't get an eternity vote.

The Christianity I was raised in dismisses my kind of faith as folly or condemns it as heresy. Christian friends concerned for my soul challenge me by saying, "The gospel demands a response." Agreed. But I would counter that *all* sacred texts demand a response; the very nature of Scripture is that antiphonal quality—a call for reaction, action, engagement, and devotion to plumbing the Big Questions. To miss or deny this fact, and to use the Bible as a proof text for itself in that regard, strike me as naive and myopic. Of course what my friends are really saying is that my response is unacceptable and my children's religious education damningly insufficient. How can I answer satisfactorily?

The gospel is near to my heart, but faith, belief, and *knowing* are separate and distinct conditions. The Christian tendency to conflate the three leaves people like me shipwrecked. So it has been a long and fraught journey into trust, a covenant with God to which I am held as I investigate the divine mystery of life and my relationship to my creator. And as I strive to guide my children toward...something true.

One belief I firmly hold is that the truth is altogether more complex and infinitely simpler than church doctrine dictates. I don't mean to be glib; that's the only way I can articulate my conviction that God blesses the exploration I am on and that it's okay if it takes me my whole life to work it out.

Surely at the moment of our death our creator knows, as s/he has always known, each one of us better than we know ourselves and is intimately familiar with the true desire of every heart, the intricacies of each person's spiritual path.

What it means to be saved I don't pretend to understand. I think it's misguided to try to work it out in much detail.

All I can control is how I live. Do the work I'm called to do and let the results go. I'm humbled by the people out in the world's trenches, truly laboring to bring about the kingdom irrespective of their creeds. My own goals are both lofty and shamefully modest; I'm just trying to seek truth, parent well, and, as an artist, tell important stories and ask vital questions. I want to dwell in love, receptivity, and intentionality in the process of becoming—not just to believe out of fear. I want to instill spiritual appetite and courage in my kids. What happens after this—how God manages the immortal soul of the greatest saints or the vilest sinners or a workaday sparrow such as myself—I must release. Eternity is here and now. No one—*no one*, I don't care what he or she says—really knows what, if anything, awaits us on the other side.

And so it's not—it cannot be—the point.

One luminous October afternoon a few years ago, my beloved grandfather passed away. He was a man of tremendous faith who lived every hour in pursuit of Christlikeness, and his belief in heaven was profound and detailed. That evening I tucked my children into bed and walked to a late yoga class. It was chilly and clear, one of those rare New York City nights without a trace of urban haze, when the sky is black and the few visible stars burn with an intensity that declines to be dimmed by even by the lurid glow of Times Square. Suddenly I felt that the sky was all around me, and I was engulfed in a sense of internal and external expansiveness, a vastness of peace, promise, and the presence of the infinite.

In yoga there's a concept called *bhava*; it's a blissful awareness, even if fleeting, of the higher realm, a moment when your spirit and psyche are opened to transcendence. It's like what Frederick Buechner describes as a simple "clack-clack" of two tree branches signaling "the approach of the approach of splendor." The practice of yoga can be devotional (and nondenominational), intended to cultivate that sacred openness. Moving your body through a bunch of funny, sweaty, strenuous shapes helps free your mind from the tyranny of quotidian clutter—the grocery list, the dentist appointment, the smartphone—to create space, one cell at a time, you can breathe with God. It aligns your spirit as it aligns your spine. I find this compelling for soul reasons, but also because, for an artist, those moments are the core of the creative state.

I know my fundamentalist grandfather was uneasy about my yoga practice, but I also know he believed that reality comprises more layers than we perceive while we exist in this mortal coil; that we see, as it were, through a glass darkly. Part of his great faith stemmed from times he had glimpsed the *bhava* realm, experienced what he believed to be miracles or angelic intervention.

I had a *bhava* moment that night and an epiphany: whatever it is that we pass on to after this life—that which my grandfather lived in faith of attaining—that night, *he knew.* He was having the ultimate cosmic *bhava* experience. I understood profoundly that whether he was standing at actual pearly gates in robes of white or whether his bright spirit had just been scattered across the universe to kindle that night's extraordinary stars was entirely beside the point. I received a deep awareness that the shimmering tranquility I felt right then was a tiny taste of the eternal and a little communion with Grandpa.

God loved me enough to give me that solace in my grief on my way to yoga. And to offer me that resource to comfort my son after his nightmare.

A theologian I'm not. I'm a ponderer, a seeker, who has received an embarrassment of riches in terms of grace. I'm still a worrier. I've sort of made peace with revolving doors, but I'm categorically phobic when it comes to spiders; and a good friend once said to me, "Jenny, if I ever knew anyone who might actually spontaneously combust, it's you."

Grace is that I met, at the age of twenty-one, at a conservative Christian college, a husband, a father for my children, who has since then, miraculously, navigated a theological road parallel to my own. It seems so much more likely that one partner's pathway of spiritual evolution would have veered far from the other's familiar orthodoxy, and pulled us apart. We don't always agree on how to teach our children about faith, but we agree that you can't go wrong to start with gratefulness.

I admit there are times when I've panicked and been tempted to urge my kids to utter a hasty salvation prayer, just in case. But I believe that's what it is: *temptation.* Over and over the Bible says it—*be not afraid.* I will not be afraid to say I don't have absolute answers; I will not be afraid of allowing my children to perceive faith as an extended adventure; I will not fear for their souls in the meantime; I will try not to come unglued and proffer too much too soon. I pray that spiritual life unfolds for them as a joyful, mind-blowing, deeply personal process. Of course the wild card is that my loaded childhood religious experience was probably the springboard for the journey I'm on; perhaps I cannot simply hand my kids the type of faith I have discovered. But I'm convinced that all they require of religious instruction right now is assurance that they are unconditionally, divinely loved and that they can talk to God—and us—without fear about anything at any time.

My children, my little sparrows, Jesus loves you, this I . . .

trust. And this I *know*: you are not meant to have hollow spiritual birthday cake. God wants your soul to have abundant loaves and fishes, manna from heaven, a mansion in the kingdom.

Growing up, I believed the only thing more lamentable than blatant nonbelief was the frankly pharisaical practice of attending worship services only on Easter and Christmas. But I confess that's what we do. For now. My children are otherwise unchurched, and though we pray together daily, talk a lot about God and how we should live, and read some easy-to-digest narratives from a progressive book of children's Bible stories, they've had no formal introduction to religion.

And yet...

We have stunningly profound theological discussions, led solely by their inquiries, their instinctive yearning for big truths.

My six-year old daughter has an uncanny zeal for the old hymns; she was belting out multiple Wesley and Runyan verses from her baby carriage. (I know! Brilliant!) And my cool urban surfer dude of an eight-year old, upon receiving a goody bag of candy, crayons, and stickers from an usher at our Episcopal cathedral's Easter service, promptly peeled off a large decal of a purple cross on which HE LIVES! was written in a bold yellow rock-and-roll font (I know! A little uncouth!), enthusiastically stuck it to his skateboard, and pronounced it "awesome."

Such is the faith of a little child, untarnished by dogma or doctrine, unconnected to fear: the universe crackles with divine mystery and the sacred is everywhere.

Seek and it just finds you.

If we only open them up to receive that, we can't screw it up.

Just this morning, as I was brooding over how to conclude this chapter, the kids interrupted my coveted writing hour, clamoring for breakfast. Resigned, I dragged them out for a bagel and a neighborhood stroll. Walking past the General Theological Seminary, my daughter asked, "Is that a church?" I explained that there is a chapel there, but it's really a school where people study God.

My son said, "I think I'd like to go there someday." And then, unprompted, he said something that made me gasp afresh at the astounding synchronicity, the almost comical simplicity, of grace.

"Hey, Mom," he said. "This is the best way to teach your kids: just tell them what you know, only make it very easier."

Awesome indeed.

Scriptural Cherry-Picking

Amy Julia Becker

All Scripture is God-breathed and is useful for teaching,
rebuking, correcting and training in righteousness...
—2 Timothy 3:16 NIV

One summer in college, I decided to read through the Bible
from start to finish. I had a lot of time on my hands, with a part-
time job babysitting two kids down the road and a boyfriend
who commuted into New York City from the Connecticut suburbs every day. While I don't remember many of the specifics,
I was intrigued by the prophets, surprised by the vitriol within
some of the Psalms, and bored by page after page after page of
historical information I didn't understand and geography I had
never learned. But every so often, a verse seemed to appear
in bold print, as if some celestial being had marked it with a
bright pink highlighter and arrows and a flutter of wings and
an admonition: "Pay attention. This one is for you."

There were the words from Isaiah in the midst of my anxiety about returning to college that fall: "For I am the LORD your
God who takes hold of your right hand and says to you, Do not
fear; I will help you" (Isa. 41:13 NIV). The words from Jeremiah

as I was trying to discern what I would do once I graduated: "Stand at the crossroads and look; ask for the ancient paths, ask where the good way is, and walk in it, and you will find rest" (Jer. 6:16 NIV). The promise from Romans 5 that I read in the midst of a serious illness: "We glory in our sufferings, because we know that suffering produces perseverance; perseverance, character; and character, hope. And hope does not put us to shame" (v. 3–5 NIV). The list of verses and stories that sustained me, challenged me, and transformed me went on.

Years later I learned that cherry-picking verses without regard for their historical, cultural, and literary context is a Bible-reading no-no. But at the time, those verses came as direct messages from God.

In time, verses leaped off the page less often, and I began to get a greater sense of the sweeping story that runs throughout Scripture, the overarching narrative of creation and sin and redemption. If once I had treated the Bible as a map that would guide me to the buried treasure of words written just for me, eventually I began to understand a broader scope to God's work in the world and my small but significant place within it. But in both cases, the question of the Bible's "inerrancy" trotted around behind me like a stray dog. I had become a Christian through a theologically conservative parachurch ministry, and I had taken it on faith not only that "all Scripture is God-breathed and is useful for teaching, rebuking, correcting and training in righteousness" (2 Tim. 3:16 NIV) but also that "God-breathed" meant "without error," without any contradiction or factual inaccuracy, as if Scripture were the work of a reporter from *Time* magazine.

But this whole business of inerrancy bothered me, and it impeded my ability to receive Scripture as God's word. First came the realization that when Paul was writing to Timothy the Scripture he referred to was the Old Testament, since the gospels and epistles hadn't all been written yet or compiled into that which we now call the New Testament. There were stories that seemed like myths to me; I wasn't confident that Jonah had been swallowed by a large fish and spit up onto dry land or that Noah's ark really contained two of every animal. There were the horrific abuses recorded in the Old Testament, such as the murder of a daughter by her father to carry out an oath (Judg. 10–12). And then there were quirky passages, such as Matthew's account of "many holy people" coming out of their tombs after Jesus was resurrected (Matt. 27:52–53) and Jude's reference to Michael the archangel fighting with the devil, and I wasn't sure what to take from those words.

Moreover, there was my roommate in college, who had no interest in Christianity whatsoever, because it had oppressed women. I could have pointed her to plenty of Scripture that might have persuaded her otherwise, but I had to admit my own questions when it came to verses about women being silent in the churches (1 Cor. 14:34) and being saved through childbearing (1 Tim. 2:15). I didn't know what to do with those passages. And I didn't know whether my discomfort with them was simply a matter of my own cultural conditioning or whether there was a different but still faithful way to read these texts.

Beyond all that, though, was my sense that the doctrine of inerrancy didn't emerge from Scripture itself. A friend had once pointed out that neither the Apostles' Creed nor the Nicene Creed mentions anything about the Bible, which is to say that for the early Christians and throughout church history our most basic confession of faith remained silent when it came to Scripture. I also learned that the doctrine of inerrancy had emerged a few centuries back in response to a cultural shift away from the Bible's authority and toward science as an authority. Conservative Christians, it seemed to me, had dug themselves into a hole, insisting that this multifaceted, mysterious book of stories was just like a science or history textbook. Applying twenty-first-century critical standards to a book written in vastly different times and places just didn't make sense to me.

I continued to believe that the church had set these particular books apart as scriptural through the guidance of the Holy Spirit. I still believed God had whispered to me time after time, even if I did pluck verses out of their original context and apply them to my life with self-centered disregard for the author's intention. Beyond my personal commitment and gratitude, these stories and poems and historical accounts had demonstrated their enduring significance within our faith community, and I needed to continue to wrestle with the parts that I didn't like or didn't understand. They offered an authoritative guide to God's enduring presence and involvement in our world.

Two concepts in particular eventually helped me to read Scripture as a complex book that offered personal application, theological insight, and challenging words with which to understand myself and our culture. First came the idea of reading Scripture literally versus reading it "literalistically." *Literalistically* isn't a real word, but it helped me to start to take books of the Bible on their own terms rather than the terms imposed upon them. I started by considering the basic distinctions between history, poetry, story, and letter. Each offered a different type of writing with different intentions and conventions.

To use a contemporary analogy, if I wanted to learn about flowers, and I consulted an E. E. Cummings poem and a biology textbook, they would both offer helpful and truthful information, even though they have different purposes and use different linguistic conventions. Similarly, the Bible tells us important truths about creation and human nature, though it and contemporary scientific texts do so for different purposes and according to different literary and cultural conventions.

I have often wondered if the story of Adam and Eve describes two real human beings in a garden a long time ago or if it offers representative types through which we understand the human proclivity to turn away from God even in the face of God's good provision. The literary clues offered in the Genesis accounts suggest the latter. In Hebrew, "Adam" means "human," and "Eve" means "mother of all the living." Now, perhaps there were two human creatures wandering around in Eden, but my faith and my understanding of Scripture don't hinge upon the physical reality of these two people. The text itself seems to give permission for a wide interpretation.

In other places, however, the text seems only to invite a historical interpretation. Luke introduces his gospel, for example, with assurances that he has taken it upon himself to provide "an orderly account" of what happened when Jesus walked the earth. John and Matthew both mention doubters after Jesus' resurrection; Luke offers stories to demonstrate Jesus' physicality after his resurrection; and later Paul invites eyewitnesses to stand up and be counted (1 Cor. 15). All suggest a common assumption that the resurrection was a moment in time and space rather than a legend with some truth that we can apply to our own lives.

In other words, some Scripture is factually specific and offers truth for us to apply. Other parts of Scripture might not be factually specific and still offer truth that affirms the overarching themes of human rebellion and God's redemption.

With all this said, however, I don't feel the need to be sure. Adam and Eve may well have been two human beings wandering around a luscious garden in the Middle East. Jonah may well have been swallowed by a big fish. God can do miraculous things. But my faith in the God of the Bible and my posture toward Scripture as the authoritative witness to God's work in our world do not depend upon an answer to these particular questions.

The second concept that has helped me approach Scripture in what I hope is both a faithful and intellectually honest way is the idea that God demonstrated humility in allowing humans to write the books of the Bible. In this line of thinking, the Bible is a manifestation of the humility of the Holy Spirit, just as Jesus coming to earth as a baby demonstrates the Son's humility, and the act of creating a potentially rebellious humanity indicates the Father's humility. God is humble, and entrusting his word to human beings offers us a sense of that humility.

God's humility offers us an invitation to receive the word with similar humility. Even though I have questions about the Bible's historical accuracy, complaints about the treatment of women and children within its pages, and concerns about the vitriolic nature of God's wrath as it is portrayed, I trust that these books we call the Bible are the living, active, transformative, and authoritative word of God.

I don't have all the answers. I don't know what role raw humanity played in writing these books. I don't understand the particulars of how the Holy Spirit intervened. I don't know whether it is accurate to call these works inerrant, though I suspect that term is unhelpful at best.

But what I do know is that this collection of books tells a true story, a story upon which I have staked my life, a story of a people who lived without God and a story of a God who comes to live with them at great cost to himself. A story of infinite love. A story I return to again and again, with thanks.

Women:

Be Silent?

Sarah Heath

For God is a God not of disorder but of peace. (As in all
the churches of the saints, women should be silent in the
churches. For they are not permitted to speak, but should
be subordinate, as the law also says. If there is anything they
desire to know, let them ask their husbands at home. For it is
shameful for a woman to speak in church. Or did the word
of God originate with you? Or are you the only ones it has
reached?)

—1 Corinthians 14:33–36 NRSV

The B-I-B-L-E! Yes, that's the book for me!"

I still remember singing that song as a child, as I am sure
many who grew up in or around the church did. I was (and
am) a horrible speller, so this song was something I sang
proudly. At least I could spell the word *Bible* right—well, at
least most of the time.

I can't recall precisely when I began to consider that the

song might *not* apply to me. Was the Bible really "for me"? I wasn't sure. It may have been when I moved from Canada to Mississippi at the age of fourteen. During my childhood I went to church with my parents and brother most Sundays. We attended a church that was part of the denomination known as the United Church of Canada. Growing up, I remember two pastors: one was a gentleman who should have won an award for putting up with my questions during children's time; the other was a wonderful woman who led our church during my teenage years.

I must admit that at the time, I didn't think there was anything unique about having a woman as pastor. As I looked around the "world" (as churchy people call it), I saw women leading in all areas. In my own home my mom and dad were models of equality. Nothing was designated "men's work" or "women's work." I really didn't believe a glass ceiling existed back then, except for the fact that girls weren't allowed in Boy Scouts. (This frustrated me; they had cool knives.)

So you can imagine my surprise when I began to read the Bible a little more closely in high school and found troubling passages about the role of women. I had begun working at a Christian camp in Canada during the summers. I was taking my faith more seriously and engaging more deeply with it. But Saint Paul's letters utterly confounded me: What do you mean, women should "be silent"?

It didn't take much asking around to discover that many people seemed to think this meant that women were not fit for the job of teaching—and definitely not fit for leading—within the walls of a church.

Wrestling with Saint Paul's words led to years of intensive study and eventually took me to Europe, where I'd follow the apostle's footsteps on a pilgrimage. I fell in love with the writings of a man I once saw as one of the church's biggest bigots. How that happened is a long story—one that gave me much disquiet.

You see, Saint Paul's words in 1 Corinthians didn't make sense, and they made even less sense as I read them in relation to what seemed to me to be Jesus' radical attitude toward women. Jesus walked the earth at a time when women were treated as possessions (or worse), and he seemed to stand in opposition to the status-quo beliefs about the "fairer sex." Jesus spoke often with women and lifted them out of their circumstances toward wholeness. In one gospel account, Jesus reveals himself first to two women after the resurrection, making them the first preachers of the good news. They were to testify to Christ's triumph over death and the grave at a time when women weren't even permitted to testify in court.

I would have thought Saint Paul, as a follower of Jesus, would see the value of women and their participation in the work of the kingdom. And you can imagine the further confusion Saint Paul's words caused me when at the age of twenty I felt a deep calling to use the gifts and graces that God had given me to go to seminary.

Before deciding that I would follow what felt like the Holy Spirit's guidance into ordained ministry, I had been leaning toward a profession in medicine, so I'd studied psychology and biology as an undergraduate. It was in one of my upper-level biology classes that I revealed to a friend that I intended to enroll in seminary. Her response: "But you're a girl, and that isn't okay." She later shared my news with one of our Baptist Bible study leaders, who from then on gave me the coldest shoulder I think I have ever felt. I don't know what I expected the reactions to be when I shared my seminary news, but shock and awe weren't it.

I didn't want my life to be a feminist statement. I just wanted to be faithful to using what I really believed God had given me. It wasn't about pushing boundaries or trying to make people uncomfortable. I didn't understand the call— even today I am not sure I totally do—but I didn't want it to be about trying to prove a point.

As I engaged with Scripture and my own sense of calling, I was left wondering how I could reconcile what Saint Paul wrote about women being silent with what I had seen and experienced. I jokingly told people who asked about my understanding of Saint Paul that I had broken up with the apostle long ago and we didn't talk that much anymore—only occasionally about our mutual friend Jesus.

After I became a seminarian, Saint Paul continued to confound me. Wasn't he the one who said that in Christ there is neither Jew nor Greek, neither male nor female (Gal. 3:8)? To help me understand this confusing aspect of Pauline theology, I took a class entitled simply "Paul." I attended a stridently academic seminary and was, therefore, hoping to hear an academic view of Saint Paul. The professor did not disappoint. I kept waiting for him to explain that Paul had a bad relationship with his mother and had experienced a bad breakup in college and was unable to appreciate women. I may not have learned about Saint Paul's pathology, but I did learn that he was a product of hellenization and was aware of (and in some ways subject to) Aristotle's understanding of women as inferior.

Aristotle himself was subject to what he learned from his own mentor, Socrates, a philosopher who considered women to be halfway between animals and men. (Sounds like the kind of guy with whom I wouldn't have gone past a first date.) The views of these two "great thinkers" permeated all of culture in Saint Paul's day. The Greeks didn't allow women into many parts of the public realm, including the agora, or open market.

On a recent visit to Greece, I learned that there were female gladiators. Images of Xena the Warrior Princess danced in my head! And Athens actually is named after the Greek goddess of wisdom. So while there were some women who were able to break through the hellenistic gender boundaries, generally speaking, women were not leaders in the public realm. Such a cultural milieu surely influenced new Gentile converts to the Christian faith at the time of Saint Paul.

At the same time, Jewish converts to Christianity were subject to past rabbinic interpretations of the Torah. I have read many of the great rabbinic teachers and their appraisal of women and women's roles. Their opinions vary widely. Some of the rabbinic dialogue was quite appreciative of the women of the Torah; others were much less likely to promote the participation of women in civil and religious society.

One of the foundational beliefs I read again and again was that the relationship between Adam and Eve should be used as a model for gender interplay. Many rabbis asserted that because Eve was created second she was inferior and to be ruled and guided by Adam. That logic perplexed me. If such logic plays out, then humankind should be subject to cattle and birds, both of which were created first in the Genesis creation narrative.

God created Adam and then saw that he needed an *ezer*. The translation of *ezer* is "helper"—not in the sense of a slave but rather of an equal companion. Scripture employs a different word for "slave," and it is not used to describe Eve. Perhaps more than Adam's temptress and naive sidekick, Eve was his equal partner.

You can imagine that when these two groups (former Gentiles and traditional Jews) came together to form the early church, there was quite a hullabaloo about how—or even whether—women could participate in worship and the life of the faith community.

Which brings me back to my old friend Saint Paul. When I looked at his history with women and the actual words he chose to employ when writing about them, he and I began to take some baby steps toward reconciliation.

Many of my discoveries were supported when I read a fabulous book entitled *What Paul Really Said About Women: An Apostle's Liberating Views on Equality in Marriage, Leadership, and Love* by John Temple Bristow. The thesis of the book is that much of what we have understood to be direct translation of Saint Paul is actually a matter of word choice on the part of the translator.

This made so much sense to me.

Any interpretation—including misinterpretation—begins with our own already formed opinions. I am guilty of this myself, having always read Saint Paul's writings with more than a small measure of skepticism and bitterness, deeming them the ramblings of a misogynist.

As I reexamined Saint Paul's teaching, I was struck by the fact that, when he had been called Saul, he had persecuted those he believed were the most influential Christians. He attests to arresting both men *and* women (Acts 8:3, Acts 9:1–2, Acts 22:4–5.) So if Saul arrested only those he believed were leaders of the rebellious Christian sect, and they included women, it stands to reason, then, that he understood the value of women *before* his conversion.

So the question is: *Did that change?*

As I looked more deeply into Scripture for answers, I found

many compelling passages that are too often neglected. Saint Paul's first European convert, for instance, was a woman named Lydia. Lydia was the first in a series of people whom the apostle would lead to Christ. When I recently retraced Saint Paul's journeys on a trip to the Middle East, one of my most powerful experiences happened in the area where Lydia is believed to have been baptized. We stopped and held a baptismal remembrance service. Standing in the place where, it could be argued, the church in Europe began with the baptism of a woman was transformational.

In his recorded letters, Saint Paul wrote often about and *to* women. In his letter to Philippi he asks two women— Euodia and Syntyche—to end their dispute for the sake of the kingdom. He seems to recognize the women as leaders of the church in Philippi and doesn't tell them to stop leading, just to stop fighting. In verses 2–3 he also mentions them as being among those who have struggled alongside him for the sake of the gospel. He mentions Priscilla (often translated "Prisca") and her husband, Aquila, as leaders of the church of Corinth (1 Cor. 16:19). Notice that he doesn't scold Priscilla for taking a leadership role and that he actually mentions her name before that of her husband.

In Romans, Paul speaks about twenty-six church leaders who are worthy of praise. Eight of them are women, including Phoebe, who is referred to as a "deacon," using the masculine form of that word—precisely the same way he describes male church leaders.

In 1 Corinthians 11:4–5 Saint Paul lays out some rules about how women should pray and prophesy. Wait a minute! If he is articulating rules without caveats, could that mean it was simply understood that women *would* be doing this regularly and that it wasn't the prophecy or the public prayer that was the issue but rather the way in which they were engaging in the act that was ruffling dear Saint Paul's feathers?

If so, how did we get to "women should be silent"? (And remember, I am a stakeholder in this, because every Sunday I get up on the podium and am far from silent.) The word the apostle uses for "silence" in 1 Corinthians is *sigao*, which is the kind of silence required when a room is disorderly. This kind of silence is *voluntary*, not demanded. Although women had previously not been welcome in public gatherings, the proscription had been lifted by the time Paul wrote 1 Corinthians, and women's newfound freedom may have led to public gossiping that in turn created a ruckus in church.

Which raises the question: Is Saint Paul demanding *silence* or *orderliness*? I read one account that speculated that women were yelling at their husbands across the aisle, as the congregation was separated by gender.

Whatever the truth of the situation, I look at Saint Paul's writings (and those attributed to him) in their entirety now. I don't see a lady hater but rather someone who, when compared with the culture at the time, was lifting women up in ways that were actually revolutionary.

The ongoing "disquiet" I've felt when reading about Saint Paul's admonition that "women should be silent" has been vital to my faith. It causes me to question, look deeper, and not just glaze over what I read. Study is a deep form of worship, and even when I question God I am drawing closer to God. My faith is growing and being stretched.

In the great rabbinic tradition of midrashic reading, asking questions—even the toughest, thorniest, most disquieting ones—deepens my faith. And for that, I am thankful to Saint Paul.

Tommy Bahama Plays "Melancholy Baby"

Anthony Platipodis

And he was three days without sight, and neither did eat nor drink.

— Acts 9:9 KJV

I parked in the alley and entered the Studio City bookstore through the back door. It was difficult to get the door open; the guys spilling from the back of the peep-show theater blocked it. My objective was to grab a few magazines, a DVD featuring lantern-jawed, gay-for-pay jocks, and go home.

The trip was born of content fatigue—it was the early 2000s, and bandwidth was anemic. Tube sites featured pixelated twinks resembling Fraggles engaged in Turkish wrestling.

I deserved better porn.

While debating the merits of *Freshmen* magazine, I realized I was being watched. A Naugahyde-tan, middle-aged man resembling a Tommy Bahama model had followed me through the aisles of the store. Unnerved, I grabbed a magazine and headed to the register.

I jogged back to my car, with Tommy trailing close behind. Before I peeled away, Tommy managed to rap his knuckles on my car window.

My panic simmered. *What did he want?* To return a quarter that fell from my pocket? A tantric awakening behind the Dumpster? A handy? This man saw my face. I was gay, and he knew it. The clock on my sexual disclosure was ticking.

I was in my twenties, living in Los Angeles, bobbing in the wake of Dubya's second term. Leggy news analysts were dividing the country into red and blue states. No one hated Mel Gibson yet, and Paris Hilton was paving the road for the Kardashians with each nipple flash and crotch shot. Self-disclosure—engineered by Mary-Ellis Bunim, Mark Burnett, and Oprah—was priming the pump for a future culture of Facebook porn. No one's secrets were secret anymore.

I worked hard to maintain my biggest secret: my sexuality. I kept my big social circle from discovering my sexual identity in the ways many nondisclosed gays do—by being the center of attention. Toeing a line that's "edgy" for a loosely orthodox environment. Camouflaging my "struggles" with evangelical language of "wounding." Marketing a suffocating depression as an angle of repose.

Worse, everyone bought the act, or—as though it were a bowl of canned cranberry sauce at Thanksgiving—they accepted it for what it was and didn't go near it.

Throughout my life, anxiety and addiction to narrative allowed me to create Frankensteins of all shapes and sizes. I now had created another—Tommy Bahama in a seafoam sweater. This monster wouldn't destroy me in the traditional sense. Instead he'd show up at the grocery store, across the desk at a job interview, or at the gas station. Tommy would recognize me, cock his head, and ask me why I couldn't pick a side.

He'd ask me why I was attached to a dogma that was making me miserable. Why I couldn't get over myself and jump into the deep end with the others. I convinced myself that Tommy would expose me before I had time to create a life free of ambiguity, consumable for everyone inhabiting my actual world and the imagined narrative I was slipping into with each passing year.

I had to hide from Tommy. Once I got home from the bookstore, I shaved my goatee and sideburns. I cut my hair with a set of clippers and took out an old pair of glasses and switched them for the black hipster frames I was wearing. I examined my face in the mirror. Old Naugahyde would still be able to pick me out of a lineup, I decided. I drove to Lens-Crafters and got fitted for contacts. They had to special-order what I needed, and I'd have to wait anxiously for a few days for the final piece of my guise.

The physical change was bread and circuses; I wanted change from within. Two married college friends lived across the street from me, and their small storefront church was conducting a fast that weekend. From Billy Graham to the pope to the pastors in the churches I grew up in—they all said the same thing: "Take it to God. When in doubt, fast."

Fasting would get me answers for Tommy's questions. Fasting would gift me with Enlightenment. Surely it'd show God I was making an effort.

So I fasted.

Each day of the fast was punctuated by glasses of water and some kind of worship service. It didn't matter where I went, but I knew I had to go. The first service was a prayer meeting at a storefront church in Pasadena. The South African pastor nonchalantly dropped anecdotes of spiritual warfare, including one that involved soldiers levitating in their barracks. I don't do well with those stories. I once saw Linda Blair in San Diego and got flush with fear of catching residual bad juju as we crossed paths.

The experience affirmed my fear that the universe worked as it did in "Time Enough at Last," a *Twilight Zone* episode I'd watched with my dad. If I lived out my sexuality, I would be the Henry Bemis, a man whose deepest desire to read his books undisturbed was granted. He became the lone survivor of a Cold War apocalypse, surrounded by his books, only to have heaven flipped to hell when his reading glasses were crushed in a moment of carelessness. For me, living out my sexual identity would mean all manner of disease, the ruin of my family, and broad spiritual fallout. I'd spend the rest of my life like Danny Torrance, speeding away from the twins on my Big Wheel.

Toward the end of the prayer meeting, a tall girl in denim shorts told a story about her father. She described how he would send her home with a gallon of milk whenever she visited him. He wanted her to be taken care of, and it was the best way he could think of to show it. She said she knew God felt the same way about all of us. God was a loving father who takes care of his children. For a split second I forgot about Henry Bemis.

God loves me and just wants me to have the gallon of milk.

The message seemed too good to be true, so instead I told myself:

God loves you enough to break your glasses if you fuck up.

The next day I went to a megachurch, also in Pasadena. The pastor interrupted himself midsermon.

"Look, we can talk about theology all day. But the main thing is just to focus on Christ. His sacrifice. His *love*."

I considered trusting the message.

Considered.

On the way back to my car from the service, I crossed the street against a traffic signal. From nowhere a police car rolled alongside me as I dashed across the street. The cop stuck his finger out and wagged it at me.

"Careful, now," he said.

On Sunday morning I went to a contemporary service in a rented Hollywood soundstage. I watched four men who were around my age stand two rows in front of me, arms around one another. As the reverb of "Holy, Holy, Holy" buzzed in my sinuses, the four men began to weep. The touch between them was tender and intimate. The tallest one had buried his face on top of another man's head. He clenched his jaw, his face wet with tears.

I couldn't yet call myself gay, but I knew that they were. And this wasn't a gay-friendly church. Why were they here? Why were they crying? They wept and held one another while the pastor intoned with his SoCal *o*s: "Gohd lohves you soh much. He lohves you."

The fast was soon over, and my takeaway was that overall God loved me and that I had to toe the line. God had employed agents to remind me that I was on the brink of a suffering I couldn't understand. The quartet of hysterical gays. The cop. Tommy Bahama.

This was Enlightenment.

A few days later, while getting dressed for work, I noticed that the patch of dry skin I'd developed during the fast was getting bigger. It stretched around my stomach all the way to my back. It ached, and it was beginning to blister. The next morning, I sat in a medical exam room. The doctor entered, I lifted my shirt, and his hands immediately recoiled from my stomach.

"Oh, wow," he said, pulling on a pair of gloves. "You have shingles,"

Touching the blisters, he eyed me from above the rims of his glasses.

"You're awfully young for this. It's a weakness in the immune system."

Then abruptly, "Are you gay?"

I glanced around the room for cameras.

He stared straight at me: "Are you sexually active?"

"No."

"Are you a homosexual?"

I took too long to answer. "No."

"When was the last time you were sexually active?"

"Never."

"Never?" he asked, raising an eyebrow. I ran through the file directory of every half-baked moment of sexual contact I'd had in my life. Encounters with men now married with kids to touching the door handle at the bookstore in Studio City.

"Never."

Home again, on the couch, hopped up on Vicodin and repeated screenings of *Crimson Tide*, I got a call that my contacts were ready to pick up. On the drive out to the mall, I remembered when I was twelve years old and had brought a tray of snacks to my mom and her friend Marla, a woman she knew from her Bible study. I arranged cookies on a shiny red metal tray emblazoned with the Budweiser logo and a huge *A* for Anheuser-Busch. Marla took a look at the tray and smiled at my mom.

"You can run," she said to my mother with a wink, "but you can't hide."

At LensCrafters, a mustached brunette brought me down the hallway to a Temple of Doom. She assisted me as I put in my contacts. The right lens popped in fine. The second contact didn't go in as easily, and it dried out on my finger. My Frida Kahlo squeezed solution onto my finger to wet the lens.

When I pressed the lens into my left eye, a thousand fire ants set my eye ablaze. I stuck my finger into my eye to pull out the lens, unable to keep the lid from slamming shut. When I finally got the lens out, Frida blamed the contact and placed another drop of solution into my eye. And with that, a raging inferno incinerated the ants scouring my eyeball.

"What are you doing?" I hollered.

Frida had mistakenly picked up the overnight solution used for gas-permeable hard contacts and doused the lens— and my eye—with it. Twice.

At the Sherman Oaks Hospital ER, the nurse saw my swollen eye, the white shrouded by crayon red, and guided me back to a bed. I took off my shirt, revealing a trench of shingles. I heard "Oh, wow" come from the mouth of a medical professional for the second time that week.

I lay on the bed and was fitted with a pump to flush out my eye, the solution spilling from my face. I got rid of my own glasses before God could smash them, and the retaliation was the white-hot contacts.

This was Enlightenment.

As I lay there, the doors to the ER flew open, and an overweight man on a gurney was rushed into the empty bay next to mine. A flurry of scrubs flew about him. My nurse looked at me and grimaced, then pulled the curtain to keep me from seeing what was happening.

While the cool saline soothed my eye, trickled down my face, and slid between the tiny amber blisters on my stomach, I listened to the doctors on the other side saying things I had only heard on TV.

"He's crashing."

"Again!"

And then something I hadn't heard before.

"Call it."

The air left the room. I listened for the big moment. When the internist says, "He wants to live!" Pushing the others aside, the internist delivers CPR, slapping the hell out of the patient until he comes back to life. Just as Ed Harris did to Mary Elizabeth Mastrantonio in *The Abyss*. Instead I heard the sounds of real life. Quiet talking, the squeaking wheels of a crash cart, rubber clogs on linoleum.

An hour later, I was at my neighborhood drugstore.

"Yeah, I don't have this," the pharmacist behind the counter said, waving the green prescription ticket in his hand.

"I need the eye ointment tonight. They said it's got to be applied right away or my eye gets infected." I pointed at the swollen ruby on my face.

"I'd have to order it. It'll take two days."

"What about another pharmacy?"

"I don't have time to call *now*," he said, pointing at the line of ear infections and hemorrhoids standing behind me. "We're busy." I looked to the refrigerator case to my left. White gallons of milk sat in the racks, behind glass doors, their caps locked tight with safety seals. I realized it was just me and this stupid asshole. All things considered, he could have had the courtesy to be glib. Instead he stood slack and passively stared through me.

"Do you have a directory of pharmacies that I can call myself?" I asked.

He gestured behind him to a cordless phone mounted above a three-ring binder. I surprised us both when I opened the half door, stepped behind the counter, removed the binder from its hook, and started making calls. No one working at the pharmacy said a word.

It was getting late, almost ten o'clock at night. After twenty minutes of hearing "no" as I called down the list, I got through to a Longs Drugs in Tarzana that was forty-five minutes away. They had the eye ointment, but I had to hustle to get there.

When I arrived in Tarzana, the Longs Drugs parking lot was empty. The building itself was midcentury in design, with a pitched roof that was connected to the main structure by plate-glass windows. Through the windows I could see one string of fluorescent lights flickering blue. I assumed the store was closed. I yanked on the entrance doors, expecting them to be locked, but both flew open.

"Hello?"

"Is that Anthony?" A man's voice called from the back of the building. I followed the string of lights, which led directly to the pharmacist's counter. He was stocky, blond, and couldn't have been much older than I was. He smiled as I approached.

"Are you closed?" I asked.

He nodded. "I knew you were coming, so I stayed."

He handed me a white paper bag, the pen-size case of ointment rattling inside. I went to pull out my wallet to pay.

"No," he said, waving his hand. "You called in your own prescription."

Postscript

A few months later, I moved back to the Midwest and stored my belongings in my parents' basement. Two weeks after that, the basement flooded—the only time in the twenty-plus years my parents lived in that house that it did. We dragged my soaked mattress, books, and stereo equipment to the curb.

What I had left to prove my existence in Los Angeles was a fever dream.

It all hit me as boilerplate: suburban gay white boy plays Old Testament character, Job. Badly. It made for a passable Woody Allen film. Told in a sermon to the choir, it was a cautionary tale. When I tried to tell the story to myself I couldn't, because my life *wasn't* a story, and none of it made sense. I stood alone in my parents' kitchen and begged for God to speak. I needed God to explain, audibly, who I was and what had been happening in an explicit series of declarative and loving statements.

I said aloud to God, "Just speak."

At that moment, the house phone rang. UNIDENTIFIED scrolled across the caller ID.

My heart leaped. I picked up the phone. "Hello?"

"Hello," came back to me over the earpiece. It was a woman's voice. Clear, soft, and warm. I took in a breath.

"Hi," I exhaled. *Finally.*

She continued: "This is Suzanne Somers here, letting you know how excited I am to present my new line of Somersize chocolates, right after my jewelry trunk sale tonight on HSN..."

When my parents came home I explained that they'd have

to buy a new cordless phone, as the old one was in pieces along with the rest of the garbage at the curb.

So ten-odd years after the fast, I write this out for Tommy Bahama and the rest of the planet to read. I am gay. I date men. I haven't been to church in years, and it's cleared my head. My family hasn't handed me the sword and asked for seppuku. Mom has placed the Budweiser tray back in rotation.

Nothing got better until I stopped using a mercurial interpretation of God's will to craft an "enlightening" narrative around my life. It's hard work, taxes my patience, and allows me to stop inventing Tommy Bahamas faster than I can run from them. At times I'll relapse. I'll daisy-chain events in hopes of uncovering a pattern, to predict the future or to redeem the past. But like a rhinestone-studded Ed Hardy shirt, my invented narratives are costly, baroque, and fall apart when washed in anything other than the gentle cycle.

Orthodox icons illustrate enlightenment as a gold-foil blast around the head of a jaundiced saint. I don't know much about gold foil. When true enlightenment comes, it happens fast and uninvited. It's followed by the rush you get from ripping off a Band-Aid. It looks like a gallon of milk and sounds like Suzanne Somers asking you to eat her chocolate. Enlightenment flickers from a fluorescent bulb controlled by a pharmacist in Tarzana who waits patiently at night for the arrival of the blind and the sick.

Rereading God's Lessons

Jeff Tacklind

"Hear, and I will speak;
I will question you, and you make it known to me."
I had heard of you by the hearing of the ear,
but now my eye sees you...
    —Job 42:4–5 ESV

I've heard it said that you are what you read, and at first glance that seems true enough. Reading brings out the thoughtful contemplative in all of us. It slows down the processing of ideas to a pace at which digestion can take place.

But actually *becoming* what we read would seem to require more than just a once-through. True transformation takes time, repetition, and commitment. It takes redundancy. It is that oft-quoted line from Aristotle: "We are what we repeatedly do."

And so maybe it could be more accurately put as: "We are what we reread."

Now, if that were true, it probably would make me a hobbit. I've read Tolkien's Lord of the Rings trilogy all the way through at least a half dozen times. But what stands out even more than the repetition of rereading alone is the way the text has intersected with so many points along my own time line.

I can remember my dad reading Tolkien's books to me as a child before bedtime and feeling scared to pieces that the Black Riders would catch Frodo. I remember sneaking one of the books into church in fourth grade and reading about the wolves attacking the fellowship when I was supposed to be listening to the sermon. The older I got, the richer it became: the language, the history, the complexity, and the nobility. Every time I came to the final chapters, it would be with such heaviness. I didn't want it to end.

Tolkien isn't the only author I've reread many times; I'm more than just a hobbit. Because of Dostoyevsky, I'm also a guilt-ridden Russian pseudointellectual. Because of Thomas Merton, I'm an ex-Communist turned Trappist. And because of Flannery O'Connor, I'm a hillbilly Thomist. Last but not least, I'm a bit of a Buddhist motorcycle mechanic. Robert Pirsig's *Zen and the Art of Motorcycle Maintenance* has been one of those books that has strategically intersected my life story through the years.

I remember the first time through, devouring Pirsig's philosophical explanation of the classic and romantic and the way these two ways of seeing came together in quality. The second time through, I lingered over the story—the complexity and the sadness, the difficulty of mental illness, and the fleeting nature of time. With each reading, the story has grown deeper and more tender to me. But this last time through was the dearest of all.

This past summer, my son turned eleven—the same age as Pirsig's son in the story. The father and son are on what he calls a chautauqua, a kind of spiritual pilgrimage. They embark on a road trip on the back of his motorcycle, exploring and revisiting the places of his past and rediscovering memories that have been forgotten.

In somewhat similar fashion, my son, Gabe, and I took to the Sierras for his first real backpacking trip. It had been years since my last one, and, as Pirsig describes in his book, many forgotten memories, sensations, and smells from past experiences flooded me. I recalled trips I took with my father when I was a child, climbing peaks with friends, and going on retreats to beautiful lakes with youth-group kids. Backpacking sets you free from all the conveniences and luxuries that only seem to dull the senses. It allows a sort of reacclimatizing with reality. I threw an old paperback copy of Pirsig's book in with the rest of my gear.

As we hiked, Gabe asked what I liked most about backpacking. I thought about that for a moment, and then I told him that I think it is where I most experience God. I can see God so clearly and hear him so distinctly in the absence of the regular clutter of life. When I'm backpacking, life is reduced to its most basic elements. What a great lens through which to process and to get clarity and perspective on the divine.

Pirsig writes, "What makes his world so hard to see clearly is not its strangeness but its usualness. Familiarity can blind you too." And I desperately was in need of some clarity. I was at one of those points in life where I found myself reevaluating. I'd come to the edge of my map, so to speak, and the trail ahead was feeling unfamiliar. Or maybe too familiar.

I'd been down this way before, but this felt different somehow. Maybe it was because of this young man traveling next to me. He served as a reminder of where I'd been, the youth I'd left behind, and the added responsibility of preparing my son for his own journey. That responsibility becomes overwhelming when you realize you're navigating your own life on the fly.

Pirsig writes, "You look at where you're going and where you are and it never makes sense, but then you look back at where you've been and a pattern seems to emerge. And if you project forward from that pattern, then sometimes you can come up with something."

But recognizing the pattern takes some work. I wonder if this is what Jesus meant when he said in Matthew 13, "Those who have eyes to see, let them see." It is there for those who look with the eyes of their heart. But it is often subtle. His voice is like a whisper. It comes in ways we refuse to recognize, unwilling to yield or surrender to these subtle leadings.

The trip was harder than Gabe and I expected. Lots of elevation gains the first day meant almost continual switchbacks for the first five miles. And the mosquitoes were still going strong; the repellent didn't even cause them to flinch. Pretty soon we found ourselves retreating to the safety of the tent. And then it started to rain.

Now, there is something pretty great about being bundled up and warm in a tent as a summer rain shower comes down. But this wasn't letting up. Gabe had brought along his mom's Kindle, but I had rolled over in the tent and elbowed it. The screen was a spiderweb of cracks. He looked at me and innocently asked, "What do we do now?"

I wasn't sure. I'm really good at self-entertaining but not so good at coming up with something fast and fun on the fly. I looked through my pack and pulled out my journal and pen. This little book is pretty sacred to me. It is filled with all my unfiltered thoughts, insecurities, and longings. On a whim I said, "Draw me a cartoon!" He's always doing that on his own, showing me these quick sketches. (Honestly, they're good.) He started to draw, and one after another we began coming up with themes and ideas he would flesh out. We were giggling away. I love the way his mind works. It is quirky and a little twisted, like his dad's. Pretty soon the rain stopped, but we kept on going with our game.

The next day was his birthday. We fished all morning, and he got three beautiful golden trout, his first fish. We laughed about the comics and spent some more time goofing around and drawing. That night, after dinner, we had freeze-dried crème brûlée with eleven candles lit on top of it. My friend Tom and I sang happy birthday off-key as Gabe stood there smiling sheepishly.

I don't mean to make it all sound so rosy. There were blistered heels and sore knees. There were plenty of dull moments and irritations. But then there were these moments of serenity. Sitting on a rock above our campsite with my son, watching the incredible glow of a Sierra sunset, is about as good as it gets.

At one point Pirsig writes, "Sometimes it's a little better to travel than to arrive." I agree. And it is even better to travel with a child. But it is also harder. You carry more weight. You change your pace. Your patience is continually being tried.

Just like life. When we start figuring out how to manage our own lives with some consistency, along come these children who constantly disrupt our plans. But their timing is brilliant and divine. It is one of God's patterns to send us people and things to disrupt us. He loves doing that. In fact, it is one of his greatest compliments to humanity.

Without God's disruptions, we'd spend our lives perpetually striving for our own self-promotion. It is God's way of protecting us from ourselves. The allure of having things all figured out, all under control and mapped out, proves too great a temptation, and we willingly ingest the poison. But God's disruptions prove to be the antidote, the opportunity to stop building according to our plan and start giving according to God's.

As we packed our tent for the final hike out, I asked Gabe how he liked the trip. He said he liked seeing the ways I heard and saw God in nature. He asked what my favorite part of the trip was, and I told him it was when he caught his first fish. He smiled, and I asked him the same question. He paused and then said, "I just liked being with you."

In that instant—there in the eyes of my son—I saw a whole new side of the Father. As Gabe and I shouldered our packs for the final descent, I felt changed. Not an ounce of added clarity as to where I was going, mind you, yet feeling a whole new level of security and intimacy.

It reminds me of Job's famous words: "'I will question you, and you make it known to me.' I had heard of you by the hearing of the ear, but now my eye sees you."

As I continue to live out this story here on earth, I am content to keep reading and rereading the lessons God has. Each time they get deeper and sweeter. Even in the sadness and the loss, they feel somehow weightier. As I release myself to God's disruptions, what I find is intimacy with God.

And that, my friends, is my favorite part.

The Eeyore of Christians
Learns to Pray

Melody Harrison Hanson

Rejoice always, pray without ceasing, in everything give
thanks; for this is the will of God in Christ Jesus for you.
— 1 Thessalonians 5:16–18 NKJV

Walking along the path through the forest, I see a feather
on the ground and pick it up. It is my habit to save things—
colorful stones, shells, a piece of bark. These things become
tokens that commemorate particular moments. I keep them;
they remind me of the way I've come to a resolution about
a question that had preoccupied me for months. I longed to
know: What could the apostle Paul have meant when he commanded us to *pray without ceasing*?

Stopping to stare up at the cobalt blue sky, I know that
prayer is about Yahweh loving me. Prayer is a walk in the garden at dusk, the aroma of flowers. Prayer is being, not doing.
It is observing the birds, the sky, a butterfly dancing at my
feet, the whisper of the wind in tall grasses, trees rustling. All
are gifts. All are prayers. All speak.

Prayer is setting aside the ebb and flow of my thoughts. Being aware, in this silence, of a world filled with God's noise. My search has given me a holy awareness, a belief that a creator God is listening. God waits for me.

For decades, I was agnostic about prayer, making me an immature Christ follower and rendering my progress into a deeper spirituality glacially slow. Although I wanted closeness with God, I remained in the desert plains, in between faith and disbelief. I knew my skepticism was a hindrance and saw a powerful connection with God in others. It was a connection I didn't have. The fact that we cannot prove prayer works, whether we do it unceasingly or infrequently, swelled inside me, a barrier, a conundrum.

The command to "pray without ceasing" seemed, of course, nothing less than impossible.

Addressing my agnosticism was frightening. I started slowly by reading contemporaries and ancients. I spoke to prayerful people, asking about their experiences. I poked and prodded at the concept of prayer, wondering about that verse in 1 Thessalonians.

I examined how I'd been praying.

As a child, I never uttered prayers aloud. I prickled at the sound of my own voice, and in my teen years the silence continued. On returning home from a youth group meeting, hidden under the covers, I'd whisper the words that I might have said if I was plucky enough. "Dear God..."

In my adult life, my prayers have been one-liners, quickly muttered expletives when I failed or hurt others.

"Shit," I'd pray. "How'd I do that again, God?"

Now fully into the middle part of life, with teenagers, an elderly parent, retirement looming, and a family with a good share of mental health concerns, life has taken on an unexpected level of gravity. I have often felt utterly helpless.

"Oh, God," I'd pray, feverishly. Almost *unceasingly*. But I wasn't sure God heard me.

Sitting in the company of others in the act of prayer, I'd whisper along: "Yes, please." But I never tried it alone—not really.

I was the Christian who didn't really believe in prayer, and I don't think I'm alone. Many people seem to "do" prayer by turning God into a candy machine. They put the coin in, expecting a shiny red gumball of help.

"Any time soonish, God. Things are really falling apart here."

I didn't want to be one of those Christians who think God cares about locating their parking spaces. And I wasn't sure about God's love for me at all.

My father was dangerously hurtful and skewed my notions about God. An angry, verbally abusive man, his raging was surreptitious, never seen by anyone outside of our home. He was a ministry head, respected for his winning intelligence and charming personality. To me, he was sometimes a monster.

Growing up was a schizophrenic kaleidoscope of mixed messages, wrecking any chance I had to see God as a good and gracious father. My faith has been gnarled and weedy, rooted in fear. God was surely a secretly cruel being waiting for me to let down my guard, waiting for my trust, planning to swoop in and destroy me.

My dad was mentally ill, but I grew up feeling like *I* was the crazy one. The ripples of his rage pushed me into chronic depression and alcohol abuse. Although in recovery from the latter, I still feel the echoes of his rage in the currents of my life as a wife, a mother, a friend. Sometimes I feel like I'm letting Team Christianity down as the Eeyore of the faith.

Undoing the idea that God the Father is an asshole has been a time-consuming and tremendously difficult spiritual exercise. By the grace of God, I have begun to accept that I am the one Jesus loves. I found a new understanding of God by reading the full narrative of Yahweh in Scriptures, from end to end. A loving husband and sweet, sweet mercy has drawn me to Christ.

I hear his gentle voice as Jesus says, "Go into your closet and pray." There, alone—where it's impossible to be a pretender, where I cannot fail—I fall down on my knees, physically saying with my body what I cannot utter aloud: "Jesus loves me, this I *finally* !#%**# know."

I have come to believe that if it is possible that we *can* pray without ceasing, it is less of an effort or an articulation and more of a ceaseless inclination toward God. Maybe it's to be willing, more often than not, to suspend fear and disbelief in order to imagine that God wants to hear from us and will speak to us.

Though I am torn up and often confused, of course I pray. My mind and heart spin with longing, leaning in to hear the holy whispers of God. I pray because I need to be healed and transformed even as I can't reconcile the question of *how* it works—this communication with God.

I know I can hear God speak through teachers and preachers.

I know God speaks in nature.

I believe that God speaks in the Bible.

The verses in 1 Thessalonians end with "in everything give thanks," implying, by its placement, that if you have joy and you're praying without ceasing, you will be grateful.

Most days I fall before God, bone-weary, aware of my deficiency, knowing intellectually the simple truth that God's presence eventually heals—if I sit still long enough. Praying without ceasing is a constant practice of trust, of saying: "Lord, help me."

Prayer doesn't have to be audible or done in a certain posture or place. None of these is essential, or we couldn't do it without ceasing. Prayer is a way to know God. And to be known.

I long to know Jesus' presence without ceasing. I hope someday to approach God with the confidence of a cherished daughter. I yearn to live in constant gratitude and awe.

But for now, I'll keep aching for more of the Holy One. That longing, that leaning, wherever I am and whatever my sorrows and anxieties are—that truly is how I've come to pray without ceasing.

You Must Be Born Again

Carla Barnhill

Now there was a Pharisee, a man named Nicodemus who was a member of the Jewish ruling council. He came to Jesus at night and said, "Rabbi, we know that you are a teacher who has come from God. For no one could perform the signs you are doing if God were not with him." Jesus replied, "Very truly I tell you, no one can see the kingdom of God unless they are born again." "How can someone be born when they are old?" Nicodemus asked. "Surely they cannot enter a second time into their mother's womb to be born!" Jesus answered, "Very truly I tell you, no one can enter the kingdom of God unless they are born of water and the Spirit. Flesh gives birth to flesh, but the Spirit gives birth to spirit. You should not be surprised at my saying, 'You must be born again.' The wind blows wherever it pleases. You hear its sound, but you cannot tell where it comes from or where it is going. So it is with everyone born of the Spirit."
—John 3:1–8 NIV

Like so many others here in my Midwestern homeland, I grew up in the Lutheran church. I was baptized at the tender age of six weeks, and I was confirmed at the age of thirteen after memorizing all of *Luther's Small Catechism* and reciting it back to my teachers, one doctrine at a time. Did you know that there is an expanded version of the Ten Commandments that includes an explanation of what each one means? Lutherans know. I took communion, I said the creeds, I knew all the words in the sung liturgy because it was "meet and right so to do."

I was an excellent Lutheran.

So imagine my chagrin when I headed off to Baptist Bible camp with my Baptist cousin only to discover that I was missing out on what was evidently a very important part of being a real Christian.

I was not, as far as I could tell, born again.

Wanting to fit in and being more than a little concerned that I'd maybe missed Luther's explanation of this step in the Christian faith, I prayed the prayer, got some extra attention from my counselor, and went back home with the reassurance that I did indeed know where I would end up "if I were to die that very night."

A few years ago, my oldest daughter headed off to the same Baptist Bible camp of my youth with one of her friends. My husband, who had visions of the documentary *Jesus Camp* flashing through his head, worried that our daughter was about to fall prey to the kind of evangelical indoctrination he had experienced in college and from which he had spent a good twenty years trying to recover. To ease his concerns, we held what we now refer to as the pre-briefing, a short conversation in which we explained the ways of the evangelical to our child.

We tried to remember every "altar call" message we'd ever heard (or had, to be honest, delivered) in our collective years of youth group meetings, campus ministries, and camp counseling. We labored to decode them for our ten-year-old. We told her she absolutely had Jesus in her heart and always had. We told her she didn't need to do anything or say anything or pray anything to change her standing before God. We wanted to make sure she wouldn't sit on the same pine bench I'd sat on three decades earlier and wonder why no one told her she was in danger of being left behind because she hadn't been "born again."

I don't want to come down too hard on the Baptists here—they certainly aren't the only ones to put their own spin on what it takes to call oneself a real Christian. Luther himself promoted the idea that we had to believe *and* be baptized in order to claim salvation. And maybe we do. I don't know. But what I do know is that any doctrine that puts the onus of salvation in the hands of human beings strikes me as fishy.

Jesus certainly seems to be drawing up some requirements when he tells Nicodemus that "no one can see the kingdom of God unless they are born again" and "no one can enter the kingdom of God unless they are born of water and the Spirit."

And yet that's not what the rest of the Bible tells us. I mean, just a few verses later, Jesus tells Nicodemus that God loved the world so much that all we have to do is believe and—*bam!*—eternal life is ours.

Let's also not forget that Jesus is doing all this talking while he's still alive. In other words, there is no resurrection for Nicodemus to buy into and no sinner's prayer to pray. It's frankly a little unclear what exactly we are supposed to believe about Jesus in order to get in on this eternal-life thing.

So what in the world is Jesus talking about? It's no wonder Nicodemus fires back at Jesus and tells him just how ridiculous he sounds.

But what if Jesus isn't being prescriptive but *descriptive* here? Maybe instead of reading Jesus' words as a scold, we need to see them as an acknowledgment that Nicodemus has already cracked the code. What if instead of telling Nicodemus what he needs to do, Jesus is naming what Nicodemus has already done?

Nicodemus starts the conversation by acknowledging that there's something divine about Jesus. Clearly God is with this man. He even calls Jesus Rabbi. He's no doubter, this Nicodemus. He's on Jesus' side here. That little shift in perspective has the potential to change *everything* about what Jesus says next.

Most of the Jewish leaders of Jesus' day were loath to admit that Jesus might be someone they needed to pay attention to. But Nicodemus comes right out and says to Jesus, "You're kind of the real deal, aren't you?" And Jesus says, "Yep. And you noticed because you are willing to put aside your tradition and make room for something new. *Nicely done.*"

Nicodemus doesn't need to *do* anything. He already did it when he started to see Jesus, to recognize that this rabbi brought the presence of God with him. It was Nicodemus's openness to the new thing God was doing that led Jesus to say he was "born again."

And that might have been exactly what it felt like for Nicodemus to push off from the traditions and stories of his Jewish heritage. It might have been very much like a rebirth of sorts.

But here's the thing: Nicodemus didn't know it had happened, and he certainly didn't make it happen. Whatever it was that opened him up to seeing Jesus as more than a pain in the ass for the religious establishment of the day, salvation wasn't something Nicodemus brought on himself. He didn't pray a prayer or acknowledge his sin or say some mystical incantation that would switch him from Team Hell to Team Heaven. He recognized God in the person of Jesus. He saw, he noticed, he believed. These weren't steps toward rebirth.

They were signs that rebirth had already happened.

Jesus' use of a birth metaphor tells us something else about what he was getting at in this weird conversation. Even with everything that modern science can tell us about fetal development, even with all the ways we can intervene in labor and delivery, the whole process of birth still starts with a chemical wash that's triggered by the baby. But no one really knows what that involves or how the baby knows when to start things moving. It's a grand mystery, and I hope they never figure it out.

Maybe Jesus meant exactly what so many evangelicals think he meant. Maybe we do have to make some kind of decision and change something in our hearts for God's love and grace and mercy to take hold. But for me to believe that would mean pushing aside all the evidence I see that tells me that faith is as mysterious a process as birth.

When we told our ten-year-old that she already had God in her heart, it was because she did. I could see God breathing in and through her from the moment she was placed, fearfully and wonderfully made, into my arms. The same was clear when her brother and sister were born. Every day of their lives I see God in them. I see the spirit of God in them. I see the kingdom of God in them. It doesn't make sense to me that God is waiting until they pray a prayer, take a dunk, or assent to a promise to become fully embedded into their minds, hearts, and souls.

And if the evangelicals (or other groups, for that matter) hold the secret code to life with God, what about all of those good folks who came along before them? You know, like

Luther? What about my dear Lutheran grandparents, who never, as far as I know, made a personal decision for Christ or asked Jesus into their hearts or did anything extra to solidify their salvation? Are they in or not? Because if they aren't in, then I don't know if I want to be in, either. I don't know that I want to be involved in a faith that puts ritual, doctrine, and human effort above the expansive, embracing, inviting love of God.

We Christians love our systems, rituals, and orderly patterns. It's nice to have four spiritual laws and a simple sinner's prayer to help us make sense of something utterly incomprehensible. But Jesus says this wind of the spirit blows wherever it pleases. It doesn't follow our systems. It doesn't conform to our patterns. It probably doesn't limit itself to our churches, our camps, our country, or our faith.

I think that's great news. I don't want a faith that hinges on a decision I made for mostly the wrong reasons when I was thirteen years old. I don't want a faith than hinges on me, period. I want a faith that's continually being reborn and remade even when I'm not doing anything to make it so. I want to be surprised by the way the wind of the spirit blows through my life and through the world around me. I want to notice God in places I never expected God to be.

I want to be open—always open—to having the doors blown off the little boxes and rooms and compartments I stuff my experiences into in an effort to have some kind of coherent narrative for my life.

I want to be born again and again and again.

The Greatest of These

Brian D. McLaren

And now these three remain: faith, hope and love. But the
greatest of these is love.
  —1 Corinthians 13:13 NIV

I was just a teenager, a freshly minted disciple, and somebody
told me it was a good thing to do. But nobody told me exactly
how it was supposed to be done. So I just decided to give it
a try—flying blind, so to speak. I have no idea where I got
the idea to do it the way I did, but my idiosyncratic approach
became absolutely formative in my life.

The "it" was reading the Bible (almost) every morning on
my own, and my blind flight involved reading the same two
chapters every day (almost), week after week, month after
month, for several years. I don't know how I chose 1 Corinthians 13 as one of those two chapters, but I'm glad I did. (If
you want to know what the other chapter was, I'll tell you.
Sometime.)

It turns out that 1 Corinthians 13 was famous for being
read at weddings. But at that point, I was just below the age
where my friends were getting married, so I hadn't been to

many weddings, and I hadn't paid attention to the Scriptures that were read at the few weddings I did attend.

Neither do I recall hearing 1 Corinthians 13 being preached at my church. We read chapters 11 and 14 obsessively, because they focused on women being silent in the churches and wearing head coverings when the church was gathered, and we were faithful—unlike Southern Baptists and other liberal denominations—in literally obeying the word of God. Let "the liberals" pay attention to all that fluffy peace-and-love stuff in chapter 13. We would remain focused on serious fundamentals of the faith—like literal six-day creation, virgin birth, the pre-tribulational Rapture, a literal hell, penal substitutionary atonement... and women keeping silent in the churches, with their heads covered, as Paul commanded.

Anyway, in spite of my church background and my lack of wedding experience, I stumbled across 1 Corinthians 13 in between 11 and 14, and somehow I decided it was a chapter I would do well to read (almost) every morning.

A few years later, when I was a freshman in college, I was sitting between classes one sunny afternoon on the quad— the large open area in front of the old library. A few students were cramming for tests, but not me. A few were sleeping in the sun, but not me. Some were throwing Frisbees to golden retrievers wearing red bandannas—red bandannas being the neck attire of choice for golden retrievers back in the mid-1970s. But I had neither dog nor bandanna. The sweet scent of marijuana rose into the breeze from little huddles of my peers around me, but I was not among them.

I was reading my Bible.

I was still specializing in 1 Corinthians 13, but I had ventured out, trying to read the whole Bible.

I had come to the story about Solomon being told in a

dream he could ask any one thing of the Lord (1 Kings 3), and he asked for wisdom. As I read, I suddenly felt that the Holy Spirit was inviting me to ask one thing of the Lord—right there on the quad, with golden retrievers catching Frisbees and THC molecules wafting by.

Having been so deeply immersed in 1 Corinthians 13 for so long, I decided to match Solomon's request and up it even higher: "Lord," I said, "like Solomon, I would like wisdom, but above all, I want to ask for love, because without love, even wisdom is a noisy gong or clanging cymbal. So my one great request is for wisdom and love, both together."

Forty years later, I'm still echoing that prayer. I don't read 1 Corinthians 13 every morning these days. By now I would hope it's in my veins and nerves. But even after all these years, I still feel like a freshman at putting it into practice.

Some of my friends think of me as a patient and kind person. But without forty years of meditating on 1 Corinthians 13, I'm sure I would be a lot less of either. I still struggle with jealousy—not for fancy cars or houses but for knowledge and other more internal capacities. So when I catch myself wishing I knew as much as *he* or had read as widely as *she*, I preach 1 Corinthians 13:4 to myself: love is not jealous.

In my line of work, with someone calling me a heretic or infidel every day or two, it's easy to respond defensively, which usually involves bragging, being arrogant, being rude, seeking personal advantage, being irritable, and keeping an account of how often I have been unfairly reviewed. But in each case, I hear 1 Corinthians 13 reminding me: love isn't like that.

When my harshest critics suffer some setback or humiliation, I might be tempted to think they deserve it—at least a little. But no, love never rejoices with evil, but rejoices only with the truth.

When I sink into a seat on a plane, desperately needing to recharge my drained introversion tank, and my seatmate is chatty and curious, I remember that love bears all things.

When I feel myself sliding into cynicism, I hear a whisper in my ear: love believes all things and hopes all things. And when it feels like humanity wants to take 2.9 steps back for every three steps forward, I try to remember that love endures all things.

The only kind of maturity that really matters, 1 Corinthians 13 has taught me, is maturity in love. The only strategy that never fails, I have come to understand, is love. Not that I live this as I should . . . but thanks to Paul's most famous chapter, at least the goal has been defined.

I remember hearing about a fellow who was celebrating the one-year anniversary of his conversion as an adult to committed Christian faith. "How has this first year been?" someone asked. "It's been good, but a little confusing," he answered. "I feel like I'm bowling, but nobody will let me see the pins." I think that's what 1 Corinthians 13 did for me: it showed me the pins.

I've lived long enough to see a lot of religious fads come and go. My name has even been associated with a few of them. But I've also come to see the truth of what I've believed since I was a teenager reading 1 Corinthians 13 every morning: only three things remain: faith, hope, and love, and the greatest of these is love.

There's a lot of great stuff in the Bible. It would take many lifetimes to mine its depths. But I'm glad I've spent most of this one particular lifetime concentrating on this one particular chapter. When I master it, or get bored with it, or give up on it, I'll move on to another. But don't hold your breath.

Acknowledgments

From Cathleen:

First of all, deep bows of gratitude to all the wonderful women and men who contributed essays to this book. Thank you for opening your hearts (and a vein) to write about what confounds and delights you about this wonderful, difficult, living, breathing book we call the Bible.

For their unfailing love and support, my greatest thanks goes to my husband, Maury; my son, Vasco; and my sister-from-another-mister, Jennafierce.

For all my chosen family, particularly Allen and Ina; Kelley; Linda, Tripp, and Trish; Adam; Timmay; Madame C. Adams; Sandi; Jimmy Jam and Jennifer; all the ONE Moms; Ginny and Jeannine; and my beloved Hobbits of the Shire—Uncle Veen, Sissi, Iris, Glennco, Mini Rev, Kitty and Rob, Jeff and Patty, Lori, Jeannette, and the Burchis—I love you and thank you for your generosity of spirit, creativity, and companionship.

For the intrepid Chris Ferebee, who is the proverbial wind in my sails.

For all the Falsanis, Pages, and Alois for their kinship and support.

For B, who ever inspires my spiritual and artistic pursuits.

And for Linda Richardson, for giving me wings all those years ago.

From Jennifer:

In the foreword to this book, Eugene Peterson writes, "Stories are verbal acts of hospitality." I want to thank all of *Disquiet Time*'s contributors for their huge-hearted generosity in sharing these and crafting them so carefully.

Thank you, Cathleen, for your friendship, for giving me a nickname that emboldens me and makes me smile (*Jennafierce!*), and for collaborating with me on this project.

I also want to thank our agent extraordinaire, Chris Ferebee, an excellent listener and lover of good stories.

Thank you to everyone at Jericho who has worked on this book, including Chelsea Apple, Laura Wheeler, and Joey Paul.

Thank you, Rachel Klooster, for your excellent (and long-suffering) administrative help.

Thanks, too, to all my good-humored, brilliant, and faithful friends in the Okay Jesus Fan Club. You know who you are, and I hope you know how much your abiding friendship and support means to me.

Last and never least, I owe thanks to my husband, David, and our children, Theo, Ian, Isabel, and Mia, who patiently bear my absences (physical and otherwise) when I am deep into the writing of a book. I hope this one will inspire good conversations and spiritual curiosity among you for many years to come.

About the Authors

General Editors:

JENNIFER GRANT is the author of four books, including *Love You More: The Divine Surprise of Adopting My Daughter*, *MOMumental: Adventures in the Messy Art of Raising a Family*, and *Wholehearted Living*, a daybook for women. She also writes for *Sojourners' God's Politics* and *Christianity Today's Her.meneutics* blog for women. She lives in the Chicago suburbs with her husband, four children, and German shepherd mix mutt—all of whom she madly adores. She's a proud member of the Episcopal Church and of INK: A Creative Collective. Find her online at jennifergrant.com.

CATHLEEN FALSANI is an award-winning journalist and author specializing in the intersection of faith and culture. She is the author of five books, including *The God Factor: Inside the Spiritual Lives of Public People*, *Sin Boldly: A Field Guide for Grace*, *The Dude Abides: The Gospel According to the Coen Brothers*, and the forthcoming *Papa Frank: Why We Love Him and Why It Matters*. She is the principal of Incubate:Spirit, a creative consultancy in Laguna Beach, California, where she lives with her husband, the Pulitzer Prize–winning journalist and author Maurice

Possley, and their teenage son, Vasco Fitzmaurice Possley. You can read more about Cathleen at godgrrl.com.

Contributors:

INA ALBERT is coauthor of *Write Your Self Well . . . Journal Your Self to Health*. As she grows older, she counts being a good listener as one of her best qualities. Her children's book, *Granny Greeny Says . . . Listen Louder*, tells us how it's done. Ina is a life transitions coach, certified Age-ing to Sage-ing® seminar leader, and adjunct instructor at Flathead Valley Community College. She writes a monthly column for *Montana Woman* magazine. She has published in numerous online and print publications, including a chapter in *The Art of Grief*, edited by J. Earl Rogers for Routledge Press. Ina lives in Whitefish, Montana, with her husband, Rabbi Allen Secher, and their dog, Kugel.

CARLA BARNHILL is the author of numerous articles and several books, including *The Myth of the Perfect Mother, Shaping Your Family's Future*, and *Blessings Every Day*, which has sold more than a half million copies and was awarded the 2002 Gold Medallion Award. The former editor of *Christian Parenting Today* magazine, Carla has also edited many books on topics ranging from leadership to Christian community to worship. She also teaches writing to college students, a job that keeps her on her toes in every way. Carla is the mother of three and the wife of one. She and her family live in Minneapolis, Minnesota.

AMY JULIA BECKER is the author of *Small Talk: Learning from My Children About What Matters Most* (Zondervan); *A Good and Perfect Gift: Faith, Expectations, and a Little Girl Named Penny* (Bethany House), which was named one of the Top Books of 2011 by *Publishers Weekly*; and *Penelope Ayers: A Memoir*. A graduate of Princeton University and Princeton Theological Seminary, she blogs regularly for *Christianity Today* at *Thin Places*. Her essays have appeared in the *New York Times* online, *The Atlantic* online, *The Christian Century*, *Christianity Today*, *The Huffington Post*, and Parents.com. Amy Julia lives with her husband, Peter, and three children, Penny, William, and Marilee, in western Connecticut.

TRACEY BIANCHI is a pastor/preacher who lives in the Chicago area and serves at a big-ish church where she leads the contemporary worship community. She's married to an honest and forgiving man named Joel. They have three young children, so she spends much of her time as "that suburban mom." Tracey is a freelance writer and speaker and has written two books and various articles and serves on a few boards and stuff. You can read more about Tracey at traceybianchi.com.

DEBBIE BLUE is one of the founding pastors of House of Mercy, a church in St. Paul, Minnesota. She is the author of *Sensual Orthodoxy*, *From Stone to Living Word*, and *Consider the Birds: A Provocative Guide to the Birds of the Bible*. Blue's sermon podcasts are listened to by subscribers around the world and her essays have appeared in a wide variety of publications including *Geez*, *The Image Journal*, and *The Christian Century*. Debbie and her family live with friends on a farm near Milaca, Minnesota. Find Debbie online at houseofmercy.org.

ANNA BROADWAY is a writer and web editor living near San Francisco. The author of *Sexless in the City: A Memoir of Reluctant Chastity*, she is also a contributor to the anthologies *Faith at the Edge* and *Talking Taboo*. She holds an MA in religious studies from Arizona State University and has written for TheAtlantic.com, *Books and Culture, onFaith, Christianity Today, Paste, The Journal of the History of Sexuality,* and the *First Things* and *Sojourners* blogs, among others. She also contributes regularly to the *Her.meneutics* blog.

STEVE BROWN is the founder of Key Life Network, Inc. (keylife .org) and a Bible teacher on the national radio program *Key Life.* Steve is professor emeritus of preaching and pastoral ministry at Reformed Theological Seminary, Orlando, Florida; Atlanta, Georgia; and Washington, D.C. He is a popular speaker and has authored numerous books including *Three Free Sins: God's Not Mad at You.* Steve is a member of the board of directors of the National Religious Broadcasters and Harvest, USA.

The Reverend VICTOR H. CONRADO is assistant rector for Spanish-language ministries at St. Mark's Episcopal Church in Glen Ellyn, Illinois. Prior to being received into the Episcopal Church in 2011, Father Victor was a Roman Catholic missionary priest and worked for eleven years in Kenya. Victor holds a bachelor's degree in philosophy from the St. Bonaventure University in Colombia and completed a masters in divinity from the Jesuit School of Theology in Nairobi, Kenya (a constituent college university of the Pontifical Gregorian University in Rome).

IAN MORGAN CRON is the bestselling author of *Jesus, My Father, the CIA, and Me: A Memoir...of Sorts* and *Chasing Francis: A Pilgrim's Tale.* He is also a Nashville-based songwriter, a free-range Episcopal priest, and one of the founders of the Wild Goose Festival. Ian, his wife Anne, and their two Portuguese water dogs live in Tennessee or in Dorset, Vermont, depending on the heat index. Find Ian online at iancron.com.

ALICE CURRAH is the cook, baker, writer, and photographer for
SavorySweetLife.com, and the author of the cookbook *Savory
Sweet Life: 100 Simply Delicious Recipes for Every Family Occasion*. She also writes a weekly food column for *PBS Parents*
and hosts a cooking series on the PBS Digital Studios network
featuring great food and authentic interactions from a three-
generational Korean-American family. Alice has been married to Rob for fourteen years and has three of the greatest
children a mother could ever have hoped for, Abbi, Mimi, and
Eli. She loves technology, traveling, food culture, eating out
with friends, exercising, and quiet meditation through prayer
and reflection (Jeremiah 29:11).

CALENTHIA S. DOWDY, PhD, is associate professor of youth ministry and anthropology at Eastern University. She also serves
as director of faith initiatives at an HIV/AIDS organization.
Born and raised in Philadelphia, the city of love, Calenthia
brings an intersectional analysis of urban life, culture, race,
gender, and faith to her work. She also enjoys co-facilitating
workshops with the Roots of Justice anti-oppression analysis
team and admittedly struggles with the ways and means of
church folk and church life.

DAVID B. FLETCHER works in ethical theory and bioethics,
including such developments as the genetic, biological, and
technological enhancement of human beings and justice in
access to health care. He is interested in the "private vices" of
gambling, alcohol, drugs, and tobacco as matters of personal
ethics and social policy. Dr. Fletcher has an interest in liturgy
and enjoys playing guitar, travel, theater, history, and humor.
He serves on a hospital ethics committee. He lives in Wheaton,
Illinois, with his wife, Joyce, a college professor and counselor.

Originally from the United States, GREG FROMHOLZ has lived in Dublin, Ireland, since 1990 working with artists, archbishops, and students; and globally collaborating, creating, drinking coffee, and risking innovation—all in an attempt to find and inspire hope. Greg is the author of *Liberate Eden*, a groundbreaking, interactive iPad book app; a music video director; a cofounder of the faith and culture think tank Rubicon; and the creative director and a founding member of Holy Trinity Church, Dublin. Greg is married to Alexandra, and they have a lovely girl named Chloe, two brilliant boys named Joshua and Eden, and a hyper dog named Mr. Bojangles.

DALE HANSON BOURKE is president of PDI, a marketing and communications strategy firm, and the author of ten books. Her most recent book is *The Israeli-Palestinian Conflict: Tough Questions, Direct Answers*. Previously president of the CIDRZ Foundation and senior vice president at World Relief, Bourke has also served as publisher of Religion News Service and was a nationally syndicated newspaper columnist. A graduate of Wheaton College, she holds an MBA from the University of Maryland. She has served on the boards of World Vision US, World Vision International, International Justice Mission, *Sojourners*, ECFA, and Opportunity International. She currently serves on the board of MAP International. The mother of two grown sons, she lives near Washington, D.C., with her husband, Tom, and is a member of National Presbyterian Church.

MELODY HARRISON HANSON lives one day at a time, one word at a time. Melody found her way back to faith through leaving ministry for motherhood, finding feminism, choosing sobriety, and fighting chronic depression, all the while discovering the grace of Jesus. She is published in *Not Alone: Stories of Living with Depression, Not Afraid: Stories of Finding Significance,* and *Finding Church.* She writes about grateful sobriety, renewed faith, and slow healing at logicandimagination.com, a contemplative blog with poetry, essays, and original photography.

JACK HEASLIP spent the first twenty years of his working life in education—teaching English and ministering as a guidance counselor and chaplain in Mount Temple Comprehensive School in Dublin, Ireland. He moved into full-time parish ministry in the Church of Ireland as an ordained Anglican priest. He has been the spiritual advisor for the band U2, traveling with them as they have toured worldwide. He is married to Patricia. Together they enjoy their family of two adult children, two children-in-law, and four beautiful granddaughters.

The Reverend SARAH HEATH is an ordained elder and currently serves at Shepherd of the Hills United Methodist Church in Southern California as the preaching pastor for the Rancho Santa Margarita site. She received her masters of divinity from Duke University in 2005. From 2005 to 2011 Sarah served as a youth pastor/campus minister for UCI in Irvine, California. Sarah has written for several publications about the struggle to find your place within the faith. She has a passion for music, traveling, acting, sports, and creating art. Her biggest blessing is her talented friends and her amazing dog, Tenor.

STEPHEN HENDERSON is a freelance writer whose work has been published in the *New York Times,* the *Washington Post,* the *Los Angeles Times,* the Baltimore *Sun, House Beautiful, Elle Décor, Town & Country, Food & Wine, Gourmet, Men's Health,* and *New York Magazine.* After working for a week as a volunteer cook at the Gurudwara Bangla Sahib, which feeds twenty thousand men, women, and children each day in Delhi, he got the idea to write a book about what he terms "gastrophilanthropy." Chapters of this work-in-progress, which looks at the fascinatingly different ways by which poor and hungry people are fed around the world, can be found at www.cookingforoth ers.com. Henderson lives in New York City and is married to James LaForce, his partner of twenty-five years. Find Stephen online at stephenhenderson.com.

CHRISTOPHER L. HEUERTZ has spent his life bearing witness to the possibility of hope in a world that has legitimate reasons to question God's goodness. After twenty years of international anti–human trafficking work, Chris and his wife, Phileena, launched Gravity, a Center for Contemplative Activism. Named one of *Outreach* magazine's 30 Emerging Influencers Reshaping Leadership, Chris is a curator of unlikely friendships, an instigator for good, a champion of collaboration, and a witness to hope. Chris fights for a renewal of contemplative activism. His most recent book is *Unexpected Gifts: Discovering the Way of Community*. Join @ChrisHeuertz on Twitter in his attempts to love on the margins.

GARETH HIGGINS was born in Belfast in 1975, grew up during the Northern Ireland Troubles, and lives in North Carolina, where he was the founding director of the Wild Goose Festival and now works as a writer and storyteller. Movies (and a theatrical mother) made his imagination come to life, and he is a grateful inheritor of the gifts of queer theology, nonviolent activism, and Anabaptist patriotic skepticism. He writes and speaks about connection to the earth, cinema and dreaming, peace and making justice, the gift of fear, and how to take life seriously without believing your own propaganda.

TRIPP HUDGINS is a PhD student at Graduate Theological Union in Berkeley, California, a preaching pastor, Baptist cantor, liturgiologist, ecumenist, writer of articles, ethnomusicologist (hon.), and grateful husband. His work is an exploration of sonic theology, mandodoxy, found objects (like grace, time, timbre, or other holy scrap), and some good old-fashioned "sangin." Find Tripp online at anglobaptist.org.

SUSAN E. ISAACS is an actor, comedienne, and author with many credits in film and TV (including *Planes, Trains & Automobiles, Seinfeld,* and *Parks and Recreation*) and an alumna of LA's Groundlings comedy troupe. Susan's memoir, *Angry Conversations with God*, was named a top religion book of the year by *Publishers Weekly*. She has since mounted a full-length production of her solo show and tours it nationally. Susan earned her MFA in screenwriting from the University of Southern California and has taught graduate screenwriting at Pepperdine University. She currently teaches a variety of subjects at Azusa Pacific University, including screenwriting, sitcom acting, and her favorite: sketch comedy writing and performance.

JAY EMERSON JOHNSON, a theologian and Episcopal priest, is a lecturer in theology and culture at Pacific School of Religion (PSR), a member of the core doctoral faculty of the Graduate Theological Union, and academic director at the Center for Spiritual and Social Transformation at PSR. His publications include *Dancing with God: Anglican Christianity and the*

Practice of Hope (Morehouse, 2005); *Queer Religion* (two volumes, co-edited with Donald L. Boisvert, Praeger Publishing, 2012); *Divine Communion: A Eucharistic Theology of Sexual Intimacy* (Seabury Books, 2013); and *Peculiar Faith: Queer Theology for Christian Witness* (Seabury Books, 2014).

TIMOTHY KING is chief strategy officer for *Sojourners* in Washington, D.C. A New Hampshire native, he is a graduate of North Park University in Chicago, and holds degrees in both theology and philosophy. He enjoys helping out on the family farm and afternoons on the porch with his banjo. Timothy has been a guest on many radio shows and has been interviewed for various print and online publications, including ABC News, *Time* magazine, CNN, *Christianity Today*, *The Christian Post*, and *The Daily Beast*. He writes regularly about the intersection of faith and politics for *Sojourners' God's Politics* blog at www.sojo.net.

BRIAN D. MCLAREN is an author, speaker, activist, and networker among innovative Christian leaders. His dozen-plus books include *A New Kind of Christianity*, *A Generous Orthodoxy*, *Naked Spirituality*, and *We Make the Road by Walking*. He and his wife, Grace, live in Florida and have four adult children and four grandchildren.

LINDA MIDGETT is an Emmy Award–winning writer, producer, and director. She has supervised more than six hundred hours of programming for networks such as NBC-Universal, the History Channel, PBS, the Weather Channel, and Discovery. Her credits include *Starting Over*, the Emmy-winning syndicated daytime reality series; the History Channel's groundbreaking series *Gangland*; and Investigation Discovery's *FBI: Criminal Pursuit*. Linda opened her own production company, Midgett

Productions, in 2012. Her most recent project is a documentary on immigration reform. Linda lives in Charlotte, North Carolina, with her husband, two children, and two cats, John Calvin and Frank.

BILL MOTZ is an Emmy-winning screenwriter living in Burbank, California. He's worked for Walt Disney Studios, Warner Bros., Sony, Cartoon Network, Paramount Pictures, Nickelodeon, and FOX. With a BA in Christian education from Wheaton College, Bill worked as a youth director at a church after graduation and then in the media department of Youth for Christ USA for a few years before pursuing work in the entertainment industry. Bill and his family are part of an eclectic little Presbyterian church where they regularly laugh and play and study and struggle and worship with a diverse group of friends who challenge them to be more authentic in faith and life.

LAVONNE NEFF has taught French, history, English, journalism, religion, and Lamaze childbirth classes. She has also worked in publishing as a marketer, copy editor, book editor, magazine editor, acquisitions director, editorial director, consultant, writer, and reviewer. Of more interest (to her, at least), she has one husband, two daughters, two sons-in-law, two granddaughters, and two grandsons. In her spare time she collects small dogs and masters degrees. Read her blog at livelydust.blogspot.com.

ELLEN PAINTER DOLLAR is the author of *No Easy Choice: A Story of Disability, Parenthood, and Faith in an Age of Advanced Reproduction* (Westminster John Knox, 2012). Her articles, blog posts, and book chapters have been published by the *Christian Century*, the *New York Times Motherlode* blog, the Osteogenesis

Imperfecta (OI) Foundation, the American Medical Association, *Christianity Today*, *GeneWatch* magazine, *The Huffington Post*, and more. A lifelong Episcopalian with a few detours into evangelicalism, she blogs about faith, family, disability, and ethics at Patheos.

JACK PALMER hails from the Sceptered Isle across the ocean (a.k.a. the UK), where he drinks tea, discusses the weather, and stands in a perpetual queue. When he's not busy doing these things, he works as a political advisor for the Archbishop of Canterbury and is studying for a masters degree in anthropology. After graduating with his bachelor's degree, he spent a year living and working in Washington, D.C., as communications assistant at *Sojourners* magazine, where he was lucky enough to work with Cathleen Falsani.

CHRISTIAN PIATT had a Bible (literally) thrown at him when he was kicked out of his youth group for asking too many questions. After painstakingly regaining his faith, Christian is committed to reconciling what Christianity claims to be with what it's intended to be. Christian is the creator and editor of the Banned Questions book series, and the author of a memoir on faith, family, and parenting called *PregMANcy* and a novel called *Blood Doctrine*. He is also the author of *postChristian: What's Left? Can We Fix It? Do We Care?* For more, visit christianpiatt.com.

ANTHONY PLATIPODIS had a math teacher who once chided, "It's a long way to Broadway when you can't pass geometry." Realizing New York would reject him due to his failure to grasp the Pythagorean theorem, Anthony chose to work as a writer and actor in Chicago and Los Angeles. It is possible to see Anthony chewing scenery on Cinemax TV shows and furniture commercials—or wandering the grocery store looking for chocolate Chex (harder to find than you'd think). You can follow Anthony on Twitter @platipod.

CAROLYN REYES was born in Miami and raised there by her Cuban grandmother with a fifth-grade education who read the newspaper cover to cover and watched *The Price Is Right* daily. At twelve, she fell in love with Jesus after a church softball game and the two have remained good friends since their amicable breakup several years later. She has spent the past dozen years as a really bad Zen student. Carolyn lives in Oakland, California. She represents kids in legal proceedings and does reform work regarding LGBT youth when she is not reading or building Lego things with her daughter, Kairos.

CARYN RIVADENEIRA is a sought-after writer and speaker. She's the author of four books: *Shades of Mercy: A Maine Chronicle*, *Known & Loved: 52 Devotions from the Psalms*, *Grumble Hallelujah*, and *Mama's Got a Fake I.D.* Caryn is a regular contributor to *Christianity Today*'s *Her.meneutics* blog for women as well as a columnist for *Think Christian*. She lives in the western suburbs of Chicago with her husband, Rafael, her three kids, a rescued pit bull terrier, two hermit crabs, and several tanks of who-knows-what-kind-of-fish. Caryn and her family are members of Elmhurst Christian Reformed Church where Caryn is on the worship staff.

JENNY SHEFFER STEVENS lives in New York City and, intermittently, Los Angeles, with her husband, Eric, and kids, Hutch and Violet. She's an actress, writer, yogi, moderate health nut, immoderate talker, and shameless shoe enthusiast, chronically torn between conflicting identities as ardent urbanite and closet hippie beach bum, who likes her city Atlantic but her ocean Pacific. She holds a BA in English literature from Wheaton College; an MFA in acting from the University of Alabama / Alabama Shakespeare Festival; and multiple yoga teaching certifications. Jenny spearheaded the Three Jennys artists' collective, 2012 recipients of the Lincoln City Fellowship, a generous grant from the Speranza Foundation.

MARGOT STARBUCK, a writer and speaker, is the author of five books. Though she does wrestle with many of the tricky bits of faith, she's pretty certain that, in Jesus, God is *with* us and *for* us. She lives in Durham, North Carolina, with her three amazing kiddos. Learn more at MargotStarbuck.com or connect with Margot at facebook.com/margot.

RACHEL MARIE STONE is the author of *Eat with Joy: Redeeming God's Gift of Food* (IVP, 2013) and *The Unexpected Way* (Peace Hill Press, 2014). She's a blogger for Religion News Service and a regular contributor to *Christianity Today*'s *Her.meneutics* blog. Her writing also appears in *Books and Culture, The Christian Century, Sojourners, PRISM*, and *Christianity Today*, among others. She has also worked as a labor doula in the United States and in Malawi, Africa. She and her husband, Tim, a professor of Hebrew Bible at Eastern University, have two children.

KAREN SWALLOW PRIOR, PhD, is an award-winning professor of English at Liberty University. She is the author of *Booked: Literature in the Soul of Me* (T. S. Poetry Press, 2012) and *Fierce Convictions: The Extraordinary Life of Hannah More—Poet, Reformer, Abolitionist* (Thomas Nelson, 2014). Prior is a contributing writer for *Christianity Today, Think Christian*, and *The Atlantic*.

She is a member of INK: A Creative Collective and the faith advisory council of the Humane Society of the United States. She and her husband live in rural Virginia with sundry dogs, horses, and chickens.

The Reverend JEFF TACKLIND is lead pastor of Little Church by the Sea in Laguna Beach, California, where he has lived and served for the last twelve years with his wife, Patty, and three kids, Gabe, Mia, and Lila. Jeff holds a masters degree in philosophy from the Talbot School of Theology and a doctorate in semiotics and future studies from George Fox University. In the gaps, Jeff spends his time reading, surfing, getting beaten at chess, and searching for the perfect cup of coffee. He is physically incapable of preaching a sermon without quoting C. S. Lewis or Thomas Merton (or both) at least once.*

The Reverend KENNETH TANNER is pastor of Church of the Holy Redeemer in Rochester Hills, Michigan, where with his wife and their seven children they have a home. His writing has appeared in Books & Culture, *The Huffington Post*, *Sojourners*, *National Review*, *Christianity Today*, and *RealClearReligion*. Follow him on Twitter @kennethtanner.

DAVID VANDERVEEN is a husband, father, avid waterman, follower of Jesus, and sinner. He has published letters, columns, essays, and short stories in the *Wall Street Journal*, *Mars Hill Review*, *Laguna Beach Independent*, *Sojourners*, and *The Huffington Post*. David recently wrote and edited *The Love Wins Companion* with Rob Bell. In his spare time, he is a global

---

* That last bit is from Cathleen, who has had the great joy of being pastored by Jeff since 2009.

energy drink entrepreneur and disco dancer. He lives in Laguna Beach, California.

Karen Walrond is a nationally recognized author and photographer. For most of her adult life Karen worked in corporate America, most recently as a lawyer, and before that, as a structural engineer. Yet her friendship with her Nikon camera began to blossom, and today she is an award-winning blogger, photographer, and author who has spoken around the world, appearing on CNN, TEDxHouston, and *Oprah*. In *The Beauty of Different*, her blog *Chookooloonks*, and her online courses and ebooks, she reminds us that our uniqueness, skills, and most mundane stories have the power to connect. Learn more about Karen at chookooloonks.com.

Katherine Willis Pershey is an associate minister of the First Congregational Church in Western Springs, Illinois. Ordained in the Christian Church (Disciples of Christ), Katherine was one of the founding editorial board members of *Fidelia's Sisters*, a publication of the Young Clergy Women Project. She has contributed to publications such as *The Christian Century, A Deeper Story, Comment, Gifted for Leadership*, and *The Art of Simple*. She is the author of a memoir, *Any Day a Beautiful Change: A Story of Faith and Family* (Chalice Press, 2012). Katherine and her husband, Benjamin, have two daughters.

Copyright Acknowledgments

"Evangelical Blues, Genograms, and the Sins of the Fathers, or The Stories We Tell Ourselves" copyright © 2014 Jennifer Grant

"A High Tolerance for Ambiguity" copyright © 2014 Steve Brown

"Women and Children First" copyright © 2014 Linda Midgett

"The Necessity of Solitude" copyright © 2014 Christopher L. Heuertz

"Mary and Martha; Mom and Me" copyright © 2014 Stephen Henderson

"God Breathed" copyright © 2014 Gareth Higgins

"Willing and Doing" copyright © 2014 David B. Fletcher

"The Bible: Full of Sound, Fury, Sarcasm, and Poop Jokes" copyright © 2014 Susan E. Isaacs

"The Starlit Way: Confronting Doubt with Jesus" copyright © 2014 Anna Broadway

"Stillness" copyright © 2014 Alice Currah

"Broken and Bent" copyright © 2014 Ellen Painter Dollar

"SLUT!" copyright © 2014 Cathleen Falsani

"Apocalypse Later" copyright © 2014 Jay Emerson Johnson

"Daydreaming of Bed Linens" copyright © 2014 Bill Motz

"Early-Morning Matters" copyright © Jack Palmer

"The Miracle" copyright © 2014 Timothy King

"Running from 'Healing' to Healing" copyright © 2014 Calenthia S. Dowdy

"The Good Shepherd" copyright © 2014 Victor Conrado

"Move Down, Clean Cup!: Pulling Back the Covers on Revelation" copyright © 2014 Christian Piatt

"Womb Work and the Uncomfortable Idea of Redemptive Suffering" copyright © 2014 Rachel Marie Stone

"This Is Buddha" copyright © 2014 Carolyn Reyes

"A Tale of Two Mottoes" copyright © 2014 Jack Heaslip

"Seekers and Sparrows and Sunday School" copyright © 2014 Jenny Sheffer Stevens

"Scriptural Cherry-Picking" copyright © 2014 Amy Julia Becker

"Women: Be Silent" copyright © 2014 Sarah Heath

Copyright Acknowledgments